LOUIS XV
THE MONARCHY
IN DECLINE

LOUIS XV
from a painting by F. H. Drouais

LOUIS XV

THE MONARCHY
IN DECLINE

G. P. GOOCH
C.H., D.Litt., F.B.A.

LONGMANS, GREEN AND CO
LONDON · NEW YORK · TORONTO

LONGMANS, GREEN AND CO LTD
6 & 7 CLIFFORD STREET LONDON W I
BOSTON HOUSE STRAND STREET CAPE TOWN
531 LITTLE COLLINS STREET MELBOURNE

LONGMANS, GREEN AND CO INC
55 FIFTH AVENUE NEW YORK 3

LONGMANS, GREEN AND CO
20 CRANFIELD ROAD TORONTO 16

ORIENT LONGMANS PRIVATE LTD
CALCUTTA BOMBAY MADRAS
DELHI VIJAYAWADA DACCA

First published 1956
Second impression 1956

Permission has been given for this
book to be transcribed into Braille.

PRINTED IN GREAT BRITAIN
BY WESTERN PRINTING SERVICES LTD BRISTOL

Absolute monarchical government is excellent under a good King, but who will guarantee that we shall always have an Henri Quatre? Experience and nature prove that we shall get ten bad ones to one good.

D'ARGENSON'S JOURNAL, 1751

PREFACE

THIS volume is designed as a pendant to the author's trilogy on the Enlightened Autocrats of the eighteenth century. While Frederick the Great, Maria Theresa and Catherine the Great laboured without intermission at the onerous task of governing their peoples, Louis XV, well intentioned but indolent, reigned but never ruled. Dynastic autocracy requires for its successful operation an unbroken succession of supermen, or at any rate of monarchs of good ability who dedicate their lives to their work. Since experience shows that this essential condition cannot be fulfilled the system has disappeared, its place being taken either by free institutions or totalitarian rule. No monarch in modern times has contributed so largely to its collapse as Louis XV. Great empires, declared his majestic predecessor in a memorandum for his grandson Philip V of Spain, are only preserved by the methods by which they are acquired—vigour, vigilance, and hard work. The least estimable of the Bourbon Kings recognised the validity of this maxim but made no attempt to carry it out.

Keenly interested though he was in foreign affairs, Louis XV lacked the courage to stand up to his Ministers, and the secret diplomacy to which he resorted was an utter failure. In domestic issues he pursued the line of least resistance, allowing his country to drift, glaring abuses to continue, deficits to increase, discontent to spread. His best qualities were negative: he was never vindictive and he had not the slightest desire for military glory. Throughout his life he suffered from paralysis of the will. It was the misfortune of France not merely that he was temperamentally unfitted to rule but that no institutions existed which could share the burden. History supplies no more cogent argument for the superiority of constitutional monarchy than this long and inglorious reign. No modern ruler has been less respected, less loved, less feared or less mourned.

His insufficiency as a ruler was matched by his unworthiness as a man. Inheriting the pathological sensuality of Henri IV and Louis XIV, he made no attempt to preserve the dignity of the crown. In a dissolute age, in which few members of the nobility were faithful husbands, the bestowal of his favours on the three Nesle sisters and Mme de Pompadour was not seriously blamed; but when he established a private brothel at the Parc aux Cerfs and picked Mme du Barry out of the gutter the limits even of French tolerance were passed. The orgies of the Regent Orleans at the Palais Royal were even more disgraceful, and the loveless debaucheries of the Duc de Richelieu, the champion rake of his time, were equally scandalous, but neither of them was the ruler of France. Louis XV lacked all sense of responsibility, the acid test of men in the highest posts. The greater the sinner, the greater the sin.

The purpose of this volume is to portray the ruler, not to supply yet another narrative of the reign; but in an autocracy the character of a monarch is a vital factor in shaping the destinies of his country. Inheriting the immense prestige of *Le Roi Soleil*, which rested on his military glories, his imposing personality and the splendour of his court, his great-grandson found his war-weary and overtaxed subjects ready to love him and prepared to continue the system in which they had been reared. As late as 1744 his desperate illness at Metz aroused a surge of emotion and earned him the title of *Louis le Bienaimé*, but it was the last occasion on which all his subjects cared whether he lived or died.

Though the economic situation of the country slowly improved over the decades, his subjects became increasingly impatient of the outworn pattern of political institutions and class privilege. The *Philosophes*, captained by Voltaire and the editors of the *Encyclopédie*, encouraged their readers to criticise, to hope, and to plan. The principal feature in the intellectual life of western Europe was the steady decline of authority. The middle class arrived in France in the eighteenth century as it had arrived in England in the seventeenth, and found the relics of the feudal era barring its way. The first task of a prudent monarch was to facilitate the transition from the old world to the new. Louis XV was by no means destitute of intelligence, but, lacking resolution, ideas and ideals, he could do nothing for his subjects: aware of his shortcomings he asked as little as he gave. It was his misfortune, not his fault, that he was no superman; but there is no answer to the charge that he let his country down and never lifted a finger to effect even the limited reforms which he vaguely sensed to be necessary. Though by the unexacting moral standards of his age he was not a bad man, he was beyond comparison the worst of the Bourbon monarchs and he qualifies for the title of the chief gravedigger of the *ancien régime*. 'I found the crown of France in the mud,' explained Napoleon; 'I picked it up and put it on my head.' It was Louis XV who let it fall.

Students of the court of Louis XV are well supplied with contemporary evidence, such as the voluminous journals of the Marquis d'Argenson, the sober diary of the Duc de Luynes, the snapshots of the Duc de Croy and Comte de Cheverny, President Hénault and Marquis Valfons, while Barbier recorded the life of the capital and Mme du Deffand, as indefatigable a correspondent as Mme de Sévigné, commented on events to Horace Walpole, the Duchesse de Choiseul, and other friends. Though none of these chroniclers approached the stature of Saint-Simon, their testimony provides a picture pulsing with life. We have merely to close our eyes to visualise the well-dressed crowd which thronged the gilded galleries at Versailles.

Portions of this volume have appeared in the *Contemporary Review*, and the author expresses his thanks for permission to reprint.

G.P.G.

CONTENTS

PLATES

I

THE LEGACY OF LOUIS XIV

I

THE principal legacy of Louis XIV was a powerful and
centralised France. Though *Le Roi Soleil* was no superman
in the sense that he would have fought his way to the front had
he not been of royal descent, he gave his name to the greatest
era in French history and his rays penetrated to every corner of
Europe. He owed his success to the combination of his political
heritage and his personal qualities. Frederick the Great saluted
the French of the age of Louis XIV as the Romans of the modern
world. The founder of dynastic autocracy was Richelieu, who
broke the power of the feudal nobility and the Protestants and
by the creation of Intendants asserted the authority of the Crown
over the whole country. So decisive was his achievement that
the Fronde was little more than a straw fire, and Condé was the
last of the *Noblesse de l'Épée* to draw his sword against the throne.
The most sordid episode in the history of seventeenth-century
France left the Monarchy stronger than it found it, for the angry
disgust it aroused led to a national demand for the curbing of
anarchy by a firm hand at the helm. The *Noblesse* and the *Parlements* had discredited themselves, and Mazarin steered the ship
of state into calmer waters without shedding blood. *Le Grand
Siècle* had begun.

If Richelieu's edifice was to outlive its architect it demanded
rulers of ability and industry. Louis XIII, the most colourless

of the Bourbon monarchs, preferred hunting to politics and left
the management of the state to the mighty Cardinal. There was
no need for Anne of Austria to anticipate the injunction of another
royal widow a century later, 'George, be a King.' Though but
a child during the hectic years of the Fronde, Louis XIV never
forgot the humiliations of the Royal Family during the dark days
of the Fronde, the early morning flight from the Palais Royal,
and the thunder of Condé's cannon in the Faubourg St. Antoine.
Even before the death of Mazarin he had resolved to be his own
master, to allow no minister and no favourite, male or female, to
shape his course, to make the nobility the ornament instead of
the rival of the throne. His veto on the duel, which had taken
heavy toll of the aristocracy during the reign of his father,
embodied his desire to preserve the *Noblesse* while abolishing
its power. Its chief function, as he saw it, was to contribute to
the splendour of the Court and the prestige of the Crown. Landowners of limited means who vegetated on their estates, called
Noblesse de Province, were disapproved, and when their names
came up in conversation he curtly remarked: 'C'est un homme
que je ne connais pas.' 'I intend to be my own First Minister,'
he announced, and he kept his word. Court posts naturally went
to the *Noblesse de Cour*, but the business of state was largely
transacted by lawyers and other capable *roturiers* who owed
everything to the sovereign. The King demanded from his
people obedience, not collaboration. Never for a moment did
he question his capacity to fulfil the task allotted to him by
Providence, and the incense by which he was surrounded confirmed his massive self-assurance. His ability was above the
average, his industry unique in the annals of the Bourbon
dynasty. Even under the shock of military disaster or domestic
sorrow he remained calm and dignified, though at times when
alone with Mme de Maintenon tears came to his eyes. He was
the first and last demigod to occupy the throne of France.

'There was nothing to be compared to him at reviews, fêtes,
every occasion on which the presence of ladies created a tone of
gallantry, a gallantry always majestic,' testifies Saint-Simon, a
rather unfriendly observer, saluted by Sainte-Beuve as the Tacitus
of France. 'Sometimes there was gaiety, but never anything misplaced or indiscreet. His slightest gesture, his walk, his bearing,

his countenance, all was measured, appropriate, noble, majestic but quite natural. Thus in serious matters such as the audiences of Ambassadors and other ceremonies no one was ever so imposing. One had to get used to him in order to avoid embarrassment when speaking to him. His replies on these occasions were always brief and to the point, rarely without some obliging or even flattering remark when the occasion demanded. In every company his presence imposed silence and even fear.' Never was any human being more obviously born to be a King. Nothing suggests more vividly the awe he inspired than the suicide of the unhappy cook when the fish for dinner on a royal visit to Condé at Chantilly failed to arrive, and the confession of one of his Generals on entering the royal presence: 'I never trembled like this before Your Majesty's enemies.' Like other autocrats he made costly mistakes, but his devotion to his task is beyond challenge. He believed in the system bequeathed by Richelieu as implicitly as he believed in himself. If Henri IV was the most popular of the Bourbon rulers, his grandson earned the maximum prestige. That the longest reign in French history was also the most illustrious is the conviction of Frenchmen who agree in little else. It was a glittering vision, the splendour and strength of which aroused the envious admiration of the world. With such a monarch there seemed no need for the States-General. The army was without a rival in Europe, and the navy, the most enduring of his creations, was double the size of the British fleet. Under the fostering hand of Colbert industry and commerce grew apace. The master of twenty million Frenchmen was the richest and most powerful prince in Europe, and scarcely anything seemed beyond his grasp. Since Charles II of Spain was childless, he reflected, perhaps a Bourbon might soon replace a Hapsburg at Madrid. In the technique of kingship he was not only unrivalled but unapproached. 'He was born prudent, moderate, friendly, and just,' testifies Saint-Simon; 'God had given him enough to make him a good King and perhaps a fairly great King. All the evil came from elsewhere.' The ceremonies of the *lever* and *coucher* recalled the solemnity of a religious cult.

The essence of Richelieu's system was the concentration of authority. It was said of the Hohenzollern Empire after the fall

of Bismarck that in the most elaborately organised of European
states there was anarchy at the top. The young Louis XIV was
resolved that there should be no flicker of anarchy, no thought
of challenge to his will, no division of power. The Cardinal's
Testament Politique, published in 1687, uttered a solemn warning
against nerveless rule: better too much severity than too much
lenity, for weakness was the ruin of the state. The Memoirs of
Louis XIV, first published in full in 1860, were at once a summary
of the first decade of his personal rule and a manual of political
instruction for his son. He portrays himself as the effective ruler
of his kingdom and a jealous guardian of the prestige of the
Crown, while fully realising how much is expected from an
absolute sovereign. Here are a few of his precepts.

It is essential for princes to master their resentments. In scheming
to injure someone who has caused us trouble we may injure ourselves. Exercising as we do a divinely appointed function we must
appear incapable of the agitations which might lower the standard.
If it is true that our heart, knowing its frailty, is conscious of the
emotions of the common herd, our reason ought to conceal them
directly they threaten the public weal for which alone we are born.
A King must hold the balance between the many people who strive
to tilt it to their side. So many pay court to us for personal reasons
under specious phrases. You cannot satisfy everyone. Do not
assess the justice of a claim by the vigour with which it is pressed.
The result of the decision is more important than the merits of the
claimants: the greatest of rulers would soon be ruined if he granted
everything to deserving cases. Since those of our rank are never
forgiven we must weigh our words. Kings are absolute lords and
have full authority over all people, secular and ecclesiastical; use it
according to the needs of the state. Never hurry. Take long views.
The King must know everything. Empires are only preserved by
the same means by which they are created, namely vigour, vigilance,
and hard work.

So far we seem to have been listening to the calm accents of
the father of the gods on the summit of Olympus, but the young
ruler goes on to admit the temptations of the flesh. Princes, he
declares, can never live too prudent and innocent a life. To reign
happily and gloriously it is not enough to issue orders if they
do not regulate their own conduct. He had felt it right to

recognise his daughter by Mlle la Vallière by granting a title to her mother.

> I could have passed over this attachment as a bad example, but after drawing lessons from the failings of others I could not deprive you of those you could learn from mine. The Prince should always be a perfect model of virtue, all the more since he lives in a glass house. If, however, we yield in spite of ourselves we must observe two precautions as I have always done. First, that the time allotted to a *liaison* should never prejudice our affairs, since our first object should always be the preservation of our glory and authority, which can only be achieved by steady toil. Secondly—and more difficult to practise—that in giving our heart we must remain absolute master of our mind, separating the endearments of the lover from the resolution of the sovereign, since the influence of a mistress is much more dangerous than that of a favourite.

Despite this frank admission of human frailty, the whole of this *Testament Politique* breathes the robust conviction that absolute monarchy is the best form of government and that the author is a blessing to his country and a pattern to the world.

Never for a moment after the death of Mazarin left him a free hand did Louis XIV allow a minister or a mistress to deprive him of a fraction of his authority. The Chancellor, who kept the royal seal, the Controller General of Finance, the Ministers of State without portfolio, and the departmental Secretaries of State, were merely executants of his will. The three successive *maîtresses en titre*, La Vallière, Montespan and Fontanges, possessed no political influence, and there is no ground for the belief that the course of events in the closing decades was deflected by the virtuous Mme de Maintenon. The concentration of power which formed the core of his political faith involved unlimited responsibility before his subjects and posterity. When a Minister apologised for referring decisions to the King on the ground that he was still new to his job, he was informed that he would never have to decide about anything and that his only duty would be to obey orders. Business was transacted by four principal Councils, three of which he regularly attended. The small *Conseil d'État*, the nearest equivalent to a Cabinet, discussed and decided the great issues of national policy. The *Conseil des Dépêches* dealt with internal affairs, the *Conseil des Finances* with taxation. The *Conseil Privé*, consisting of lawyers and rarely attended by the King, was the highest judicial court in France. None of the Councils possessed any statutory rights, and they were regarded as purely advisory bodies. When Colbert and Louvois were gone the era of supermen was over, and during the closing phase he had no one on whose judgment he was inclined to lean. Never did he attempt to shield himself behind a subordinate when things went wrong; that would have been beneath his dignity. Like Mazarin, he imposed his authority without shedding blood. *L'État c'est moi* was his slogan, even if he never coined the phrase. Of all the princes in modern Europe Louis XIV and Frederick the Great came nearest to the ideal of father of the country, the first servant as well as the master of the state.

Every potential focus of opposition to the royal will was neutralised if not removed. The *Parlement* of Paris, which had roughly challenged the court during the turmoil of the Fronde, was paralysed by a veto on its traditional privilege of recording remonstrances against the decisions of the crown, and no further trouble arose while Louis XIV was on the throne. It was a high-handed proceeding, for the magistrates regarded themselves —and were widely regarded—as guardians of the fundamental laws. The *Parlement*, an offshoot from the old Curia Regis, could boast of centuries of service as the Supreme Court of Justice, dealing especially with appeals from lower courts. At its foundation by Philippe le Bel the President and Councillors were appointed yearly, but they were usually reappointed. As business increased it was divided into the *Chambre des Enquêtes*, dealing with most of the appeals, the *Chambre des Requêtes*, with petitions on points of law, and a third chamber with criminal cases. The most important decisions were reserved for the *Grand Chambre*. Twelve provincial *Parlements* were instituted during the following centuries. In addition to its judicial functions the *Parlement* of Paris was required to register the royal edicts, but under Louis XI it claimed the power of remonstrance and delay, and the claim grew into a recognised right. The ruler, however, could override opposition by a *lit de justice*, and Louis XIV was determined to keep the magistrates strictly to their legal duties. The Estates still met occasionally in various Provinces but were allowed little power, and the Provincial Governors, the

French equivalent of the English Lords Lieutenant, were merely ornamental nominees of the King. The work of administration was carried on by the thirty Intendants, usually chosen from the bourgeoisie, who took orders from and reported to the King and his Councils at Versailles.

In 1692 Louis XIV abolished the right of the towns to elect their functionaries and further reduced their prestige by the sale of municipal offices in order to raise money for his wars. The local tribunals were no less dependent, for their decisions could be overruled by the King. The Intendants could prevent cases coming into court and could sentence to the galleys or imprisonment. What Richelieu had begun was completed by *Le Grand Monarque*, who had no scruples about using his power to the full. Blackstone bracketed France and Turkey as the countries where civil rights were most unreservedly at the mercy of the Crown, for in the absence of Habeas Corpus or trial by jury an innocent citizen had little chance of securing his rights.

With equal determination Louis XIV clipped the wings of the Church by reaffirming the principles of Gallicanism first formulated by Francis I, the essence of which was the supremacy of the Crown except in matters of belief. The celebrated Four Articles of 1682 drafted by Bossuet threw down a ringing challenge to the Pope and the Jesuits. 'Kings and princes,' declared the first article, 'are not by the law of God subject to any ecclesiastical power nor to the keys of the Church with respect to their temporal government. Their subjects cannot be released from the duty of obeying them nor absolved from the oath of allegiance.' Even in the field of doctrine the power of the Vatican is strictly circumscribed. 'The Pope has the principal place in deciding questions of faith,' runs the fourth article, 'but his judgment is not irreversible until confirmed by the consent of the Church.' The Declaration, signed by thirty-four Bishops and thirty-four lesser clergy, was registered by the *Parlement* at the command of the King. An edict was issued prescribing that the Four Articles should be taught in all universities and accepted by all professors of theology, and the Archbishops and Bishops were summoned to enforce the decree. Though the angry Pontiff considered the issue of a formal censure of the articles, no action was taken against Gallicanism, for the King, with the nation behind him, was too powerful to be coerced. Such influence as the Church retained could only become operative with the consent of the Crown.

His ideal was a homogeneous nation, looking up with pride, affection and gratitude to its head. This monolithic conception of the state left no place for religious minorities, and when he turned *dévot* under the influence of his Jesuit Confessor and Mme de Maintenon his zeal for uniformity became an obsession. The revocation of the Edict of Nantes was as much an assertion of the principle of national unity as an affirmation of the Catholic faith. Richelieu had been content to destroy what little political influence the Huguenots retained after the Wars of Religion, and at the opening of his reign Louis XIV paid public tribute to their loyalty during the Fronde. That these orderly and industrious citizens asked only for a quiet life was recognised by all. The clergy had always detested the Edict, and their Quinquennial Assemblies demanded its abrogation or at any rate its drastic modification. Twenty years of mounting persecution, including the closing of churches and schools and the nightmare of the *dragonnades*, led thousands of Huguenots to seek shelter abroad and thousands more to avoid almost intolerable suffering by nominal conversion. Declaring that it was his duty to convert all his subjects and extirpate heresy, and encouraged to take the final plunge by his Confessor Père La Chaise, Harlay Archbishop of Paris, and Louvois the ruthless Minister of War, he revoked in 1685 the Edict of his grandfather. In a frenzy of fanaticism he exclaimed that he would complete the conversion of the Huguenots even at the cost of his right hand, and the greatest of French ecclesiastics piled incense on his altar. 'Let us make known the miracle of our times,' exclaimed Bossuet; 'let us make known what we feel about the piety of Louis; let us raise our acclamations to the skies; let us say to this new Theodosius, this new Charlemagne: Here is the supreme achievement of your reign. It is this which gives it its true character. By your deed heresy exists no longer. God alone has wrought this miracle.' Huguenot ministers were ordered to leave France within ten days or go to the galleys, but laymen were forbidden to cross the frontier. Churches were demolished, services in private houses forbidden, meetings held in the mountains; children were to be baptised by

Catholic priests and brought up as Catholics. Hundreds of thousands defied the fury of their persecutors till the Revolution established equality before the law. The greatest crime of the reign was also the gravest blunder, for the thousands of skilled artisans who streamed across the frontiers before and after the Revocation weakened France as much as they strengthened England, Holland, Prussia and other Protestant states in which they found a new and happy home. A few even sought refuge in South Africa. The ferocious onslaught transformed the bolder spirits into rebels, and during the War of the Spanish Succession the bloody guerrilla struggle in the Cevennes added to the anxieties of the Crown.

The King's detestation of the Jansenists was scarcely less vehement than that which he entertained for the Huguenots, though the repression was less severe. The precise nature of their doctrinal deviation was beyond him, for he was no theologian. What stirred his anger was the thought that so many of his subjects, including a section of the clergy, continued to hold Augustinian ideas on grace proclaimed by Jansen, Bishop of Ypres, and popularised in France by Saint-Cyran and Antoine Arnauld. Five propositions concerning predestination in Jansen's *Augustinus* were declared heretical by Innocent X in 1653; and the Jansenist hostility to the Jesuits, which inspired Pascal's flaming *Lettres Provinciales*, increased the determination of the King to enforce uniformity. It was no easy task since the Jansenists were widely respected for their piety and austerity. Their attitude was restated in Quesnel's *Réflexions Morales sur le Nouveau Testament* which enjoyed immense popularity and led to new measures of repression, culminating in the expulsion of the inmates of Port Royal des Champs, the demolition of the convent buildings, and the issue of the Bull 'Unigenitus' in 1713. It was not the end of the struggle, but the old King died in the belief that another focus of opposition had been removed.

Compared to the fierce battles against Huguenots and Jansenists the Quietist controversy was a storm in a teacup. An extravagant variety of mysticism taught by Molinos, a Spanish priest, and commonly described as Molinism, was embraced with fervour by Mme Guyon and with greater circumspection by Fénelon. The aim of Quietism was to rise above ceremonies, sacraments and dogmas into a rapturous vision of the Divine Essence by the *via negationis*, self-annihilation, an emptying of the soul from all thought, feeling and will. That such a rejection of external authority and direct moral responsibility might degenerate into antinomianism was obvious, but Fénelon believed that much could be learned from this gospel of renunciation. His attitude was defined in his *Maxims of the Saints*, a devotional treatise saturated with mystical theology. Like all the great mystics from St. Theresa and St. John of the Cross to Molinos, his goal was complete surrender of self: all that mattered was to love God. At this stage Bossuet, the national champion of orthodoxy and authority, entered the lists and fulminated against the new heretics. When Fénelon appealed to Rome the Pope condemned his book and the author submitted. Regarding himself as the guardian of orthodoxy, the King deprived him of his post as Preceptor to the Duc de Bourgogne and excluded him from the Court. Mme de Maintenon, who counted him and Mme Guyon among her intimate friends, bowed as usual to the royal will. In one of his temperamental outbursts Saint-Simon complained that the Court vomited hypocrisy. In his later years the King was a gloomy fanatic, but hypocrisy could no longer be laid to his charge. The last of his Jesuit Confessors, Le Tellier, incarnated the spirit of intolerance which contributed to the growth of anti-clericalism at least as much as the shafts of Bayle and Voltaire. Even during the later years of the *Grand Monarque* there was a good deal of unbelief in high circles. In 1699 the Duchess of Orleans reported to her German relatives that faith was extinct and that every youngster wanted to be an atheist. Doubtless she was thinking of her son, the future Regent, who made no pretence of sharing the beliefs of the Royal Family. Regarding the Church as a pillar of the throne, Louis XIV never worried about anything except an open challenge to its authority which he regarded as an indirect challenge to his own.

II

The political ideology of Louis XIV was formulated by the most eloquent preacher of the age. In his massive treatise

La Politique tirée de l'Écriture Sainte Bossuet spoke for France
with the same authority as Locke and Halifax interpreted the
England of 1688. As in his better-known *Discours sur l'Histoire
Universelle*, compiled for his pupil the Dauphin, the Bishop of
Meaux draws his arguments from scripture, history and reason
in support of the system of dynastic autocracy. The Bible, he
argues, is the touchstone of truth in the political no less than in
the religious sphere. Sharing the conviction of Hobbes that by
nature men are wolves to one another, he reaches the same conclusion that absolute power, preferably exercised by hereditary
monarchy, is needed to keep them in order. He rejects the
Aristotelian maxim that man is a political animal, and attributes
the creation of society to the instinctive physical need for self-
preservation. To fulfil his duty of securing the public welfare
the sovereign must possess unfettered authority; his right once
established, all other rights fade away. '*O rois, vous êtes des dieux.*'
Private rights are valid only if recognised by the law which the
ruler decrees. Having entrusted all their power to a single
person, the people can do nothing against him: even their lives
are in his hands and in case of disobedience he may take them.
Bad princes, even tyrants, possess the same right to obedience
as good ones, and the early Christians performed their duty in
praying for Nero. If opposition is permitted for any purpose,
the state is in peril for public order is threatened. The ruler is
no less under an obligation to maintain his authority unimpaired
than his subjects to obey his commands, for its diminution would
paralyse his capacity to keep the peace: the best government is
that which is furthest removed from anarchy. All benefits
should derive from him alone. It is right that he should be loved
but he should also be feared. Caring nothing for political or
religious liberty, Bossuet denies both the need and the value of
constitutional guarantees, for it is as easy to sign a scrap of paper
as to tear it up. Hereditary monarchy has proved the best system,
for in working for his state the monarch is working for his own
children.

So far Bossuet's premises and conclusions are pure Hobbes,
but as the argument develops vital differences emerge. While
the freethinking publicist is an incurable pessimist about human
nature, the pious Bishop sees the stars shining in the heavens

since Christian ethics point the way to a better life. Though
subject to no terrestrial authority the ruler is under the moral
law, and is in duty bound to maintain ancient institutions, fundamental laws and inherited privileges. Tradition, which meant as
little to Hobbes as it was later to weigh with Bentham, possessed
for Bossuet an authority which he dared not and had no wish to
ignore. He believed in the wisdom of our ancestors, and in his
eyes the passage of time gradually legitimised conquest. If, however, the ruler neglects his duties—even if he openly flouts the
laws of God and orders his subjects to do the same—he could be
neither punished nor resisted: like the early Christians they must
if necessary suffer and die. While the system of Hobbes rested
on the fear of punishment, the political edifice of Bossuet was
theoretically cemented by love. He was too fine a spirit to flatter,
and his paean to the ruler breathes genuine devotion.

> A good subject loves his prince as the embodiment of the public
> weal and the safety of the state, as the air he breathes, as the light
> of his eyes, as his life and more than his life. He is more than the
> head of the state and the fatherland incarnate. Next to the love of
> God comes love for the prince, and how greatly must he love his
> people in order to retain their love! All men are brothers and
> should love each other like brothers. If he fears the people, all is
> lost. If he fears the great nobles, the state is weak. He must fear
> God alone. The more exalted the office, the greater the severity of
> the divine judge: mercy is for the little man, torments for the
> mighty. Without the divine judgment-seat absolute authority
> degenerates into arbitrary despotism.

Both as a believer in an all-powerful executive and as a pillar
of the Catholic Church, Bossuet rejects liberty of conscience as
a challenge to the true faith and a threat to the spiritual solidarity
of the state. As an embodiment of the *mystique* of absolute
monarchy on a Christian basis in seventeenth-century France
Bossuet's treatise ranks with the writings of James I and the
Divine Right teachings of High Church theologians in the reign
of Charles I. Its purpose was to convince the heir to the throne
that a Christian prince was the representative of God on earth
with all the powers, privileges and obligations appertaining to
the post. Written when *Le Roi Soleil* was at the height of his
glory, it breathed boundless confidence in the strength and

stability of the Bourbon monarchy. As, however, the reign moved towards its close an atmospheric change, arising from the almost unceasing wars and the ever-increasing frustration and resentment, stimulated a search for alternatives.

The critical spirit of a younger generation found its most eloquent expression in Fénelon who, like Bossuet, was appointed to train an heir to the throne, though he was allotted a more promising pupil. No preceptor could have struck sparks from the indolent and mindless Dauphin, but the qualities of his son, the Duc de Bourgogne, seemed to authorise the highest hopes. Saint-Simon's portrait of Fénelon is one of the gems in his gallery. 'This prelate was tall and thin, well proportioned, with a big nose, eyes from which fire and intelligence poured like a torrent, and a face unlike any I ever saw and which, once seen, could never be forgotten. It was full of contradictions, yet they always harmonised. There were gallantry and gravity, earnestness and gaiety; there were in equal proportions the teacher, the Bishop, and the Grand Seigneur. His whole personality breathed thought, intelligence, grace, measure, above all nobility. It was difficult to turn one's eyes away.' For Saint-Simon the Archbishop of Cambrai was the most dazzling ornament of the Court. No French ecclesiastic except Richelieu has left such a legend of personal distinction; no Frenchman of his time looked so far ahead and gave his contemporaries such sound advice. In Acton's words he was the first who saw through the majestic hypocrisy of the Court and knew that France was on the road to ruin. A century before the Revolution he proclaimed that the pyramid must rest not on its apex but on its base, and two centuries before the League of Nations he pleaded for an interdependent world. It was characteristic of this practical idealist that his earliest publication was a plea for the higher education of women.

Télémaque, like *Gulliver's Travels*, is a *roman à thèse*, a political tract in fictional form: everyone realised that it was a broadside against autocracy in general and Versailles in particular. Translated into many languages, it was read with delight by the King's enemies, including the persecuted Huguenots at home and abroad. Mentor is the oracle, Télémaque, the son of Ulysses, the eager pupil. Every incident contains a moral or implies a criticism. 'Love your people, Telemachus,' declares Mentor, 'as if they were your own children. A good King is all-powerful over his people, but the laws are all-powerful over him. His power to do good is absolute, but his hands are tied when he would do ill. The laws give him the people in trust as the most precious thing they can bestow on condition that he looks on himself as their father. He should live more soberly, less luxuriously and with less outward magnificence and pride than others.' Mentor's sharpest arrows are aimed at the craving for fame and the wars of conquest to which it led. Though he scarcely ranks with his contemporaries William Penn and the Abbé Saint-Pierre among the pioneers of a League of Nations, he denounced the slogans of arrogant nationalism with equal vigour. 'The whole race is one family. All men are brothers. Say not, O ye Kings, that war is the path to glory. Whoever puts his own glory before the dictates of humanity is a monster of pride, not a man.' A meeting of kings should be held every three years to renew their alliance by a fresh oath and take counsel together. Not merely wars but the trade barriers of Colbert's mercantilist system were an offence against the unity of mankind. War was the costliest of royal follies, but the building mania was not far behind. Believing that all people and all nations are brothers, he paints a picture of the Elysian fields, a Christian Utopia, a land of peace and joy. 'Peu sérieux,' commented Bossuet, 'et peu digne d'un prêtre.' Though the Eagle of Meaux had powerful wings he lacked originality and never soared into the upper regions of the sky. He was the greatest of conservatives before Joseph de Maistre, Fénelon the greatest liberal of his age.

The attack on the principle and practice of autocracy was developed in an unpublished *Lettre à Louis XIV* so vehement in tone that its authenticity might be challenged but for the survival of the autograph manuscript, doubtless a first draft. 'All your Ministers,' begins Fénelon, 'have abandoned all the old maxims in order to glorify your authority. People no longer speak of the state, only of the King and his good pleasure. They have raised you to the skies; but absolute power is only a sham, for real power resides with the Ministers, who have been harsh, arrogant, unjust, violent, false.' The King's worst fault was his passion for war, and the Dutch War had unleashed all the misfortunes of France. 'Your Majesty was driven into it to enhance

your glory, but such a motive can never justify a war.' A terrible
and obviously exaggerated picture is drawn of the plight of
France in 1691.

> Your peoples are dying of hunger. Agriculture is almost at a stand-
> still, all the industries languish, all commerce is destroyed. France
> is a vast hospital. The magistrates are degraded and worn out. It is
> you who have caused all these troubles. The whole kingdom having
> been ruined, everything is concentrated in you and everyone must
> feed out of your hand. The people which loved you so much is
> beginning to withdraw its affection, its confidence and even its
> respect. Your victories no longer arouse delight. There is only
> bitterness and despair. Sedition is boiling up. You do not love
> God; you only fear Him with a slavish fear. It is hell you are
> afraid of. Your religion consists of superstition and ceremonies.
> You relate everything to yourself as if you were God on earth.

That the letter was read by the proud monarch is inconceivable.
   The death of the Dauphin in 1711 turned all eyes to the Duc
de Bourgogne who might be expected to succeed his septuagenarian grandfather at any moment; and then, it seemed, was
the chance of the ardent reformer at Cambrai. 'Our trouble,' he
wrote to the Duc de Chevreuse, 'is that this war has been the
personal enterprise of the King, who is ruined and discredited.
It should be made the concern of the whole nation which must
save itself.' Since he might perhaps be called to power, he felt
bound to draft a new policy for the new reign. After prolonged
discussions with his old pupil's closest friends, the Duc de
Beauvilliers, his ex-Governor, and the Duc de Chevreuse, he
formulated maxims in which he approached closer to practical
issues than ever before. The first tasks were to overcome the
active or passive resistance of the Court, abolish sinecures, curb
the building craze, introduce simpler furniture and cheaper
apparel. Such austerity could only become effective if the people
joined in the reforming campaign. For this purpose it would
be necessary not only to summon the States General which had
not met for a century, but to integrate it into the life of the
nation, meeting every three years and sitting as long as circumstances required. Since the members would doubtless be as
moderate and loyal as the Estates of Languedoc and Brittany,
they could discuss every aspect of policy at home and abroad.

In his anxiety to limit the power of the ruler he argued that
Gallicanism was no longer necessary since the authority of Rome
had so sharply declined. Give the Church a little more freedom
and let the parishes have *curés* of their own choice. The most
conspicuous omission in this generous programme of reform is
the absence of any reference to liberty of conscience, for Fénelon
approved the revocation of the Edict of Nantes and had no use
for the Jansenists.

A few other points are made in a little essay, *Examen de conscience des devoirs de la royauté*, which urges the sovereign to inform
himself in detail of the state of the various classes and the working
of central and local institutions. Above all he must have no
favourites and must strive to avoid war, the mother of misery;
if forced to fight, he should observe the laws of war. 'He is the
cleverest and the most fantastical head in the kingdom,' grumbled
the old King. Had he peered more closely into that scintillating
brain he would have recoiled in anger at the audacity of its
schemes. That the Duc de Bourgogne never came to the throne
was the tragedy of Fénelon's life and was a major misfortune for
France, for the first seeds of revolution were sown in the closing
years of Louis XIV.

A scarcely less formidable critic of the *régime*, though he
attacked on a narrower front, emerged from a different camp.
Among the Marshals whose triumphs built up the renown of
Louis XIV none occupied a loftier place in the regard of his
countrymen and the Court than Vauban. Though Condé and
Turenne were his superiors on the battlefield, he was the prince
of military engineers whose fortresses on the eastern frontiers
remained the admiration of Europe long after his death. He was
also a man of noble character whose interests embraced the problems of peace no less than war. Staggered by the revocation of
the Edict of Nantes, he deplored in a letter to Louvois the blow
struck at industry and commerce and the revival of religious
strife. He forwarded a copy to Mme de Maintenon, but the
appeal fell on deaf ears. The decision, he argued, weakened
France by the loss of industrious citizens and strengthened her
enemies. Kings were masters of the life and property of their
subjects but not of their opinions, and they should not press
their prerogative too far.

His next venture was more ambitious and might appear to have more chance of success, for the financial plight of war-worn France was notorious. The Peace of Ryswick in 1697 was merely a truce after a generation of continuous struggle which emptied the treasury and almost beggared the people. The Intendants were instructed to investigate and report on the condition and needs of their districts. It was the wrong method of approach, for they were likely to minimise the evils and in some cases to conceal the causes which brought them gain. Far weightier was the counsel of Vauban who had studied conditions on the many journeys and marches of his long life. No one since Sully had displayed such deep and unflagging interest in the peasantry which he regarded as the backbone of the state. When the return of peace afforded him ampler leisure Vauban summarised his conclusions in *Le Dîme Royale*. Since France, he estimated, could support 24 millions but contained only 19, there was no over-population; the climate was temperate, the soil good, the peasantry thrifty and industrious. Why then was there such misery? Taxation was heavy but not unbearable if the burden were fairly distributed. The fundamental cause was that many contributed too much while the nobility and the clergy were exempt. The privilege of the former was an inheritance from feudal times, when the landed proprietors were expected to aid the Crown from their own resources in time of war. The exemption of the clergy was equally a survival from the ages when the Church was a law to itself. These financial entrenchments Richelieu himself had not attempted to storm. The gross injustice was resented by the *Tiers État*, but there were no channels through which it could express discontent. Every year the King's Council fixed the sum required from the several districts, and the local collectors required police protection. If the taxpayer could not meet the demand, his animals, agricultural implements, and even his furniture might be seized. The knowledge that a substantial portion of the yield never reached the coffers of the state increased the smart.

Minor changes, argued Vauban, were useless and a new deal was required. A tax should be levied on all citizens, ranging from 5 to 10 per cent according to the needs of the state, in place of the existing *taille*, local *douane* and *aides*. The idea of a tenth was

C

familiar to the Jews, the Greeks, the Romans, and the early French kings. The Church tithe aroused little complaint and involved no corruption. The hated *taille* was not adjusted to the capacity to pay, since the value of properties changed and gross favouritism was rife. To avoid the *taille* peasants often concealed their resources and went about in rags. Comparing the yield of tithe and *taille* in some fifty parishes, he discovered that the former yielded the larger sum. The *Dîme Royale* would be assessed on land, houses, mills, fisheries, salaries, pensions, and every other source of income, concealment of assets being punishable by confiscation and doubling the demand. Manual workers should only pay a thirtieth, since they were frequently unemployed and their standard of life was low. Passing to changes in indirect taxation, the author proposed the reduction of the salt tax which many were too poor to pay, and an extra charge on wine supplied in cabarets, a measure which might help to keep peasants at home and not waste their money on drink. The new system should be introduced gradually so that the whole country could witness its benefits. It was not intended to increase the total yield of taxation but to diminish the burden on those least able to bear it. Vauban expected opposition from the 'leeches and harpies'. He accepted autocracy but declared war on the swarm of parasites up to the highest levels.

The old soldier wrote, not to inflame the public, for his book was not on sale, but to convert the King and his council, expecting that his record of service would ensure attention if not gratitude. A manuscript copy was sent to the King who, if made aware of its contents, cannot have resented it, for the author was promoted a Marshal two years later. When, however, it was printed anonymously in 1707 without seeking the usual permission of the police, which he feared would be refused, a storm blew up. Though the book was presented only to a few influential friends the authorship was no secret, and it was denounced by the tax farmers and other vested interests. A demand was raised that the audacious reformer should be sent to the Bastille and his book destroyed. The shock was too much for the old warrior, who died of a broken heart. When the King heard the news he exclaimed: 'I lose a man greatly attached to my person and the state.' Perhaps he may have felt a momentary twinge of conscience that he had not held his shield over a faithful servant who was saluted by Saint-Simon as the best of Frenchmen. Three years later he was vindicated when the King imposed a special war levy of a tenth for three successive years.

On the same day, March 14, 1707, which witnessed the condemnation of the *Dîme Royale*, another formidable indictment of Government action and inaction was suppressed by decree. Speaking with inside knowledge of provincial administration Boisguillebert, a respected official in Normandy, described the sufferings of the people without sparing his superiors. While his *Détail de la France*, published in 1697, had been mainly statistical, his *Factum de la France*, published ten years later when the sky had become even darker, clamoured for the reform of taxation and the liberation of agriculture, the dominant industry of the country, from the stifling restrictions on purchase and sale. His appeal, like that of Vauban, fell on deaf ears, and the courageous critic was disgraced and transferred to the centre of France. The *ancien régime* had scarcely reached its zenith than it began its slow decline. Unfettered absolutism leads to the abuse of power, and the abuse of power to resistance, at first in thought and later in deed. Yet the pace was very slow and nothing could be done till the middle class, steadily increasing in numbers, wealth and self-confidence, took matters into their own hands. During the reign of Louis XIV far more *roturiers* dreamed, like Molière's *Bourgeois Gentilhomme*, of buying their way into the privileged classes than of attempting to alter the social stratification which reserved the highest prizes for the chosen few.

III

Louis XIV lived too long for his reputation, and during the last two decades of his reign he forfeited much of the respect he had enjoyed in his prime. The Augustan Age of French history had been as brief as it was brilliant. The change from the major to the minor key was recorded by many witnesses, with Saint-Simon and Madame, Duchess of Orleans, at their head. He himself was growing old and weary, though he put a brave face on his misfortunes. The distress which had inspired the composition of Vauban's *Dîme Royale* rapidly increased as the latest, longest, and fiercest of his many conflicts, the War of the Spanish Succession, dragged on year after year, with the scales turning steadily against France under the hammer blows of Marlborough and Prince Eugene. National bankruptcy was in sight. Critical pamphlets and verses began to appear for the first time since the *Mazarinades* in the days of his youth. The fruits of absolutism proved as bitter as those of feudal anarchy. In 1709 nature conspired to swell the mounting tide of misery with the cruellest and most prolonged winter in the history of France. The young Apollo who had trampled the serpent of faction under his feet and gathered the laurels of victory in a series of campaigns had withered into a disillusioned old man fighting for his life against a coalition provoked by placing his grandson on the throne of Spain.

He had always been industrious, and when Colbert and Louvois were gone he worked harder than ever. For eight or nine hours daily he presided over the Council of Ministers, studied reports from his Generals, gave audiences to Ambassadors, dictated replies and instructions, and occasionally, as in the correspondence with his grandson the King of Spain, wrote letters in his own hand. It was an exacting profession. The scandals of the early years were now a distant memory, and Mme de Maintenon had little reason to complain. The secret marriage left her official status unchanged. *La veuve Scarron*, ex-governess of the royal bastards, continued to be styled the Marquise de Maintenon, second *dame d'atours* of the Dauphine, but the royal *ménage* told its own tale. From 1685 onwards they were inseparable, and her apartments at the various palaces were connected with his own. His free moments were spent with her, and every evening he worked with one or other of his Ministers in her room. Though she took no part in the discussions she knew everything that was going on, and he discussed his many problems with a cool-headed and sympathetic woman who cared as little for money as for intrigue. 'She is a saint,' declared the King. 'She has all the perfections and plenty of intelligence, and I have none.' One day he remarked: 'Madame, a King is called Your Majesty, the Pope Your Holiness, and you should be Your Solidity.'

Döllinger's well-known description of Mme de Maintenon as the most influential woman in French history is unjust to Joan of Arc, Catherine de Medicis and Mme de Pompadour. That she took a lively interest in ecclesiastical affairs was known to everyone, but here too the King's will was her law. If he was ever influenced by any human being it was by his Jesuit confessors. Knowing the limits of her power she never dreamed of crossing the boundary, for unquestioning subordination was the condition of her hold on that wayward heart. She was fortified by the conviction that her sacrifice—she often felt it to be her martyrdom—was the will of God; she had rescued the proudest of European monarchs from a life of sin and enhanced the dignity of the Crown. She was also sustained by her love for the Duc du Maine, the Duchesse de Bourgogne, and her little girls in the École de Saint-Cyr. Romantic love she had never known, for her marriage to the semi-paralysed Scarron was a legal ceremony and nothing more, and her second venture was a *mariage de raison*. To understand her character and her trials we must turn from the caricature of Saint-Simon and the malice of Madame to her letters and to the affectionate record of her beloved secretary, Mlle d'Aumale. Saint-Simon's unscrupulous schemer was a woman of unblemished repute, unfailing tact, culture and refinement. The mud hurled at 'the old Sultana' and Mme Ordure by Liselotte does not stick. A fairer verdict was recorded at her death in the Journal of Dangeau who had studied her at close range for many years: 'a woman of such great merit who had done so much good and prevented so much harm that one cannot overpraise her.' That this tribute was denounced by Saint-Simon as 'a stinking lie' reflects discredit on the spiteful little Duke, not on the morganatic wife.

'Do you not see that I am dying of grief,' she wrote, 'and am only saved from collapse by the grace of God? Once I was young and pretty, enjoyed pleasures and was a general favourite. A little later I spent years in an intellectual circle. Then I came to favour, and I confess it all leaves a terrible void, a disquiet, a weariness, a desire for change.' The atmosphere of the Court filled her with disgust, and Mlle d'Aumale often saw her in tears. 'I witness every kind of passion, treacheries, meannesses, insensate ambitions, disgusting envy, people with hearts full of rage,

struggling to ruin each other, a thousand intrigues, often about
trifles. The women of today are insupportable, with their
immodest garb, their snuff, their wine, their gluttony, their
coarseness, their idleness. I dislike it all so much that I cannot
bear it.' Yet bear it she did for thirty years. Too reserved to
radiate very much warmth, she was respected by those who knew
her well and loved by those who knew her best. The notion that
she wished or the King wished her to be Queen is fantastic. She
possessed too much good sense, he too much pride.

Next to Mme de Maintenon the old monarch found his chief
happiness in Marie Adelaide, 'the Rose of Savoy', grandchild of
Monsieur and his first wife Henrietta of England, the child-wife
of the Duc de Bourgogne, who brought a gleam of sunshine
into the gloomy halls of Versailles and in the words of Madame,
Duchess of Orleans, made everyone feel young again, for she
was only eleven. 'She is a treasure,' reported Mme de Maintenon
to her mother, the Duchess of Savoy.

> She is the delight of the King, amusing him with her gaiety and
> pranks, though she never goes too far. One can talk seriously to
> her without being bored. She dislikes flattery and is grateful for
> advice. She gets prettier every day. She is growing a little and her
> figure is perfect. She dances well and no one ever possessed such
> grace. I never exaggerate. No one dreams of spoiling her. Per-
> haps it will not always be so. Traps are set for princes as for ordinary
> folk. I hope God will protect her. She fears and loves Him, and
> has a great respect for religion. Her education has been excellent
> and her range of knowledge is surprising.

Her only failing was a passion for the card table, which the
King unwisely encouraged by paying her debts. In her combination of youthful levity, natural charm, and warmth of heart she
reminds us of Marie Antoinette. During the first phase she
appealed more to the King and Mme de Maintenon than to her
austere husband, who disliked society and loved to shut himself
up with his books; but as motherhood ripened her character she
learned to appreciate his noble qualities, and it grew into the first
happy marriage in the Bourbon family.

When the shadowy figure of the Dauphin, his father's only
legitimate child, passed away at Meudon, few tears were shed.
The most colourless of the Bourbons had sought relief from

his lifelong inferiority complex in the pleasures of the table and the chase; 'sans vice ni vertu' comments Saint-Simon disdainfully. He had lost his Bavarian wife, and his three sons meant as little to him as he to them. His death at the age of fifty in 1711 was welcomed, not only because it removed the threat of a ruler totally unfitted for his task, but because it opened the way for a successor of exceptional promise. In dynastic autocracies the abilities, virtues and vices of the Royal Family make history. Twice in the course of the eighteenth century there seemed to be a chance of the Monarchy renewing itself, and twice the cup was snatched away by a cruel fate. When the full measure of the unworthiness of Louis XV came to be realised, the nation looked back nostalgically to the Duc de Bourgogne, the pupil of Fénelon. The King was very fond of him, testifies Mlle d'Aumale, and the whole Court adored him. He was born a terror, records Saint-Simon, and during his youth he made his entourage tremble by paroxysms of fury, for he could not bear the slightest opposition. Often there were storms so violent that his body seemed ready to burst. He was obstinate to a degree, with a passion for all kinds of pleasures—good cheer, the chase, music. He radiated intelligence. His repartees were astonishing, his answers pointed and profound, the most abstract subjects his delight. From this blend of dross and precious metal his admirable Governor the Duc de Beauvilliers, and his Preceptor Fénelon, we are told, fashioned a casket of shining gold. 'The marvel was that in a very short time their devotion made him another man, changing his faults into corresponding virtues. Out of this abyss we have witnessed the emergence of a prince affable, gentle, human, generous, patient, modest, humble and—for himself—austere. His only thought is to fulfil his duties as a son and a subject as well as those to which he is summoned by destiny.' His youthful passion for the card table had been overcome, and Mme de Maintenon, an exacting critic, described him as a saint.

Among the papers found in his desk after his death was a meditation on the call awaiting him which confirms Saint-Simon's portrait.

Of all the people who compose a nation the one who deserves most pity and receives least is the sovereign. He has all the disadvantages of grandeur without its delights. Of all his subjects he has the least liberty, the least tranquillity, the fewest moments for himself. Soldiers go into winter quarters, magistrates have vacations, everyone has periods of rest: for the King there are none and never will be. If he changes his residence, his work follows him. A day of inaction involves a crushing task next day or else everything stagnates. His whole life is spent in a whirlpool of business—a round of ceremonies, anxieties, disagreeable tasks, solicitations without end. His plans go wrong. The people, conscious of their evils, ignore his efforts to help. In appointments he seeks for merit but is deceived. He tries to make someone happy, but he reaps discontent and ingratitude. He has palaces which he has not seen and riches which he does not enjoy. He fulfils St. Paul's ideal of a Christian: he has everything and possesses nothing. Strictly speaking he is the poorest of his subjects, for all the needs of the state are his needs and they always exceed his fortune. A father is never rich when his income does not suffice for the sustenance of his children.

The Duc de Bourgogne was fortified by the counsel and affection of friends who composed what Saint-Simon calls *le petit troupeau*, which stood for piety, austerity, and reform. He needed moral support, for the disastrous campaign of 1708, in which he held a high command, had depreciated his stock. The leader of 'the little flock' was the Duc de Beauvilliers, one of the few stainless figures, *sans peur et sans reproche*, on the crowded stage at Versailles. At his side stood his brother-in-law, the Duc de Chevreuse, who shared his devotion to the heir to the throne. Both of them looked up to Fénelon, who, though banished from the Court, remained in close touch by correspondence. The youngest member of the group was Saint-Simon who in long private talks urged him to restore the political influence of the *noblesse* when he was called to the helm.

His testing time came sooner than he expected, for his father died of smallpox. During the five days of his illness the Duke and his wife held open court and were equally gracious to all comers. In Saint-Simon's glowing phrase it was like the coming of spring. Not only was the whole Court there but *tout Paris et tout Meudon* flocked to worship the rising sun. When the news of the Dauphin's death reached Versailles late at night Saint-Simon rushed out of his apartments and found *tout Versailles* assembled or assembling, the ladies emerging from their beds or bedrooms just as they were. The new Dauphin—'*tout simple*,

tout saint, tout plein de ses devoirs'—embodied the hopes of all that
was best in France. He had discussed financial reform with
Vauban and was prepared for still more fundamental measures:
the machinery of government must be transformed and a popular
element introduced. Looking beyond the walls of the palace he
longed to aid the common man and the common soldier who had
never had their chance. It was a false dawn, for within a year the
Dauphin, his wife, and their eldest son died within ten days.
For once Saint-Simon, who could love as well as hate, gave way
to passionate grief. The Duke, he declares, was born for the
happiness of France and all Europe. 'We were not worthy of
him. I wished to withdraw from the Court and the world, and
it needed all the wisdom and influence of my wife to prevent it,
for I was in despair.' To the Duc de Beauvilliers he exclaimed
after the last scene at St. Denis: 'We have been burying France,'
and Beauvilliers agreed. Their grief was shared by Mme de
Maintenon, who wrote to the Princesse des Ursins: 'Everything
is gone, everything seems empty, there is no more joy. The
King does his best to keep up his spirits, but he cannot shake
off his sorrow.' Never in the history of France has there been
such universal regret at the death of a reigning monarch or heir.
In the words of Duclos it would have been an era of justice,
order, and morals.

The Duke of Orleans, now marked out as the future Regent
for the little boy of two who was to become Louis XV, shared
some of the views of the Duc de Bourgogne, but he never
inspired the devotion and respect which had been so widely
entertained for the pupil of Fénelon. The three remaining years
of the most memorable reign in the history of France were a
gloomy time. The routine of Court life, the music, the gambling,
continued, but the sparkle had disappeared. The weary old
monarch, like Francis Joseph at a later date, plodded joylessly
through his papers. The fairest flower of the Court, the only
member of the Royal Family whom he had taken to his heart,
was sorely missed, and Mme de Maintenon, always a restful
rather than an exhilarating influence, was nearing eighty. The
victory of Villars at Denain saved the French cause on the brink
of catastrophe, and procured an honourable settlement in the
Treaty of Utrecht, for the King's grandson retained the Spanish

throne. Yet the country was exhausted by half a century of warfare, poverty-stricken and depressed, and the ruler felt that he was no longer beloved. It was time to go, and he died with the dignity which had never deserted him in good and evil times. The sun went down in a bank of dark clouds, for the heir was a delicate lad of five. The second grandson was far away in Madrid and had resigned his claim to the throne. The third grandson, the Duc de Berry, had passed away in 1714. On his deathbed the King sent for his great-grandson and addressed the little boy in words which deeply moved all who were present. 'My child, you will one day be a great King. Do not imitate me in my taste for war. Always relate your actions to God, and make your subjects honour Him. It breaks my heart to leave them in such a state. Always follow good advice; love your peoples; I give you Père Le Tellier as your Confessor; never forget the gratitude you owe the Duchess de Ventadour.' He embraced the child, gave him his blessing, lifted his hands and uttered a little prayer as he watched him leave the room. 'Not a day passed,' testifies Villars, 'without some mark of strength, goodness, and above all, piety. His instructions for the funeral were given with such clarity and self-control that he seemed to be making arrangements for someone else.'

Shortly before his last illness the King drafted instructions for his great-grandson which he requested Marshal Villeroi to hand to him on reaching the age of seventeen.

My son, if Providence allows you to shape your own life, receive this letter from the hands of the faithful subject who has promised me to deliver it. You will find therein the last wishes of your father and your King who, in quitting this world, feels such tenderness for you in your childhood that the troubles he apprehends during your minority cause him more anxiety than the terrors of approaching death. If anything can soften my pain it is the promise of good subjects who have sworn to me to watch over you and shed their blood for your preservation. Reward them and never forget them, nor the services of my son the Duc du Maine whom I find worthy to be placed at your side. This distinction will doubtless be assailed by those whose desire to rule it frustrates. If anything happens to him, or if my dispositions in his favour are set aside, I desire you to restore everything to the position existing at my death, both as regards religion and the Duc du Maine. Have confidence in him. Follow his advice. He is quite able to guide you. If death deprives you of such a good subject, preserve for his children the rank I have bestowed on them, and show them all the friendship you owe to their father who has sworn to me only to abandon you at death. Let the ties of blood and friendship ever unite you to the King of Spain and allow no reason or misunderstood political interest to separate you. That is the only way to preserve peace and the European equilibrium. Maintain an inviolable attachment to the common father of the faithful, and never for any reason separate yourself from the bosom of the Church. Place all your confidence in God, live rather as a Christian than a King, and never incur His displeasure by moral irregularities. Thank Divine Providence which so visibly protects this kingdom. Set your subjects the same example as a Christian father to his family. Make them happy if you desire happiness.. Relieve them as soon as possible of all the heavy burdens necessitated by a long war which they bore with fidelity and patience. Grant them the long periods of peace which alone can restore your kingdom. Always prefer peace to the hazards of war, and remember that the most brilliant victory is too dearly bought at the expense of your subjects' blood, which should only be shed for the glory of God. This conduct will earn the blessing of heaven during your reign. Receive my blessing in this last embrace.

The future of France was constantly in his thoughts. Addressing the courtiers and officials from his bed he commended his successor to their care. 'He is only five. He will greatly need your zeal and fidelity. I request for him the same sentiments you have often shown for myself. I advise him to avoid wars. I have made too many, and they compelled me to lay heavy burdens on my people. This I deeply regret and I ask the pardon of God.'

A briefer and somewhat similar declaration of faith was embodied in the maxims for his grandson on leaving to assume the crown of Spain in 1700.

Love your wife, and ask God for one to suit you—not an Austrian. Beware of flatterers. Esteem those who risk your displeasure, for they are your real friends. Only wage war if you are compelled, and then take command yourself. Never have a Favourite or a mistress. Be the master. Consult your Council but decide yourself. God, who has made you King, will provide all the wisdom you require so long as your intentions are good.

Having by this time dispensed with mistresses the royal moralist no longer claimed indulgence for the weakness of young rulers which he had regretfully recognised thirty or more years earlier.

The closing scene was most vividly described by his sister-in-law the Duchess of Orleans in a letter written four days before the end.

Today we have witnessed the saddest and most touching scene imaginable. Our dear King, after preparing himself for death and receiving the last sacraments, sent for the little Dauphin, and gave him his blessing. Then he summoned the Duchesse de Berry, myself, and all the other girls and grandchildren. He bade me farewell with such tenderness that I wonder I did not faint. He said he had always loved me, more than I knew; that he regretted to have hurt me at times; begged me to think of him sometimes, which he believed I should do as I had always felt affection for him. He gave me his blessing and wished me happiness. I fell at his knees and kissed his hand, and he embraced me. Then he spoke to the others and exhorted them to unity. I thought he was speaking to me, and said I would obey him in that as in everything. He smiled and said: I was not speaking to you, for I know you are too sensible; I was speaking to the other princesses. The King's self-control is indescribable. He issues his orders as if he were merely going on a journey.

Louis XIV had raised France to the highest pinnacle in the first half of his reign, but he lived long enough to destroy much of his handiwork. 'I noticed in my youth,' wrote Duclos many years later, 'that those who lived longest under his reign were the least favourable to him.' The colossal national debt resulting from many years of war hung like a millstone round the neck of his descendants, and the system of government could only be operated by a ruler of equal capacity. The population had fallen by one-fifth in half a century owing to war casualties, the expulsion of the Huguenots, and widespread starvation. Agricultural production had declined in an even more alarming ratio. Considerable areas went out of cultivation, the country swarmed with robbers, and bread riots were frequent. Direct and indirect taxes, tithes and feudal burdens were a nightmare at a time of bad harvests and dear bread. Old taxes had been increased and new ones—the *capitation* and the *dixième*—imposed. Every possible source of revenue was exploited, including forced loans, lotteries, the issue of paper money, the sale of titles and official posts, and the depreciation of the currency. France, still almost entirely an agricultural country, was sucked nearly dry. Huge annual deficits added to the national debt, and the revenues of the coming years were mortgaged to meet immediate needs. The glitter of a lavish Court offered a grim contrast to the spectre of hunger which stalked through the land. The sufferings of the people were far more grievous in 1715 than on the eve of the Revolution in 1789. Such was the price his subjects had to pay for the greater glory of the *Roi Soleil*.

2

THE REGENCY ERA

I

ON the morning of September 1, 1715, when the chapel clock
had struck a quarter past eight, Louis XIV passed away
three days before his seventy-seventh birthday, in the seventy-
second year of his reign. Only Père Le Tellier, his Jesuit Confessor, and the Duc de Villeroi, Captain of the Guard, were with
him at the end. A few minutes later an officer in a hat with a
black plume stepped out on to a balcony. Removing his hat he
shouted 'Le Roi est mort' and disappeared. A moment later he
reappeared with a white plume, doffed his hat and cried three
times 'Vive le Roi Louis XV.' Few tears were shed in the palace
or beyond its walls. Mme de Maintenon, who had never cared
for Court life, retired to her École de Saint-Cyr, where she spent
the happiest years of her eventful career among her little girls.
France sighed for a change. Everyone was tired of the old ruler
who had left an empty treasury and a mountain of debts. 'Some
hoping to play a part,' reports Saint-Simon, 'were delighted to
witness the end of a reign from which they had nothing more
to expect. Others, wearied by a crushing yoke—of the Ministers
even more than of the ruler—welcomed their freedom. Everyone
was glad to be relieved from a continual strain and hungered
for new ways.' The people, he adds, ruined, crushed and in
despair, gave thanks to God with a scandalous exuberance.
When the funeral *cortège* passed through Paris on the way to
St. Denis there was dancing, singing and drinking in the streets,

and insults were hurled at the corpse. The spell was broken. In his best days he had inspired respect and admiration, but he was too much of a demigod to be loved. Never again was the Crown to recover the prestige at home and abroad which it had known under the greatest of the Bourbon Kings.

The first public duty of the new King, accompanied by his Governess the Duchesse de Ventadour, was to receive the homage of his subjects. The pretty boy of five, with curly hair, delicate features and long plumes in his hat, combined grace and dignity, seeming, we learn from Buvat, much older than his years. His parents had been more generally liked than any members of the Royal Family for half a century, and their son inherited their popularity. The first of the nobles to greet him was Philip, Duke of Orleans, aged forty-two. 'Sire,' he exclaimed, 'I come to pay my respects as the first of your subjects.' However many sins weighed on his conscience, neglect of his duties to the Crown was not among them. He felt genuine affection for the shy lad who during the eight years of the Regency always regarded him as a friend. The belief that he wished to poison him and inherit the throne was a monstrous libel on a kindly man without much ambition. We know the gifted and dissolute Regent as we know few other eighteenth-century princes, for he lives in the voluminous correspondence of his mother and the Memoirs of Saint-Simon, the most faithful of his friends. The best feature in his complex character was his steady affection for Liselotte, who made allowance for the fact that he had not been permitted to choose his wife, and in that dissolute age no one expected him to be a faithful husband. 'He is quite crazy about women,' she reported. 'Provided they are good-tempered, indelicate, great eaters and drinkers, he troubles little about their looks.' When she complained of his choice of ugly women he blandly rejoined: 'Bah! Maman, dans la nuit tous les chats sont gris.' The orgies of the Palais Royal became the talk of Europe, but, like his uncle, he allowed his mistresses no political influence. A second failing was drunkenness, though in fairness we must remember that two or three glasses were enough to upset him. A third was his licentious talk, so gross that his long-suffering wife dared not invite decent folk to their table. A fourth was his open scorn of religion, and he was said to read a volume of Rabelais during

Mass. No wonder Louis XIV called him *un fanfaron de crimes* and dreaded his rise to power. On the credit side, however, there were some excellent qualities. He was gracious, human, generous, tolerant, open-minded, deeply interested in science and art, and fully aware of France's desperate plight. No Bourbon prince came so close to the pattern of a Renaissance ruler, combining military prowess and intellectual tastes with the unbridled lusts of the flesh. 'He has the best intentions,' reported his mother, 'and he loves his country more than his life. He works all day and wears himself out. He would like to see everyone happy. For tradition he cares nothing. He is very nice to me, shows me real friendship, and would grieve to lose me. His daily visits are a joy. His stories always make me laugh. I should be an unnatural mother if I did not love him with all my heart.' The fairies, she added, had been invited to his birth, and each had given him a talent; but one of them had been forgotten and, arriving later, remarked that he would possess all the talents except the capacity to use them. He pitied his wife, who bore him eight children, even more than himself, for he possessed compensations which she was denied.

That the most dissolute Prince of the age could win the friendship of better men is proved by the unchanging devotion of Saint-Simon. The proud little Duke had stood by him when the courtiers cut him, and when he was insulted by the mob at the funeral of the Duc de Bourgogne in the belief that he was a poisoner. Though they were almost of the same age, Saint-Simon regarded him as his political pupil and never ceased to tender advice. They spoke a hundred times of the plight of France—the necessity to break with the system of the detested Mazarin and to restore the power of the *Noblesse* which had been largely usurped by the bourgeois (*gens de rien*) and the lawyers (*gens de robe*). The Regent let his friend talk, but he was too much of a liberal to approve the restoration to power of men who had been excluded from affairs for so long that many had become mere drones. Whatever changes might be made in the machinery of government everything would depend on the Regent, whose notorious failings filled Saint-Simon with apprehension.

I was the only person with whom he could have heart to heart talks. He was gifted by nature, and his first instincts were usually right.

He never gave himself airs. He had the weakness of believing himself like Henri IV. Like Henri IV he was naturally kind, human, compassionate. He wished no harm to anyone. He loved liberty, for others as well as for himself. In England, he used to say, there were no *lettres de cachet*. He had no ambition either to reign or to rule. No one was more expressly formed to secure the happiness of France. Unfortunately he was badly educated. He had been ruined by his evil genius, the Abbé Dubois, whom his father in an unlucky hour had chosen as his tutor.

That influence was the more fatal since the pupil was a weak nature, drawn rather to the arts and sciences than to politics. He laughed at decorum. Like all the members of the Royal Family he had been excluded from affairs by his formidable uncle, and when his chance came he was too old to change. He divided Frenchmen into clever rascals and honest imbeciles, declares d'Argenson, and only the former were employed.

Another vivid portrait was painted by Duclos.

Though not tall he possessed ease and grace. Endowed with rare penetration and sagacity, he expressed himself with vivacity and precision. His repartees were prompt and gay. His first judgments were the best; second thoughts often clouded his will. A quick reader, with a good memory, he seemed rather to sense things than to study them. He had a fair acquaintance with painting and music, chemistry and mechanics. Though modest in speaking of his military valour and severe on those whose courage was suspect, he would have held high military rank had the King allowed. He was thoroughly approachable, feeling that personal distinction rendered it needless to stand on his dignity. He bore no malice, but the cause of this indifference was his contempt for mankind. He believed that his most devoted servants would have been his enemies had it been to their interest. This pose he learned from Dubois, the most corrupt of men. He was most amiable, talented, brave, kindly, but one of the worst of rulers. The Duchess possessed figure, intelligence, virtue, but she felt that she conferred no less honour on her husband than she received. Proud of her royal birth she never gave a thought to her mother, Mme de Montespan. She was jokingly compared to Minerva who, acknowledging no mother, boasted of being the daughter of Jupiter. Her hauteur fortified the taste of the Duke for a free life. Human and sympathetic, he would have had virtues if that were possible without principles, which Dubois had destroyed in him. The leading-strings in which the

D

King held him made him a great admirer of English liberty, and the liberty he desired for himself he allowed to others. If he liked people they became his equals. Despite his talents and intellectual resources he could never suffice for himself: he needed dissipation, noise, debauchery. He admitted into his circle people whom no one with self-respect would recognise as friends despite their birth and rank. Though he took pleasure in their company he did not respect them, calling them *mes roués* to their face. One evening at supper the Comtesse de Sabran remarked that when God created man a little mud remained from which was formed the soul of princes and lackeys, and the Regent laughed with delight at the *mot*. As to religion he affected a scandalous impiety. He celebrated the festivals of the Church by spectacular debaucheries and made a cult of his impiety. But in doubting the existence of God he frequented fortune-tellers with all the credulity of a simpleton. Had he been seriously ill he might well have had recourse to relics or holy water.

The most urgent task of the new era was to decide who should stand at the helm during the long minority of the King. The Royal Family, like the Court, was divided between the champions of the *Légitimes* and the *Légitimés*, captained respectively by the Duc d'Orleans and the Duc du Maine. In 1694 Louis XIV had placed his bastards, Maine and Toulouse, directly after the princes of the blood in the official hierarchy, and before foreign princes, dukes and peers. After the death of his youngest grandson the Duc de Berry in 1714 he declared that the sons of the Duc du Maine should enjoy the same honours as their father. In July of the same year he took a more important step by declaring that the *Légitimés* should inherit the Crown in default of legitimate heirs. Though the Orleans family had the better right, the old King hoped to keep the succession in the direct line. Saint-Simon was horrified, but the public was used to autocracy and the *Parlement* registered the edict without any fuss. The status of the *Légitimés*, however, was only part of the problem, for who should take control till the heir came of age? That his nephew should hold the reins of power filled the old ruler with dismay. His fears were shared by Fénelon, who regarded Orleans as enslaved by a degenerate daughter. To avert such perils the King drew up a will, dated August 2, 1714, providing for a Regency Council consisting of fourteen persons, among them Maine and Toulouse, Orleans, the Duc de Bourbon, Marshals

Villeroi and Villars, and the Secretaries of State, which should reach decisions by majority vote; no Regent was named. The education of the heir and the command of the Household troops were entrusted to the Duc du Maine, with Marshal Villeroi as Governor under his control. Louis XIV was well aware that his authority would end with his life, and he could only express his wishes.

On September 4, 1715, Orleans called a meeting of the *Parlement* of Paris—all three chambers sitting together—to hear the reading of the will. He knew he could count on its support, for he promised to restore the cherished right of remonstrance which had been withdrawn. Saint-Simon vividly describes the arrival of the bastards, smiling and confident, almost bursting with joy, since they knew what the document contained. Their satisfaction was short-lived, for Orleans was unanimously declared Regent before the will was read. 'It seemed as if the whole *Parlement* was determined to ignore the instructions,' wrote Marshal Villars in his Memoirs, 'and to make the Duke of Orleans Regent and absolute master.' That the express instructions of *Le Roi Soleil* should be set aside almost before his body was cold symbolised that the *Grand Siècle* was over and that a new era of independence had dawned. During the reading of the will Orleans intervened. 'I have been proclaimed Regent and during the minority I ought to possess the power of the King.' He was now authorised to select the members of the Council of Regency, which was to have merely deliberative powers. This decision, reports Saint-Simon, was received with such acclamation that Maine dared not open his mouth. On the following day the members of the *Parlement* complimented the King on his accession. The lad was frankly bored. 'He would be very nice,' commented Madame, 'if he would talk a little: it is difficult to extract a word. He seems to love no one except perhaps his governess.' On September 12 the solemn ceremony of a *lit de justice*, in which the sovereign attended a meeting of the *Parlement*, confirmed the new arrangements.

The Duc du Maine lacked ambition, but his spirited Condé wife resented the spectacular rebuff. Her views were shared by the King of Spain who had never ceased to feel himself French. Though he had renounced his claim to the throne, he believed

that he possessed the best title to the post of Regent. After three
years of rule the popularity of Orleans had ebbed, and in 1718
the Cellamare Conspiracy, which took its name from the Spanish
Ambassador in Paris, brought the latent rivalry to a head. The
plan of kidnapping the Regent and substituting his master was
born in the busy brain of Alberoni, an Italian adventurer who
dominated the policy of Madrid through the masterful Italian
Queen. In France the soul of the movement was the ambitious
Duchesse du Maine, granddaughter of the Grand Condé, of
whom Madame acidly remarked that if she were as good as she
was malicious, there would be nothing against her. We may well
believe Saint-Simon's testimony that her colourless husband,
ever mindful of his illegitimate birth, trembled before her. She
cuts only a slightly better figure in the Memoirs of her *dame
d'honneur* Mme Staal-Delaunay, for she had more head than heart
and inspired little confidence or affection in any quarter. When
the incriminating dispatches, which were not in cipher, were
intercepted *en route*, the Maines were interned for a year in
different places of residence.

Not a drop of blood was shed by the kindly Regent, who knew
that the conspiracy had never constituted a serious danger, and
felt some sympathy with the Duc du Maine, who had known
nothing of his wife's machinations; but the time had come to
put the bastards in their place. Saint-Simon had long urged his
friend to act. 'I was the oldest, the most attached and the most
outspoken of his servants, and he trusted me without reserve.
But he was on his guard against what he called my vivacity, my
love for my dignity which was challenged by the bastards and
the activities of the *Parlements*.' It was decided that the Regent
should announce his decision to the Council, and he assured Saint-
Simon that he would not flinch. The secret had been well kept,
and the members had the surprise of their lives when a serene
but determined voice announced that the *Légitimés* (the Duc du
Maine and the Comte de Toulouse) were deprived of the privileges granted to them under their father's will, and that the
education of the young King was transferred to the Duc de
Bourbon, head of the house of Condé. 'The Regent,' records
Saint-Simon, 'wore an air of authority that was new to me.'
Each member of the Council was asked for his opinion. There

was no overt opposition, but the faces of Villars and Villeroi told their own tale. The second act of the drama began when the *Parlement* met to register the decisions of the Council, and the young King, as was usual on solemn occasions, was present. When the ceremony was over Saint-Simon congratulated the Regent on his firmness, but his joy was clouded when he was asked to break the news of the humiliation of her brother to his neglected wife at St. Cloud. 'I am the last person for the task,' he exclaimed, 'for my hostility to the bastards is notorious.' 'No,' was the reply, 'she likes you and admires your frankness.' She had no love for her brothers, but she was sensitive about her position and her prestige largely depended on theirs. She wept bitterly and promptly drove to Paris to see her husband. Very different was the reception of the news by Madame, who rejoiced at the firmness of her son. Maine and Toulouse took their final humiliation with a good grace. The autocratic little Duchesse du Maine abandoned politics and found scope for her restless energies among the Philosophes who thronged her court at Sceaux, among them President Hénault and Mme du Deffand, Mme du Châtelet and Voltaire.

The final eclipse of the bastards filled Saint-Simon with such delight that he feared his heart would cease to beat, but the failings of his friend caused him corresponding distress. He particularly resented the influence of his old tutor, later his secretary and chief adviser, the Abbé Dubois, who had encouraged him in sin. 'All the vices competed within him for the first place: avarice, debauchery and ambition were his gods, perfidy, flattery and subservience his means. Falsity oozed out of every pore.' He was treacherous, ungrateful and malicious, a blasphemer and an unbeliever. He was no less detested by Madame. When the Regent visited her immediately after the meeting at which the will of the late King was set aside, she received him with the words: 'My son, I desire only the good of the state and your glory. I ask only one thing for your honour—a promise never to employ that arch-rascal Dubois.' Later she described him as a fox crouching for a spring on a chicken. All appeals were unavailing. Despite the hatred and contempt Dubois inspired, old ties proved too strong for the Regent, and the two men collaborated till the end. Appointed a Councillor of State,

Dubois assumed control over foreign affairs. His first task was to repair the friendship with England, his second to counterwork the intrigues of Alberoni, who was dismissed by his master after French troops crossed the frontier. The policy was better than the man, whose ambition and greed were insatiable. He demanded and received the Archbishopric of Cambrai, the richest See in France, and later a Cardinal's hat, in addition to enjoying the revenues of seven abbeys. Part of the undying odium attaching to the Regency is due to the fact that the power behind the throne was the shady Dubois.

Scarcely less painful to his mother and his friends—and far more harmful to his reputation—was the Regent's passion for his eldest daughter the Duchesse de Berry, which led contemporaries to talk openly of incest and twentieth-century scholars to leave the question open. Since the narrow piety of his eldest son was an unspoken rebuke to his evil life, the Regent centred his affections on his daughters. He visited the second, the Abbesse de Chelles, once a week, but it was only in the society of the eldest that he felt completely at home. Married in 1710 at the age of fourteen to her cousin the Duc de Berry, the youngest grandson of Louis XIV, she found herself a childless widow four years later, with a large income, a palace, a household of eight hundred, and nothing to do but enjoy herself. Her amours were as notorious as those of her father, and she was no less addicted to drink. He met her lovers at her suppers at the Luxembourg with as little embarrassment as she met the Parabère and the Falari at the Palais Royal. If we are to believe Saint-Simon, she would drink till she rolled on the floor and vomited over the guests. When drunk she would use vile language and call her mother a bastard. 'She imported into her amours an incredible frenzy, a temperament of fire.' Without a blush she called her circle *mes roués*. Like almost all members of the Royal Family she was an inveterate gambler and piled up enormous debts. The intensity of her father's grief on her early death seemed to confirm the rumour that he was drawn to her by something more than parental affection. 'There is no longer a Court,' lamented Madame. 'Would to God that the late King were alive. I found more satisfaction in a single day than in six years of the Regency of my son. Then there really was a Court, and not this bourgeois

life to which I cannot accustom myself, I who have been bred at
Court and spent all my life there.' It was typical of a freer age
that anyone could join in the Opera balls, masked or otherwise,
which the Regent inaugurated, by payment of six francs. The
Tiers État was slowly moving towards the centre of the stage.

The Regent meant well, but he was unfitted by training or
temperament for his task. He experimented with a system which
evoked high hopes but soon came to nought. It was the dream
of Saint-Simon, as it had been of the Duc de Bourgogne, to
diminish the authority of the King—and still more of his Ministers
—by restoring the influence of the *Noblesse*. The departments of
state, he argued, should be placed under the control of Councils
staffed mainly by peers like himself, whom he regarded as the
most precious element in the life of the country and the pillars
of the throne. Seven Councils were created and their Presidents
attended the meetings of the Council of Regency. The result was
disappointing, for they worked slowly and found it difficult to
reach decisions. They were abolished in 1718, and power was
once more concentrated in the Ministers.

Constitutional issues were dwarfed by the financial chaos. In
addition to the funded debt bequeathed by the wars of Louis
XIV, the floating debt was a nightmare. The Government could
only raise loans at ever-mounting interest, the *billets d'état* were
only worth a quarter of their face value, and part of the prospective yield of taxation was pledged for two years ahead. Much
of the revenue flowed into the pockets of the tax farmers who
had bought the right to collect taxes and proceeded to feather
their nests. The yield was declining while industry and commerce
languished for lack of capital. The Duc de Noailles, President of
the Council of Finance, lacked not only the drive but the vision
to cope with an emergency which threatened the existence of
France as a Great Power. Though Saint-Simon's audacious plan
for a declaration of national bankruptcy on the ground that it
would aid the many at the expense of the few was rightly rejected,
it was generally agreed that drastic remedies were required.

At this moment John Law, the gifted son of an Edinburgh
goldsmith, offered his services to the Regent whose confidence
he had won on a visit to Paris during a continental tour. Since
France, he argued, possessed a rich soil, a favourable climate, and

an industrious population, her evil plight must be due to mis-management. Industry and commerce needed more capital for development than the private banks could supply, and the state must employ its credit. The first principle of his system was the issue of paper money by a State Bank which would eliminate the usurers. Since the Regent's confidence in the foreigner was not generally shared, Law was merely permitted to establish a bank at his own risk with a limited power to issue notes. It made such a good start that two years later it was transformed into a State Bank and its notes became legal tender. The provision of money in ample quantities oiled the wheels of industry for a time, but Law's fertile mind ranged far beyond the home market. The second pillar of his system was the development of France's colonial empire, and in 1717 he founded a company working in harmony with the State Bank for the exploitation of Louisiana in which French citizens were invited to invest their savings. It was a statesmanlike long-range conception, and the Mississippi Company took over various minor enterprises in Africa and the New World; but the Company of the Indies, as it was now styled, required almost unlimited capital. Since Law's prestige was at its height the public joyfully responded and the shares soared like a rocket. He was made financial dictator of France, and the Bank and the Company were united; but the orgy of speculation got beyond control, too much paper money had been issued, shares toppled down, the bubble burst, and the wizard fled to Italy. Only the Company of the Indies survived the wreck, with its wings clipped. A few speculators had scored and many credulous moths had been scorched in the flame. It was characteristic of the Regent, a loyal friend, that he never lost faith in the man who had striven—not wisely but with good intent—to raise France from the mire.

'In all I undertake for the good of the people,' the Regent informed the *Parlement*, 'I shall be aided by your counsel and wise remonstrances.' Relations were friendly enough at the outset, but the honeymoon ended when the magistrates claimed the right to veto legislation. Declining to weaken the prerogative of the Crown during the minority of Louis XV, he dismissed Noailles and the Chancellor d'Aguesseau, who were regarded as too favourable to the *Parlement*, and appointed d'Argenson, the

vigorous Minister of Police, as Chancellor and President of the
Council of Finance, with Dubois as Foreign Minister. For the
second time the easy-going Regent asserted himself. When the
Parlement opposed Law's schemes and vetoed the issue of a new
coinage, a *lit de justice* was held and it was deprived of the right
of remonstrance, relapsing into the subordinate position it had
held under Louis XIV. It was forbidden to interfere in questions
of administration and finance, and the members were exiled to
Pontoise. A torrent of 'Philippics' was launched against the
Regent. It was a fight with the gloves off, and the cry was raised
'Tuez le tyran.' Such scenes had been unknown since the dark
days of the Fronde. A further blow for autocracy was struck by
suppressing the quasi-autonomy of the Breton Estates.

That the liberalism of the opening phase of the Regency was
merely skin-deep was further illustrated when the Government
sought closer relations with the Vatican as a means to secure the
coveted Cardinal's hat for the all-powerful Dubois. On the death
of Louis XIV the imprisoned Jansenists had been released and
the Jesuit confessor Le Tellier dismissed; there was talk of suppressing the Jesuits, and lenient treatment was ordered for the
Huguenots. The wind veered in 1717 when the Regent announced
the opening of negotiations with Rome and forbade further controversy on the Bull '*Unigenitus*'. When in 1718 the Pope ordered
entire obedience to the Bull under threat of excommunication,
all the *Parlements* protested against the revival of a claim to
authority, but their protest was in vain. When the Regent ordered
the registration of the hated Bull, the *Parlement* yielded and was
allowed to return to Paris. His injunction to stop discussing
Jansenist theology was ignored, for the Jansenists were prepared
for any sacrifice and the flood of pamphlets continued for another
twenty years. The transformation of the sceptical Regent from
a friend of the Gallicans, the lawyers, the Jansenists and the
Huguenots into a patron of the Jesuits destroyed what was left
of his popularity, and his rule ended in an atmosphere of resentful
discontent. 'Mon fils est aimé,' reported Madame in the first
year of the Regency. Neither his mother nor Saint-Simon, his
two stoutest champions, could have written such words during
the closing phase.

The year 1723 witnessed a series of events which registered

the end of an era. In February Louis XV, who had recently moved to Versailles, came of age on his thirteenth birthday, and the Regency came juridically to an end. In August Dubois passed away, and the Duke of Orleans succeeded him as First Minister. On December 2 the ex-Regent collapsed at the feet of his mistress the Duchesse de Falari and died of apoplexy without a word, worn out by his debaucheries at the age of fifty-one. After the bursting of the Mississippi bubble and the death of his daughter he had lost his *joie de vivre*. Other men, among them the Duc de Richelieu, were worse than he, but no one did so much to debase the moral currency. While Louis XIV had striven in his later years to make amends for his sins, his nephew sinned to the end. Paris had welcomed him as a relief from the stuffy Court of the old King, but in a few hectic years he squandered the heritage of goodwill and the country was glad to see him go. The only gleam in a dark sky shone from the pretty face of the boy King.

II

During the closing phase of the Regency a sombre picture of politics and society was painted by Montesquieu in his *Lettres Persanes*, the French equivalent of *Gulliver's Travels* and one of the classics of political literature. Since French travellers had recently described the ways of Persia, it occurred to the young lawyer to bring two Persian Moslems to Europe—Rica, a light-hearted mocker, and Uzbek, a more serious observer. Taken together they are the voice of the author, a complex personality in whom the *frondeur* and the *esprit fort* jostled the earnest reformer and the future author of the *Esprit des Lois*. Having no desire to explore the interior of the Bastille, he published his book in Cologne and without a name. While the majestic *Esprit des Lois* is rarely studied except by students, the *Lettres Persanes*, with their sparkling satire, remain as popular as *Candide*.

In his first letter written from Paris a month after the arrival of the travellers and dated 1712, Rica explains the institutions of the country.

The King of France is the most powerful prince in Europe. He has no gold mines, like his neighbour the King of Spain, but he is richer since he exploits the vanity of his subjects which is more inexhaustible. He has financed great wars by the sale of titles. He is also a great magician, ruling over the minds of his people and making them think as he wishes. If he has only a million crowns in his treasury and needs two, he has only to say that one crown equals two and they believe him. If there is no cash to sustain a difficult war he merely proclaims that a piece of paper is money and they are promptly convinced. He can even make them believe that illness is cured by the royal touch.

After a year in Paris Uzbek paints an elaborate and darkly shadowed portrait of Louis XIV.

The King of France is old: we have no example in our history of so long a reign. He is said to possess a rare talent for making himself obeyed, and he governs with the same virtuosity his family, his Court and his state. He has often said that of all the governments in the world he prefers those of Turkey and our own country. I have studied his character and have discovered contradictions which it is impossible to resolve. For instance, he has a minister of eighteen and a mistress of eighty; he loves his religion but cannot abide those who say it must be vigorously practised. Though he avoids the tumult of cities and is only accessible to a few, he spends the whole day in making people talk about him; he loves trophies and victories, but he fears to see a good General at the head of his troops as much as he would fear to see him at the head of a foreign army. Never, I think, has there been a prince rich beyond the dreams of avarice and yet crushed by poverty which a private citizen could not tolerate. He likes to gratify those who serve him, but he rewards the assiduity or rather idleness of his courtiers as generously as the arduous campaigns of his captains. Sometimes he prefers a man who undresses him or hands him a serviette at table to one who captures towns or wins his battles. He does not believe that his sovereign grandeur should be fettered in the disposal of his favours, and, without inquiring whether he whom he loads with favours is a man of merit, he believes that his choice renders the recipient worthy. He is magnificent above all in his buildings, and there are more statues in the gardens of his palaces than citizens in a large town.

Not all the people of Europe, the Persian visitors had learned, were equally submissive to their princes. For instance, sub-

mission and obedience were virtues to which the English paid
scant respect. 'If a prince, far from making his subjects happy,
wishes to destroy them, the foundations of obedience fall away
and they resume their natural liberty. No uncontrolled power,
they believe, can be legitimate.' Here is the germ of the thesis
of limited monarchy enshrined many years later in *L'Esprit
des Lois*.

The *Lettres Persanes* denounce the Church with no less vigour
than the Monarchy of which it was the main bulwark.

> I find here [reports Uzbek] people who talk without ceasing about
> religion, but they also attack those who practise it. They are not
> only not better Christians but not even better citizens, though
> observance of the laws, love of one's fellows, and reverence for
> one's parents are the primary duties of every faith. Is it not the
> first duty of a religious man to please the divinity who established
> his religion? The surest method is to observe the rules of society
> and the duties of humanity. Whatever one's faith may be one must
> believe that God loves men since He established a religion to make
> them happy. If He loves them, surely we please Him if we too love
> them, that is to say by fulfilling towards them all the duties of
> charity and humanity and observing the laws of the country. In
> that way we can be more certain of pleasing Him than in performing
> this or that ceremony, for ceremonies are good only on the assump-
> tion that God has ordained them. Here, however, there is much
> controversy, and we can easily go astray, for we have to choose
> between two thousand competing forms. Someone used to offer
> this daily prayer: 'Lord, I understand nothing of these unending
> disputes. I desire to serve Thee according to Thy will, but everyone
> whom I consult wishes me to adopt his own method. When I want
> to pray I know not what language I am to choose. Nor do I know
> in what posture I am to place myself: one says standing, another
> sitting, another on my knees. All these things are an unspeakable
> worry. I cannot turn my head without fearing to offend Thee.
> But I am anxious to please Thee. I may be mistaken, but I believe
> that the best way is to live as a good citizen in the society of which
> I am a member and a good father of the family Thou hast given me.'
> There is another magician, even more powerful than the prince,
> who is called the Pope, who makes people believe that three are
> only one, that the bread one eats is not bread or that the wine one
> drinks is not wine, and a thousand other things of the same sort.
> The chief of the Christians is an old idol to whom incense is offered.

In past times he was a danger to princes, whom he deposed as easily as our Sultans depose a Georgian king. Today he is no longer feared. He claims to be the successor of one of the first Christians called St. Peter, and a rich heritage it is, for he possesses immense treasures and rules over a large territory.

Throughout the book Montesquieu loses no opportunity of attacking the intolerance and the worldliness of the Roman Church.

The *Lettres Persanes* were not merely a satire but a confession of faith. Why should suicide be condemned?

When I am crushed by grief, suffering and contempt, why should anyone prevent me from putting an end to my troubles? Since society is founded on mutual advantage, why should I not renounce it when it becomes a burden? Does the prince wish me to remain his subject when I derive no advantage from my subjection? People argue that I am challenging the order of Providence. God, they say, has united your soul to your body and you separate them. But when that occurs will there be less order in the universe? Will the world have lost anything? Do you think my body, transformed into a blade of grass, a worm, a piece of turf, is less worthy of nature, and that my soul, detached from everything terrestrial, becomes less sublime?

Morality was independent of theology. 'Even if God did not exist we must all love justice, striving to resemble the Being of whom we have so lofty a conception and who, if He exists, must be just.' Compared with this attack on the Monarchy and the Church, the *Noblesse* and the *Robe*, *Télémaque* and *Le Dîme Royale* are a mere tinkle of discontent. The first well-aimed missile in the long campaign for reform of the government which culminated in 1789 had been launched.

Less scintillating but no less incisive a critic was the Abbé de Saint-Pierre, almoner of Madame, friend of the Regent, diplomat and publicist, ingenious author of more plans for the welfare of humanity than any writer of eighteenth-century France. His experiences as a member of the French delegation during the interminable discussions leading to the Treaty of Utrecht bore fruit in the earliest, most celebrated and most elaborate of his writings, *Projet de Paix Perpetuelle*. Following the model of *le Grand Dessein* attributed by Sully to Henri IV, he worked out a plan for the organisation of a peaceful Europe, renouncing war as an instrument of policy, recognising existing frontiers, and providing mediation in the event of disputes. If every state were to furnish a contingent of troops for the defence of peace, the burden of armaments could be reduced. Not till the Covenant of the League of Nations was drawn up in 1919 was so much constructive thought devoted to the integration of mankind.

When the third volume of the *Projet de Paix Perpetuelle* was launched in 1715 the Abbé turned his thoughts to the reform of the French government, and embodied his proposals in his *Traité de la Polysynodie*, published in 1718. Anticipating Bentham's maxim that institutions must be judged by their utility, not their origin or longevity, he was less interested in the form than in the working of political systems. Though less radical than Montesquieu, he shared his conviction that kings had too much power, and there is no trace of the adulation almost universal during the previous reign. The *mystique* has evaporated, and his analysis is carried out with the calm detachment of the scientist. His first conclusion is that autocracy is too heavy a burden for a single individual, even for a superman.

If princes regard the functions of government as inescapable obligations, even the ablest would find himself overtaxed, and he would be as eager to limit his dominions as he now is to extend them. Yet, far from reflecting on the penalties of power, they visualise only the pleasures of command. Since the people in their eyes are only the instrument of their whims, the more whims they desire to humour the more power they possess. The more limited their understanding, the stronger is the urge to be great and powerful.

Happily for their subjects there is a limit to human capacity.

The sovereign of a great empire is at bottom only the minister of his ministers or the representative of his agents. They are obeyed in his name, and when he thinks he is exercising his will it is he who, without knowing it, is doing theirs. That is unavoidable, since he can only see with their eyes and must therefore act with their hands. Compelled to transfer to others what is called detail—what I should call the essence of government—he reserves for himself the big things, the verbiage of ambassadors, the intrigues of his favourites, at most the choice of his masters, for masters he must have with so many slaves. What does a good or bad administration matter to him? How can his happiness be disturbed by the misery of the people he does not see, by the complaints he does not hear, the public disorders of which he knows nothing? If by a miracle some great spirit is equal to the grievous burden of royalty, the principle of heredity and the faulty education of the heir will always produce a hundred imbeciles for one real king. Minorities and illnesses, periods of delirium and passion, often reduce the head of the state to a mere shadow. Thus, since public business has to be carried on, a system is needed which can dispense with the King.

Far better than the rule of a Vizier—or of two Viziers as i.1 the time of Louvois and Colbert—was government by Councils as applied by the Regent in 1715, one for each of the leading departments. No other system was so likely to bring the best men into the public service and to ensure justice and consistency in the national policy. The councillors should sit successively on each Committee in order to obtain a comprehensive grasp of the needs and resources of the State.

Saint-Pierre proceeded from a criticism of the system of government to a frontal attack on the late ruler. 'He might well be called Louis the Powerful or Louis the Formidable, for none of his predecessors was so powerful and so much feared; but we should never allot him the title of *Louis le Grand* nor mistake great power for true greatness. Unless it is employed to benefit mankind in general and his subjects and neighbours in particular it will never deserve great esteem. In a word, great power alone will never make a great man.' This audacious passage was brought to the notice of the Academy in 1718 by Cardinal de Polignac, who demanded the expulsion of the blasphemer. Ignoring appeals from his fellow-members to withdraw his words, the author was expelled after a ballot in which Fontenelle alone opposed the decision. Though the Regent was believed to share the Abbé's estimate of the late King, he declined to annul the decree. The offender spent the two remaining decades of his long life elaborating further projects for the welfare of mankind, among them marriage of the clergy. Though old enough to be Montesquieu's father, he was no less in spirit a child of the critical eighteenth century.

The Regency era has found few champions, but the most eloquent of French historians salutes it with a cheer. A brief but creative intermezzo, exclaims Michelet, a social revolution, the breaking of fetters which paralysed the energies of France, the end of autocracy, hypocrisy and bigotry, in a word, the dawn of the Age of Reason. The power of the Church was challenged and the domination of the Jesuits ceased. Birth counted for less, ability and money for more. The Regent and his associates, despite their vices and errors, were forward-looking men, heirs of Montaigne, Molière and Vauban, forerunners of the *Philosophes,* spokesmen of reformist and humanitarian France. However much water we may have to pour into Michelet's foaming wine, it is true enough that the Regent was mildly liberal, a modern man, for whom the problem of government was a matter to be approached, not by searching the Scriptures or following precedents, but by the familiar process of trial and error. France was growing tired of autocrats. 'We laughed at his death as we had laughed at his government,' declares Voltaire in his *Siècle de Louis XV*, 'for the French laugh at everything. His only faults were his passion for pleasure and his liking for innovations. Of all the descendants of Henri IV Philip of Orleans most resembled him in his valour, his kindliness and his lack of pose, and he possessed a richer culture.' If he cannot be described as a *Philosophe* he prepared the way for a new age. 'Philosopher,' declared Mme de Lambert in 1715, 'c'est secouer le joug de l'autorité.' The *saeculum rationalisticum* had begun.

3

CARDINAL FLEURY AT THE HELM

I

THE Duke of Orleans had lost his popularity, but his death brought no relief to France. Louis XV was in his fourteenth year and no experienced helmsman was in sight. Fleury, his former tutor, might have grasped the prize had not his placid nature shrunk from strife, and he had little doubt that his hour would strike when his young master grew up. To whom then could the country look for leadership? The King was the sole legitimate representative of the direct line except Philip V of Spain, whose accession to the French throne was barred not only by his formal renunciation but by the Treaty of Utrecht. The Orleans family, which stood closest to the throne, could supply no suitable candidate, for the new Duke was only twenty and —in strange contrast to his dissolute father—preferred the study of theology to the distractions of politics. Thus the road was open for the third branch of the Royal Family, the Bourbon-Condés, descended from the uncle of Henri IV, and at the age of thirty-one the unworthy great-grandson of the Grand Condé claimed the post of First Minister as his right. There was no overt opposition. Fleury approved, keeping ecclesiastical patronage in his own hands. The King, too young to care, indicated his assent by a silent nod. He and the new Minister were close relatives, for the latter's mother was a bastard of Louis XIV. The *Conseil* or Cabinet was composed of the Duc de Bourbon, Marshal

Villars and Fleury, the latter being always present at the inter-
views of the boy King with his Ministers. Everyone knew that
the Bishop, not the Duke, was the power behind the throne.

It was the misfortune of France that no worthier figure could
be found among the princes of the blood, and the unhappy
experiment lasted only three years. The Duc de Bourbon, invari-
ably known as M. le Duc, could boast of no qualifications except
birth, wealth, and a splendid residence at Chantilly, for he
possessed neither public nor private virtues. No one had much
to say for him except the Dowager Duchess of Orleans who in
1719 credited him with plenty of qualities and friends. His main
achievement was to have accumulated millions in the orgy of
speculation unleashed by Law. Arrogant, extravagant and unin-
telligent, he cared for little but eating, gallantry, and sport.
Having recently lost his wife he was dominated by his latest
mistress, Mme de Prie, daughter of a rich financier and wife of a
Marquis who had represented his country at the Court of Turin.
'The Duke's mistress,' reported Bolingbroke, then living as an
exile in France, 'is attached to him by no inclination and is the
most corrupt and ambitious jade alive.' D'Argenson dismisses
her as a sinister meteor, the Venetian Ambassador as an avaricious
intriguer. 'So M. le Duc is First Minister,' noted Barbier in his
journal. 'He is very limited, knows nothing, loves nothing but
pleasure and sport. He is deeply in love with Mme de Prie, who
will govern the country and extract as much money as she can,
like M. le Duc and his brother the Comte de Charolais.' 'Mme
de Prie,' echoed Marais, 'has a very good opinion of herself. She
aspires to govern the Duke and with him the whole kingdom.'

Her charms are attested by many witnesses. 'She was pretty
and had a good figure,' testifies Saint-Simon, 'charming, very
intelligent, and extremely cultivated. I do not believe that a
more heavenly creature ever lived.' No one was so pretty,
declares President Hénault; 'she looked like a nymph.'

She possessed something more than beauty [testifies Duclos]; her
whole person breathed seduction. With as many graces of mind as
of body, she concealed the most dangerous stratagems behind a veil
of naïveté. Virtue seemed to her a word without meaning. Head-
strong beneath an air of gentleness and libertine by temperament,
she deceived her lover with impunity, for he believed what she told

him even when it contradicted the evidence of his senses. He was very limited, obstinate, harsh, even ferocious, and, though a prince, boastful as an upstart. His brains only sufficed to make him exploit his rank, and he was nothing but the tool of his mistress.

A recent biographer argues that she has been too harshly treated, that there is no evidence of disloyalty to her lover, and that many critics were simply jealous of her success.

Rarely has France been governed by such a mediocrity as the Duc de Bourbon, whom Saint-Simon describes as stupid, obstinate, greedy, and generally hated. He was worse than Dubois, not as a man but as a ruler, for the Cardinal, despite his private vices, had the makings of a statesman. Most of the administrative and financial business devolved on the four Duverney brothers, sons of a small provincial innkeeper, who had become rich army contractors and strove with some success to clear up the confusion bequeathed by the fiasco of John Law's schemes. Everyone from the King downwards regarded M. le Duc as a mere stop-gap, to be succeeded in due course by the King's old preceptor, who declined the glittering offer of the Archbishopric of Rheims in order to retain his strategic position at Court. Money made little appeal to a man of simple tastes, but behind the *façade* of his modest bearing he had his full share of political ambition. In the pungent phrase of Duclos his modesty was an instrument of his ambition. Counting on the unpopularity of M. le Duc, the King's dislike of new faces, and on his steady affection for himself and his former *Gouvernante*, Mme de Ventadour, the two persons whom he had known longest and liked best, he had no need to intrigue and could afford to wait.

In accordance with the wish of Louis XIV the boy King was transferred from Versailles, which was to stand empty for seven years, to Vincennes while the Tuileries was prepared for residence. Early in 1716 he migrated to Paris, where he lived for six years, and at the opening of 1722 he returned to Versailles. The delicate child of twelve had grown into a sturdy lad who looked older than his years, delighted in physical exercise, and found his greatest happiness in shooting in the Bois de Boulogne and the wooded environs of Versailles. On his visit to Paris Peter the Great had been impressed with his good looks, and he was often described as the handsomest young man in France.

Madame Palatine wrote to her German relatives of his long curling eyelashes and pretty complexion, his charming little mouth and ruddy cheeks: there was something of the delicacy of a girl about him. But looks were not everything, and a little later her verdict was less favourable. 'He has a nice face and plenty of sense but a bad heart. He loves no one but his old governess, dislikes people without reason, and enjoys making biting remarks.' At the age of twelve he could be sharp and satirical. When he exclaimed that a certain courtier was very ugly, the Bishop of Metz remarked: 'What a badly trained child!' The de Goncourt brothers, indefatigable explorers of the byways of eighteenth-century France, stumbled on the fragmentary journal of an equerry, the Marquis de Callière, covering the first half of 1722, which showed the author playing games with the lad who manifested no signs of intellectual interest. Monarchical sentiment, however, which had begun to wane during the last phase of Louis XIV, revived when the King appeared on ceremonial occasions and played his part with dignity and poise. The contrast between the saturnalia of the Palais Royal and the handsome youth who could be seen playing on the terrace of the Tuileries turned the thoughts of France to the time when a King would once more rule as well as reign. His grave illness in 1721 created a fever of anxiety, and Barbier's Journal, which records the doings and gossip of Paris, describes the festivities on his recovery. Even louder were the rejoicings during the coronation ceremonies at Rheims in the following year and the official coming of age in 1723.

Louis XIV had made precise arrangements for the care and education of his heir. The most important was that of the *Gouvernante*, Mme de Ventadour, Lady-in-Waiting to Madame Palatine, a kindly woman who mothered the orphan child, won his abiding affections, and was addressed by him as *Maman* to the end of her days. She handed the sobbing child at the age of seven to a team of men with the Regent at their head. While the Duc du Maine had been chosen by Louis XIV to take general charge of his education, he played less part in the boy's life than his Governor, the septuagenarian Marshal Villeroi, who talked without ceasing of the *Grand Siècle* and the *Roi Soleil*, coached him in Court etiquette, and impressed on him with ill-advised emphasis that he was in the fullest sense the master of everybody and everything in France. Of far greater significance was the choice of Fleury, the son of a bourgeois official, who entered the Church and became Almoner successively to the Queen and the monarch. Though appointed to the remote southern diocese of Fréjus, which he sulkily accepted, he was not forgotten, and he was recalled to become Preceptor to the little heir, the same post which Fénelon had occupied during the early years of his father. When the octogenarian Villeroi lost his post in 1722, Fleury's position was unchallengeable. First in the wings and soon in the glare of the footlights, he continued to pull the strings till his death twenty years later. 'I have complimented the Bishop of Fréjus on his prudent direction of his royal pupil,' reported the British Ambassador, brother of Robert Walpole, in 1725. 'He gives what he thinks the best advice at every turn and is rewarded by the King's affection.'

The Preceptor appointed teachers for history, geography, mathematics, Latin, and science. Lessons on government were provided by officials of the Foreign Office, War Office and Finance under the direction of Dubois, while the Regent himself occasionally took a hand. Some of the memoranda drafted for his instruction and volumes of his exercises and translations corrected by Fleury are preserved in the Bibliothèque Nationale. From the age of ten, in accordance with the instructions of Louis XIV, he was allowed to attend the *Conseil d'État*. He was an average boy, neither exceptionally idle nor particularly studious. He displayed much intelligence and vivacity, records Marshal Villars when his young master was eleven, but he had a temper. With all his good qualities he could not bring himself to speak a word except to his intimates. He made no replies to Ambassadors or even deputations from the provinces except those dictated by Marshal Villeroi, and Villars tactfully encouraged him to overcome his shyness and speak in public as part of the duty of a king. Since the return to Versailles had been a blow to officials who had taken houses in the capital, and to the interests which profited by the presence of the Court, Villars also urged him to spend the winter there, enjoying the opera and theatres, and warned him against listening to flatterers. The boy listened quietly, but the advice fell on deaf ears. His pleasures were hunting, cards, and food. So far there was little or no gallantry. Though shy with women, he was physically precocious and ripe for matrimony in his fifteenth year. Occasional bouts of fever, attributed to over-eating, aroused anxiety. Everything pointed to early matrimony. 'God has given us a King so strong that for the last year we might hope for a Dauphin,' commented Villars; 'so, for the satisfaction of his people and himself, he should be married today rather than tomorrow.'

Louis XIII and Louis XIV had married their Spanish cousins, and it was decided that Louis XV should follow their example. He was accordingly betrothed to his first cousin, though the marriage was to be postponed for ten years. The seven-year-old princess arrived in Paris on the lap of Mme de Ventadour with a doll in her hand, and was lodged in the Louvre. Since, however, the succession hung by a thread and the boy King was as eager for a wife as his subjects, she was returned to Madrid with the explanation that France could not wait so long for an heir. The Courts of Europe were now combed for a bride of suitable age and vigorous health. Among the dozens of suggestions the most eligible in rank were a daughter of the Prince of Wales and Elizabeth, afterwards Empress, daughter of Peter the Great, but in both cases the difference of religion formed an insurmountable barrier. A sister of the Duc de Bourbon was also considered. The final choice amazed the world, for who could have guessed that the proudest monarch in Europe would share his throne with the penniless daughter of a Polish nobleman who had once sat for a brief space on the shaky Polish throne? The chief contriver of the most astonishing marriage in the dynastic history of France was neither Fleury nor the Duc de Bourbon but Mme de Prie, who desired the selection of a woman with such meagre qualifications that she would blush for her unworthiness and leave the authority of her patron intact.

In 1725 Stanislas Leczinski was living forgotten in the Rhineland as a pensioner of France. Elected to the Polish throne in 1704 at the age of twenty-seven, through the influence of Charles XII of Sweden after the deposition of Augustus, Elector of Saxony, he lost the glittering prize five years later when the victory of Peter the Great at Pultowa restored the former King. The only consolation Charles could arrange was to appoint his *protégé* to the little principality of Zweibrücken in the Rhineland which had been in the possession of Sweden for half a century. Here again his tenure was brief, for on the death of the Swedish King in 1718 the previous ruler of Zweibrücken returned and the pension from Stockholm ceased. His property in Poland had been confiscated and his wife's jewels pawned. Compelled to borrow from Frankfurt bankers, and with his life in danger from agents of the King of Poland, Stanislas sought despairingly for a roof over his head. His appeal to the Regent Orleans resulted in the promise of an allowance of 20,000 crowns and a house in Wissembourg in Alsace where he maintained a skeleton court. A man of fair abilities and cheerful temperament, better suited to be a country squire than a king, he bore his misfortunes bravely. The worst of his worries was the irregular payment of the allowance from France, and the resultant inability to provide the salaries of the old retainers who had refused to desert the sinking ship. It was a dull *ménage*, for he was too poor to entertain. The ex-Queen, unlike her husband, was soured by misfortune, and an elder daughter had recently died. When all hope of a restoration to the Polish throne was abandoned, the parents focused their ambition on their surviving child, hoping that her homely virtues might outweigh the lack of princely birth and wealth. She resembled her father in her serenity, her artistic interests, and her kindness of heart. Though making no claim to beauty, she was pleasant-looking, unselfish, and generous to neighbours even poorer than herself. That she would make a good wife and mother no one who saw her in her modest home could doubt.

The fallen monarch, who continued to sign himself Stanislas Roi, had no intention of letting his beloved daughter go at less than the fair market price. Shortly before the death of the Regent her hand was sought by a marquis, a grandson of Louvois, but her father dreamed of a duke and was hurt at the refusal of his request for a Baden prince. At this moment Mme de Prie was looking round for a wife for her lover, the Duc de Bourbon, a childless widower. According to her calculations the best choice would be a bride neither too attractive nor of too high rank to challenge her position. Through the Chevalier de Vauchoux, who had served under Stanislas in Poland and now resided in

Paris as his agent, she learned that the daughter of the ex-King would fulfil these conditions. M. le Duc found his second wife elsewhere at a later date, but it dawned on him and Mme de Prie that the Polish girl might be a possible consort for the King. In the lengthy annotated list of candidates the comment attached to the name of Maria Leczinska was in the minor key. 'The parents are not rich and would doubtless want to settle in France, which would be inconvenient. Nothing is known to the disadvantage of the family.' The young King expressed no decided preference, and when he was shown a portrait which Mme de Prie had commissioned he agreed to the match. An envoy of the Duc de Bourbon described the lady as lively, natural and cultivated, sweet-natured, charitable, adored by her domestics, entirely devoid of pride, and pious without bigotry. Her reading included works of devotion, history, and geography. She danced, played the piano, and sang. In addition to Polish she spoke German and French without accent. She was abstemious and mixed water with her wine. Her health was good. Though not a beauty she was attractive in her gentleness, intelligence, and tact.

The decision of the French Government electrified the little household in Alsace. Stanislas burst into the salon where his wife and daughter sat at their needlework. 'Down on our knees in thanks to God!' 'Are you restored to the Polish throne?' 'Heaven is still more gracious: you are Queen of France.' In a moment the clouds which had hung over the exiled family melted away. As father-in-law of the proudest sovereign in Europe Stanislas would recover his prestige and live in affluence. That the modest girl was as enraptured as her father is improbable, for the prospect of a change from the twilight of Wissembourg to the glitter of Versailles was enough to alarm any woman not of princely birth. Moreover, she was seven years older than the King.

The announcement which brought joy to the shabby little Court aroused amazement throughout Europe and consternation in France. Everyone spoke of a *mésalliance*, the responsibility for which was assigned to the Duc de Bourbon and Mme de Prie. The Court, records Marais, was as sad as if the King had had a stroke. 'Monstrous,' exclaimed Maurepas, the youngest of the

Ministers. For the first time there was to be a Queen without a drop of royal blood in her veins. But the mood of depression was in no way shared by the young King who was so anxious for a wife that he cared little who she might be. Protests by his uncle the King of Spain, his cousin the Duke of Orleans, and his grandfather the King of Sardinia, were ignored. There was nothing to wait for, and the Household was promptly announced. The highest post, *Surintendante de la Maison*, was assigned to Mlle de Clermont, sister of the Duc de Bourbon, the second, that of *Dame d'honneur*, to the Maréchale de Boufflers. Mme de Mailly, the mother of five daughters of whom we shall hear more, became *Dame d'atours*. Among the twelve *Dames du Palais* was Mme de Prie herself. Paris-Duverney, the trusted factotum of the Duc de Bourbon, was nominated *Secrétaire des Commandements*, Fleury, Grand Almoner, and a Polish Confessor was allowed. Mme de Prie was dispatched to instruct the future Queen in the ways of the Court, and was quickly followed by Mlle de Clermont with a bevy of courtiers to escort the bride. A preliminary marriage ceremony was performed at Strasbourg by Cardinal de Rohan, Grand Almoner of France, in which the young Duke of Orleans deputised for the bridegroom. A second ceremony took place when the bride reached Fontainebleau. Though she had little natural charm, she earned a popular welcome by her friendly and unassuming ways. Her happy father was installed in the magnificent Château de Chambord with a smaller residence at Meudon within easy reach of Versailles. The tide of fortune had turned at last.

Marie Leczinska wrote happily to her parents, and on their first visit they were treated as sovereigns. They were lodged in the apartments at the Trianon allotted to the Queen, and at Versailles her father was allowed the use of the apartment of the Comte de Clermont, younger brother of M. le Duc. The visits of the gay and affectionate Stanislas, with his hearty laugh and unfailing *joie de vivre*, acted like a tonic. Having mistresses of his own, he never broke his heart over the infidelities of his son-in-law. 'God be praised,' he reported, 'the King's friendship for the Queen increases greatly and she has gained his confidence. Everyone is pleased with her conduct.' Nothing, he added, was lacking except a Dauphin. He drew up written instructions

warning her against the wiles of men and the temptation to
meddle in politics.

> Your whole confidence must be reserved for the King alone. He
> must be the only confidant of your feelings, desires, projects,
> thoughts. Never try to pierce the veils which hide the secrets of
> state. Authority desires no partner. Respond to his hopes by every
> possible attention. You must no longer think except after him and
> like him; only his joys and worries must be yours. Know no ambi-
> tion but to please him, no pleasure but to obey him, no interest but
> to merit his affection. In a word, you must no longer have fancies
> or preferences; your whole soul should be merged in his.

Her father's counsels echoed the promptings of her heart. It
was easier for her than for many other brides to surrender her
individuality, for there was not very much to suppress. No
element of romance lurked in her uncomplicated nature, and she
quitted her home without illusions. She knew that she was
drafted to provide an heir and for that purpose alone. No
eighteenth-century princess dreamed of a love match, and the
factor of unequal birth condemned the Polish Cinderella to a
life-long inferiority complex. Neither partner felt quite at ease
with the other, though she respected his rank and he recognised
her virtues. It was her misfortune that she lacked the qualities
required to hold the roving fancy of a man who demanded above
all the capacity to enliven his empty hours. She did her duty to
the best of her limited ability, but she could never be the friend
and companion for whom he craved. In one sphere, the most
important of all, she fulfilled his expectations, presenting him
with ten children in as many years. For a time they lived as
happily as most royal couples, and in a Court with such licentious
traditions it aroused surprise that he resisted temptation for about
seven years. When the charms of some beauty were extolled the
King gallantly remarked, 'Le reine est encore plus belle.' Her
life was rendered bearable by the joys of motherhood, by the
loyal friendship of members of her household, above all by the
annual visits and letters of her adored and adoring father who
lived to a hearty old age.

It would have been almost a miracle if the inexperienced Queen
had avoided every pitfall in her path. Gratefully aware that she
owed her promotion to the Duc de Bourbon, she assumed that

her friendly feelings were shared by her husband. Soon after her marriage she asked him which of his Ministers enjoyed his confidence so that she might know whom she could trust. 'How do you like M. de Fleury?' she inquired. '*Beaucoup*.' 'And M. le Duc?' '*Assez*.' Though the curt reply should have convinced her that the latter was out of favour, she incautiously allowed herself to be exploited by him and Mme de Prie. The King, they complained, never worked alone with his First Minister; Fleury was always present and was with him for hours on the pretext of lessons. The unsuspecting Queen sent a message asking the King to her apartment. There he found the Duke who expressed a hope that he would allow her to stay. 'Stay,' replied the King coldly. She had already reached the door and sat down as far away as possible. The tactless Duke, blissfully unaware that he was skating on very thin ice, presented a letter from Cardinal Polignac attacking Fleury. The King read it and returned it without a word.

THE DUKE: What do you say to this letter?
THE KING: Nothing.
THE DUKE: What is your will?
THE KING: Things to remain as they are.
THE DUKE: So I have the misfortune to displease you?
THE KING: Yes.

Realising his *faux pas* the offender fell on his knees and begged for pardon. 'I pardon you,' rejoined the King, and left the room. The First Minister had signed his political death warrant.

Fleury had expected some hostile manœuvre and welcomed it when it came, for it had always been his tactic to wait for the clumsy rival to break his neck. When he attempted to visit the Queen and was not admitted he ordered his carriage, leaving a brief note for the King. 'As my services appear to be useless I beg permission to end my days with the Sulpicians.' The King shut himself up and gave way to tears. 'Sire,' exclaimed the First Gentleman of the Chamber, 'are you not the master? Order M. le Duc to go and fetch M. de Fréjus this moment and you will see him back.' The Duke sulkily obeyed and next day Fleury returned in triumph. After this dramatic intermezzo it was clear that he would be in full command as soon as he wished.

He had already urged the Duke to dismiss Mme de Prie and Paris-Duverney on the ground that they injured the prestige of the State. The First Minister angrily replied that if his friends had to go, he would go too.

To spare her father's feelings Marie Leczinska concealed the atmospheric change since her ill-advised championship of her benefactor. Writing to his agent, Marshal de Bourg, Stanislas complained that Fleury exceeded his functions and was inconsiderate to the Duke: happily, he added, the King continued and increased his love for the Queen. The troubled woman consulted the veteran Marshal Villars, who declared that the King had a cold heart and advised her to seek an interview with Fleury. The Bishop, fully understanding that she had been merely an innocent tool, was kind and fatherly; but he argued that Mme de Prie and Paris-Duverney were doing harm and ought to be dismissed. They were members of her circle, interjected the Queen, and would feel hurt if they had to go. That would have to come, rejoined the Bishop, adding that the coolness of the King was not his fault. Once again she sought counsel from Marshal Villars, who again advised her to make friends with Fleury as the only way to keep the King. The same prudent counsel came from her father. Everyone knew that the days of M. le Duc were numbered, and on June 11, 1726, the blow fell. Louis XV always took time to make up his mind about the dismissal of a Minister, maintaining correct relations till the last moment and then launching his thunderbolt. The exile of the Duke to his estates was followed by a clean sweep of his entourage. To the general delight of the Court and the capital, Mme de Prie was ordered to her home in Normandy where she died in the following year, while Paris-Duverney spent a short time in the Bastille. The Queen was informed of the changes in a curt letter from the King. 'Madame, I pray you, and if necessary I order you, to receive what the ex-Bishop of Fréjus will tell you in my name as if it were myself. Louis.' Villars, to whom she showed it, found her in tears. For the next seventeen years her relations with the omnipotent Minister were sufficiently correct to avert the King's displeasure, but she never thought of him as a disinterested friend.

II

The Fleury era had begun. Since the death of the Regent he had monopolised the King's favour, and at the age of seventy-three he emerged as the unchallenged ruler of France. 'Without the title of Prime Minister,' reported the British Ambassador Horatio Walpole, 'he will have the power in a more absolute manner than it was ever enjoyed by Richelieu and Mazarin.' After the ruinous wars of Louis XIV, the fireworks of the Regency and the shoddy intermezzo of M. le Duc, his mild sway was a relief. Such mediocrities excite neither enthusiasm nor violent hostility. At the first meeting of the *Conseil d'État* after the crisis the King, aged sixteen, expressed his pleasure at the restoration of the system of Louis XIV, who never appointed a *Premier Ministre*. Requests should henceforth be addressed to himself, and stated times would be allotted to the Ministers who would transact their business in the presence of Fleury. He was deluding himself, for the change was not of a system but of men. There was no need for his old tutor to assume the title of *Premier Ministre*, for his influence surpassed that of any statesman since Mazarin. For the present there was neither a mistress in the wings nor a political rival to challenge his sway. Anchored in his pupil's confidence he could perform his task without fear of being stabbed in the back. Of all the many servants of Louis XV he alone inspired in him some measure of affection. So impregnable was his position that the discredited Duc de Bourbon was allowed to reappear at Court, and the King often stayed with him at Chantilly for the shooting. The seal was placed on Fleury's triumph by the coveted Cardinal's hat. His honours were not undeserved. The desire of France for a rest cure—peace abroad and economy at home—harmonised with his instinct for a quiet life. Since he cared little for money, disdained pomp, and bore himself modestly to all men, even hardened intriguers realised that it was useless to plot his overthrow. His advanced age tended to diminish jealousy. Standing at the helm for seventeen years he presided over the happiest phase of an unhappy reign. The young King, bored by business, was only too glad to leave the task of government in his hands and to enjoy

life in his own way. 'This detestable priest,' complains the
Duchesse de Brancas, 'had spoiled the germs of the King's good
qualities, broken the springs of his mind, and filled him with
prejudices and suspicions. A man of different character would
have saved the King and the country many misfortunes.' The
verdict was too harsh, for few believed that any preceptor could
have made very much of Louis XV.

The earliest and most significant achievement of the Fleury
régime was the stabilisation of the currency after a period when
the title of a coin indicated different values at different times. It
was now decreed that a louis (pound) was the equivalent of
twenty-four livres (francs) and the écu (crown) the equivalent
of six. The generation of almost unbroken peace enjoyed by
France between the War of the Spanish Succession and the War
of the Austrian Succession enabled the new system to take such
firm root that it remained intact till the Revolution. The new-
born confidence in the currency was a prime factor in the rapid
development of commerce since it enabled long-term contracts
to be made. In 1732 Chauvelin, Keeper of the Seals, an able
lawyer, was associated with the Cardinal as Vice-Chancellor,
with special responsibility for foreign affairs, and the two men
governed France for the next five years. The Ministers of
Louis XV were well up to the standard of other countries, but
in the absence of a driving will at the top there was little to show
for their endeavours.

Though Fleury was made for a quiet life, he could not avert
a conflict with the only institution which attempted to limit the
prerogatives of the Crown. On the death of Louis XIV the
Parlement of Paris emerged from the shadows and reiterated its
traditional claims to a share in the life of the State. Its first
victory—not over the temporary ruler of France, for in this case
the Regent was on its side—was won when the will of the late
ruler was set aside. The second challenge was to the Church
rather than to the Crown, though the former was backed by the
latter. The condemnation of Jansenism by the Bull '*Unigenitus*'
inaugurated a struggle which lasted for decades. The Jansenists
found powerful support in the *Parlement*, the stronghold of
Gallicanism, and the smouldering antagonism flared up when the
Archbishop of Paris excommunicated the clergy who rejected the

Bull. Forty practising lawyers in the capital advised an appeal to the *Parlement* on the ground that it formed the Senate of the nation and possessed supreme jurisdiction as the custodian of the law. To this audacious claim the Government retorted that all power resided in the King. The lawyers assented to the principle, while arguing for their right to intervene if an abuse of ecclesiastical authority occurred. The *Parlement* ordered the suppression of any episcopal pronouncements which denied its jurisdiction, and in 1731 it issued a decree that 'the temporal power is independent of all other authorities, that it alone has the right of restraining the subjects of the King, and that the ministers of the Church are accountable to the *Parlement*, under the authority of the monarch, for the exercise of their jurisdiction'.

Though this went no further than the traditional Gallicanism, Fleury exiled twelve of the advocates, annulled the decree of the *Parlement*, vetoed its discussion of Church questions, and declined to receive a deputation which complained of the restriction of its rights. Neither the advocates nor the magistrates were in a yielding mood, the former refusing to plead in the courts while their colleagues remained in exile, the latter threatening to resign their posts. A rebuke by the King, who summoned representatives of the *Parlement* to Compiègne, failed to break their spirit, for they condemned a new allocution by the Archbishop and forbade its publication. The new order was annulled by the King, and some of the magistrates were arrested and exiled, whereupon most of their colleagues resigned. After further threats by the Government, the *Parlement* resumed its work without surrender on either side, but the feud quickly broke out again. When a *lit de justice* to register a decree limiting the powers of the *Parlement* was ignored, 139 magistrates were exiled. At this stage Fleury, weary of the unprofitable strife, revoked the sentence of exile and suspended the declaration limiting the rights of the *Parlement*. The magistrates had triumphed. It was the first sign of political opposition, twenty years before the *Philosophes* began to count. The dispute flared up again in the fifties, when the magistrates were once more exiled to the provinces, and culminated in the suppression of the *Parlements* by Maupeou in the closing phase of the reign. Though the easy-going ruler left the initiative to his Ministers, he frowned on the *Parlements* throughout his reign.

The magistrates were fighting for themselves, not for the nation, but their spirited challenge was widely applauded as a symbol of the mounting discontent with dynastic autocracy.

The partnership of the old tutor and his royal pupil is vividly described in the voluminous journal of d'Argenson, as critical a witness as Saint-Simon and temperamentally more prone to blame than to praise.

> One of the most ridiculous spectacles of the time [he records in 1731] is the *petit coucher* of M. le Cardinal. Though he is in sole command his only title is Minister of State. All France and the whole Court crowd his anteroom. His Eminence enters his cabinet, the door is opened and you see this old priest take off his trousers, don a shabby dressing-gown and shirt, comb his four white hairs. He chats, repeats his old anecdotes, makes bad jokes interlarded with sugary commonplaces and the gossip of the town.

Yet d'Argenson was not wholly blind to his virtues. 'He loves the King and the State, is honest and sincere, and wishes to be liked.'

D'Argenson, like most Frenchmen, started with high hopes of the young ruler whose failings he was soon bitterly to chastise.

> At the moment, [he notes cheerfully in March, 1730, when Fleury was ill] he works with his Ministers, does it admirably, and reaches just decisions. He has an excellent memory for details. He displays great humanity and a sense of justice. Recently the Finance Minister proposed to discharge a debt of four years standing. Had interest been paid? inquired the King. No, replied Orry, that was not the custom. That was not fair, rejoined the King, who ordered the payment. People wonder if he will continue to work, or if his activity since the illness of the Cardinal is like the fervour of the young priest. We must remember that he is almost without passions or dominant tastes, and apathy leaves a void which has to be filled. Business is presented to kings without thorns. Their Ministers arrive with the work neatly arranged and he has merely to say Yes or No. No effort is required. He is good-natured, shrewd, extremely discreet, the son of clever parents, expresses himself well, and listens to the smallest details. He thinks as quick as lightning, but so far he has not taken in very much since he dislikes long discussions. He has been charged with idleness and indifference, yet he displayed real feeling during the recent illness of the Dauphin

and the Cardinal. He has long formed his scheme of life—amusing himself while he leaves the Cardinal to govern, knowing his probity and capacity; but when he goes he intends to shoulder the burden himself. We shall see if he keeps his word. He is a good judge of men and likes respectable folk such as the Cardinal and his valet Bachelier. His favourites are Soubise and Coigny, very decent young fellows. All this gives promise of a happy reign. God preserve him. It is hoped he will govern in person like Louis XIV, for he does not need a First Minister. He is a man of sound sense, rather lazy yet anxious for the work to go well. He is reserved and discreet as the greatest kings have been. The only person to whom he confides all his affairs is his valet Bachelier, who desires nothing for himself but all for the glory of his master, keeps his ears open, and likes to know everything. He has little taste for study, but he has picked up enough geography and politics to make conversation with the King.

Though the monarch's liking and respect for his octogenarian Minister continued till the end, he came to share the general opinion that he had lived too long. The first difference of opinion arose when the Cardinal advised the dismissal of Chauvelin, the ablest of the Ministers, on the ostensible ground that his policy involved a risk of war, but in reality because it was felt that he was striving for the first place. Yet it no longer sufficed for Fleury to express a wish.

The King [comments d'Argenson] is more independent now he has a mistress; it is astonishing how it matures princes to possess a confidant. Moreover there will never again be so dissimulating a prince. Thus the Cardinal meets with silent but firm opposition which needs a good deal of time to overcome. The King is more inclined to serious things than people think. Chauvelin just suited him, as he is extremely supple and persuasive. What has he done wrong? The King finds in him *flair* and discretion, skill in lightening the burden of business, and a wide grasp of affairs. Who could replace him?

The King finally gave way, exiled Chauvelin to Bourges, and never recalled him when he could do as he chose.

At the end of the thirties d'Argenson records a decline of Fleury's power. He notes in April, 1738:

His credit wanes from day to day, and he confines himself to ecclesiastical affairs. He is losing flesh, which comes of living too

F

long. The King puts up with him with growing impatience, and shows it by brusque replies or silence. Everyone expects the return of Chauvelin when the poor old fellow disappears. The King only sees him twice or thrice a week, and only about fifteen minutes alone. Power has sapped his good qualities, and he realises the insecurity of his tenure. The King hopes to drive him to resign by petty slights. His only real friend is the Queen. He remains because the King does not wish to seem ungrateful or to see him die of shock.

Despite his failing powers the old man clung to his post. 'Supple as a glove, he swallows all the snubs. The nearer one is to him, the less one esteems him—mediocre but adroit, not cruel but malevolent. His only supporters are a few unworthy parasites.' Severe as d'Argenson was on the Minister, he became ever more critical of the King. His greatest fault was his increasing indolence. 'He rises at eleven,' notes the diarist in August, 1739, 'and leads a useless life. He steals from his frivolous occupations one hour of work; the sessions with the Ministers cannot be called work, for he lets them do everything, merely listening or repeating what they say like a parrot. He is still very much of a child.' When this crushing and in some measure unjust verdict was pronounced the monarch was twenty-nine and his old tutor was still at the helm.

D'Argenson, like other diarists, records the impressions of the hour without any attempt at consistency. Having repeatedly noted the decline of Fleury's influence he observes without regret how the growing apathy of the King compelled the Minister to bear the burden almost alone.

He behaves like a Mayor of the Palace [January, 1740], which is even more than a Regent. He claims to decide everything and to despatch his decisions to the ends of Europe. One might think that he was a Legate governing France in the name of the Pope. At the moment he works scarcely half an hour a week with the King: two short sessions suffice, the first alone for fifteen minutes, then the Ministers enter for the signing of the documents. He began by urging the King to work and decide, appealing to his honour, and at first the King showed some interest in affairs. But the Cardinal has by degrees given rein to a tyrannical and jealous ambition such as no one has ever displayed. Neither feared nor loved by the public, he is a mean old man, a contemptible and hated priest whom a King, born virtuous, sensible and steady, allows to exercise his functions for fear of his dying of anger and jealousy. Here is a King very well informed, who showed last year during the Cardinal's illness that he knew how to rule and to rule well; but at the end of this period he has been reduced to a degrading impotence. Though modest in regard to himself and his family, the Cardinal's assumed virtues have been unmasked and the King often shows his discontent. With a council of wise men at his side as well as a mistress he will announce one day that he intends to rule and will dismiss him.

Fleury declined either to die or to resign, and as the King was unwilling to hurt his feelings, other possibilities of shifting him began to be discussed. When a vacancy at the Vatican occurred, it was suggested that the virtual ruler of France, despite his eighty-seven years, might be promoted to a still higher post. When the prize fell to Benedict XIV, some people turned their thoughts to the Duke of Orleans, son of the Regent, a man of unblemished reputation.

This wise and virtuous prince [wrote d'Argenson in September, 1740] is quite equal to the first place. He goes boldly to the King and, when necessary, speaks up in the Council. He tells him of the slack administration, the rascalities, rigours and imbecility of M. Orry, the incapacity of M. Amelot, of all the disorder and degradation which the Cardinal increases daily by his bad appointments, his lack of justice and decision, and the damage arising from this tutelage to the prestige of the Crown.

When this hope of delivery also vanished, it seemed as if the prevailing economic distress might bring him down. 'With lack of bread and rising prices in Paris, famine in the country and heavier taxation,' notes d'Argenson in September, 1740,

the Cardinal is at his wits end and his resignation is expected from day to day. When the King passed through the capital he was greeted with cries of *misère, du pain, du pain*. When Fleury drove through Paris, women seized the bridle of the horses, opened the door of his carriage, and screamed *du pain, du pain, du pain, nous mourons de faim*. He almost died of fright and threw coins to the crowd. The King was momentarily upset when he sensed the mood of the capital, and his duty to himself and his people struggled with his duty to the Cardinal. Though he does not feel bound to sacrifice his kingdom, he thinks it would kill the Cardinal to substitute his arch enemy Chauvelin. Moreover he esteems his talents, though everything is going to pieces and the Cardinal has become odious to the whole kingdom. Insensible to the public plight, more infatuated than ever with his old tutor, incapable of action, the King amuses himself and hunts, his mind a blank. Nine-tenths of the Court think him an imbecile who will never come to anything. Our nation is desperate, enervated, annihilated, and only the Farmers General are alive. The moment approaches when the King will govern himself or rather will choose the Ministers he needs and will work with them, though it needs the faith of Abraham to believe all that. Every day the dilemma is more urgent: the King counts for much or for nothing.

With d'Argenson's portrait of the young ruler as observed at close quarters we may compare the impressions of Barbier, whose invaluable journal describes the doings and sayings of the capital from 1718 to 1762. A lawyer of cold temperament, equally sparing of praise and blame, he watches the performances of the King with tolerant eyes, expecting little and thus avoiding disappointment. 'Today,' he notes in April, 1730, 'the King went for six weeks to Fontainebleau to hunt stags, which is his only occupation.' A year later he records another visit to Fontainebleau. 'His taste for hunting is unchanged, but people say it is less for the hunt itself than from an urge to move about from place to place. He has no desire to take the helm, and he places great confidence in the Cardinal, who is the real master.' If the adolescent Louis XV had been fortunate in possessing such a prudent and trusted adviser, there was also a debit side to the balance-sheet, for the period of tutelage continued long after he reached years of discretion and encouraged him to neglect the duties expected of him as ruler of France. Barbier, however, refused to despair, for the Cardinal would not live for ever.

The King is unknown to the public [he writes in August, 1732]. The Jansenists say he can neither hear nor speak, but they are greatly mistaken. He is good-natured, I am told by persons in his entourage, has an excellent memory, and is a good mathematician— no small thing for a young King to care for these sciences. He is an admirable narrator, but for that he must be in his own circle. He is very timid and dislikes showing off. His discretion amounts to dissimulation. He is blindly attached to the Cardinal, which makes one wonder if he does not fear him as much as he likes him. But if he ever overcomes his timidity we may discover the qualities of a King.

The tough old priest lived for another ten years and Barbier, like most other people who wanted nothing for themselves, was in no hurry to see him go. The monarch seemed unable or unwilling to grow up. In 1738 the diarist records a rumour that his valet Bachelier supplied him with *filles* and that he had a touch of syphilis. 'One can say without flattery,' writes Barbier when the Cardinal was ill in 1739, 'that all France dreads his death, since the government, broadly speaking, is just and mild, and foreign countries feel complete confidence in his word.' The reaction to his illness at Versailles was very different, and the problem of the succession was the topic of the day. When at this moment Archbishop Tencin received the red hat it was generally expected that he was destined to fill the vacancy, little though he was respected or liked. Others guessed that Chauvelin might return. No one at Court seems to have expected that the King, now in his thirtieth year, would take the reins into his own nerveless hand.

When France plunged into the War of the Austrian Succession in 1740, contrary to the wishes of the Cardinal, it began to be felt that he was losing grip. Among Barbier's merits was his habit of copying into his journal selections from the anonymous *chansons* of the capital which took the place of a free press. Here is a specimen composed shortly before the Cardinal's death.

> Le désordre est ici complet,
> Comme tout le monde sait;
> Qui peut donc se taire, en effet,
> De voir l'Eminence
> Dans sa décadence,
> Traiter le roi comme un baudet [donkey]
> Comme tout le monde sait?

While the King had too little to do and suffered from incurable *ennui*, the long-suffering Queen was systematically overworked. According to d'Argenson, not the most reliable of witnesses, the sorely tried woman exclaimed, 'Toujours coucher, toujours grossesse, toujours accoucher.' She bore her burden bravely, merely lamenting that she had too many daughters and too few

sons. After three years of married life she informed her father
that no one had loved as she loved, but she was deluding herself.
Louis XV was too selfish and superficial to be capable of giving
or inspiring much love, and after seven years of matrimony she
witnessed the first of a series of *liaisons* which lasted till her death.
Much as she fretted she never allowed bitterness to poison her
soul. During the King's frequent absences while she was tied
to her base by repeated pregnancies, she wrote daily to Fleury
with news and tender messages. 'Please ask him to think sometimes of a woman who loves him more than her life. My obedience is even more blind from affection than from duty.' She also
made constant inquiries about the Cardinal's health, addressing
him as 'mon très cher ami', 'mon chérissime ami', signing herself
'la meilleure de vos amies'. If ever she needed advice, she added,
she would apply to him. Her solid virtues—loyalty, modesty,
and kindliness—won recognition beyond the walls of the palace,
and the chansonniers sought more rewarding targets. Her welcome on a visit to the capital in 1728—the first by a Queen of
France for half a century—was a well-deserved tribute to the
success with which she had played her part. Critics she had in
plenty but not an enemy in the world.

The most strenuous but perhaps also the happiest phase of her
married life was the decade of child-bearing. The nursery started
in 1727 with twin girls, Louise Elizabeth and Henriette, sometimes called Mme Première and Mme Seconde, followed in 1728
by Louise Marie, who died at the age of five. The eagerly
awaited Dauphin, who appeared in 1729, was greeted with
illuminations in the capital and a thanksgiving service at Notre
Dame attended by the King. The enthusiasm revealed a heritage
of monarchical sentiment so strongly entrenched that it could
only be destroyed over a long course of years by the King
himself. The birth of a second son in 1730 caused scarcely less
satisfaction, since child mortality was as high in crowded and
insanitary palaces as in the hovels of the countryside. When the
child passed away at the age of three the need of a second prince
to secure the succession in the direct line was as urgent as ever,
but it was not to be. Five princesses appeared within five years,
Adelaide in 1732, Victoire in 1733, Sophie in 1734, Félicité, who
died in infancy, in 1736, and Louise, 'Mme Dernière', in 1737.

The younger girls—Victoire, Sophie, Félicité and Louise—were packed off by Fleury in 1738 to be educated at the abbey of Fontevrault, and it required a ruse on the part of the Queen to keep Adelaide at home. Not daring to ask her husband for such a favour, the timid mother deputed her daughter to plead her own cause. The girl proceeded to waylay the King on his return from mass, kissed his hand, and wept. The plan succeeded, but the mass migration was a sore trial, all the more since visits from or to Fontevrault were never arranged, though Nattier was dispatched to paint the girls. Félicité she never saw again, Victoire not for ten years, Sophie and Louise not for twelve. The excuse for this amputation of family life appears to have been Fleury's desire to avoid the expense of the inflated households deemed necessary for even the youngest members of the Royal Family. The King cared little for his children till they grew up. In 1739 Louise Elizabeth departed to marry a cousin in Madrid, leaving only her twin sister Henriette, the Dauphin and Adelaide at home. It is not surprising that the only surviving son held a special place in his mother's heart.

The Queen took little interest in affairs till 1733, when the death of August II, Elector of Saxony and King of Poland, afforded a possibility of her father's restoration to the throne. With its crazy tradition of elective monarchy, Poland suffered a major crisis every time a ruler passed away. Stanislas, who had nothing to lose by failure, hurried to Warsaw and was elected for a second time. Though Louis XV felt no affection for his father-in-law, he welcomed the choice of a candidate so closely tied to France, but neither he nor Fleury was prepared to play for high stakes. Despite the appeals of Stanislas to his daughter to use her influence, only a small corps was dispatched and only four million francs were supplied. 'Must we ruin the King to aid his father-in-law?' exclaimed Fleury. A policy of limited liability was clearly the wisest course, for the strongest cards were in the hands of the rival candidate, Augustus III, Elector of Saxony. Russia, who had always backed the late King, was on the side of his son, and Sweden, whose warrior King had placed Stanislas on the throne, had fallen into the ranks of the minor states. A Russian army crossed the frontier and ordered a sparsely attended Diet to elect Augustus III. Stanislas took refuge in Danzig, whence he escaped in disguise on its surrender to the Russians after a long siege. For centuries the fortunes of Poland have been decided, not by the Poles, but by her more powerful neighbours.

The fiasco was a keen disappointment to the Queen, not only for her father's sake, but because his success might have augmented her slender store of prestige at Court. The easy-going Stanislas took his latest defeat philosophically, returned to his quiet life, and soon after received an unexpected consolation prize. When Francis, the reigning Duke of Lorraine, married Maria Theresa it was arranged that he should exchange his Duchy for Tuscany, where the Medici line became extinct in 1737. Lorraine was assigned to Stanislas with remainder to France. For the rest of his life the kindly old Epicurean made his little principality one of the happiest States in Europe, fostering agriculture, encouraging industry and the arts. The revenues of the State were transferred to France in return for a fixed annual allowance, and the First Minister, nominated by Fleury, was the virtual ruler of the country. The reign of the father-in-law of the King of France was a period of transition between the complete independence of the Duchy and its total absorption in France. Stanislas welcomed to his gay and tolerant little Court of Lunéville men of letters with Voltaire and Mme du Châtelet, Montesquieu and Helvétius at their head. 'I have been ill,' reported Voltaire, 'but that is a pleasure when one is a guest of the King of Poland. Nobody takes greater care of his invalids. It is impossible to be a better King or a better man.'

France's next international commitment was a far more serious affair, for she was dragged into the long and costly War of the Austrian Succession. The Pragmatic Sanction had been laboriously negotiated in vain, for when its author the Emperor Charles VI died in 1740 the crowned vultures swooped on the feast. Frederick II inaugurated his reign by the rape of Silesia, and the indignant Hapsburgs fought four wars during the next forty years in a vain attempt to recover their property. Louis XV had as little passion for military glory as his Minister, who would have preferred to stand aloof; but the pressure of the war party led by Marshal Belle-Isle and the anti-Austrian tradition of French policy proved too strong for him. Here, it was argued, was a golden opportunity of chastening the Hapsburg foe. However they might condemn the political morals of Frederick the Great France could not wish him to be crushed by the House of Hapsburg. Fleury believed that the conflict would be brief, but England intervened and it dragged on for eight years. For reasons of economy he had let down the army and navy, and France was in no condition to fight. It was one of the ironies of history that Fleury and Walpole, two of the most peace-loving statesmen of the modern world, should have closed their career by leading their peoples into unwanted and unprofitable wars.

As he approached his ninetieth year the Cardinal began to lose grip, and it was never in him to fight stubbornly even for causes in which he believed. The Prussian Minister reported that his stomach, eyes, and hearing were wearing out. 'It is a painful task to govern mankind,' he complained in 1742; 'the news from Italy and Bohemia makes me dizzy. I almost feel that we are nearing the end of the world. With all the dark clouds on every side a far stronger head than mine is needed.' One of his last acts was to write an abject letter to the Austrian Marshal König-segg at the same moment that he was instructing Marshal Belle-Isle to make peace, whatever the price. To regard him as the principal author of the troubles in Germany, he declared, was an injustice. 'Many people know how much I was opposed to the decisions we reached, and that I was in some measure forced to consent. Your Excellency can easily guess who did his utmost to determine the King to join a league which was so contrary to my inclination and my principles.' The offender to whom he referred was Marshal Belle-Isle, who was entrusted with the negotiations. That his letter was promptly published by the Austrian Government was a shock to the distracted old man who had thereby weakened the bargaining power of France. He had lived too long; but though he died amid the thunder of the guns he ranks among the few French statesmen who strove to spare the lives and pockets of their countrymen. Many people, commented Barbier, would regret the end of an era of tranquillity. If any mortal was ever happy, declared Voltaire, it was Fleury, who retained his health and his position till his death at the age of ninety. 'It was a happy time for all the nations which vied in commerce and the arts and forgot its past calamities.' Supermen are seldom wise, little men rarely strong. Yet the passing of this benevolent mediocrity left a vacuum which was not effectively filled till Choiseul was called to the helm fifteen years later. The war continued for another five years, ending with a treaty so unrewarding that Frenchmen taunted each other with the words 'Tu es bête comme la paix.' It was at this period that the phrase *travailler pour le roi de Prusse* became current coin. Frederick had retained Silesia with the aid of an ally who was to join his foes in the next round of the boxing-match.

4

THE FACE OF FRANCE

I

THE passing of Fleury in 1743, like the passing of Louis XIV in 1715, was generally welcomed at the Court of Versailles. In the lapidary phrase of Cardinal Bernis he had lived too long for his glory. The emotions of Louis XV were a blend of relief and regret—relief at the disappearance of the only person who ever ventured to lecture him, regret at the loss of his only trusted guide. 'I owe everything to him,' he wrote to his uncle at Madrid, 'and I always felt he took the place of my parents.' The removal of the old pilot provided the opportunity to take his place at the helm if he so desired. That his subjects wished him to rule as well as reign he was well aware. 'Le Cardinal est mort, vive le Roi,' was the cry in the streets, and for a brief space it seemed as if he might emerge from the shadows. At the age of sixteen, on the fall of the Duc de Bourbon, he had declared in a circular to the Intendants and the Governors of the provinces that he would rule in person like Louis XIV, but nothing had come of it. At the age of thirty-three he renewed his resolve. 'Messieurs,' he declared at his first Council, 'me voilà Premier Ministre.' Early impressions were favourable. 'The King works hard, and takes his duties seriously,' noted d'Argenson in his journal; 'he has more brains than the Cardinal, but he is timid and retains the services of certain people through dislike of new faces.' It was too good to last. Two months later when the bright dawn had faded, he is described by the same observer as unfeeling and caring little how the kingdom was governed. The more he saw of him, the less he understood him. 'What is he like? He is impenetrable and indefinable. Sometimes excuses are found for him, sometimes he is blamed.' Admirers were few, for there was little to praise, and flatteries would have recoiled on their authors for lack of plausibility. It was not entirely his fault, for with crowds he was shy and, like his unfortunate successor, he had no small talk. 'Sometimes you could see he was longing to speak,' testifies the Duc de Luynes, 'but the words died on his lips. He wished to say something friendly, but merely asked some trivial question.' Yet though stiff and silent in public, he expanded in intimacy. The latter tribute is confirmed by the Duc de Cheverny, whose official duty was to introduce Ambassadors. 'He was kindly, gay and chatty at the *petits soupers* where formality was banished; the servants left the room and the host poured out the coffee. Then came the card games with modest stakes. In these surroundings he was delightful, easy, and courteous.' An equally pleasant picture is drawn by the Duc de Croy. 'I have often felt more at home with him than with many others. His kindness is engraved on my heart. He never grumbled or stormed.' Temperamentally he was a pessimist with a low opinion not only of mankind but of himself.

The tragedy of his life—and the tragedy of France—was that he inherited a calling which he disliked and a political system which demanded more initiative than he could supply. France possessed institutions but no constitution. Eighteenth-century English rulers and statesmen inherited laws and precedents to guide them, from Magna Carta to Habeas Corpus. The sovereign was head of the State, but with the coming of the Hanoverians he ceased to be the effective head of the government. The latest English champion of dynastic autocracy by divine right was James II, who demonstrated that it could not last. Henceforth the monarch could neither rule without Parliament nor override its settled will. Limited monarchy was the invention of seventeenth-century England and in the eighteenth it became an axiom. The British Constitution embodied Montesquieu's ideal of the separation of powers. In France, on the contrary, there could be no appeal to the past, since there were no recognised sign-posts.

Instead of freedom slowly broadening down from precedent to precedent there had been retrogression, for the States-General had ceased to meet. In claiming and exercising full sovereignty on the ground that nothing less would meet the demand for unity, internal order and national strength, Louis XIV had been thought successful, but it soon became clear that the system could only be operated by a successor as able and industrious as himself. A young monarch of average ability, good intentions and a feeble will would not suffice: the ship needed a captain, not a mere figure-head. While Frederick the Great visited every part of his scattered dominions every year, halting his carriage in the village street and talking to everyone who wished to speak to him, Louis XV migrated from palace to palace in the environs of Paris, seeing little of his kingdom and his subjects, even in the capital. Barbier records that in 1750 he passed only fifty-two nights at Versailles. 'The thievings in my household are enormous,' he confessed to Choiseul, 'but there is no remedy. Too many powerful people are interested. Calm yourself, for the evil is incurable.' Everybody stole, from the highest to the lowest. Astronomical sums were charged for such items as coffee for the King, food and candles for Mesdames, but contractors often waited for years for their bills to be paid, and the wages of the gigantic household were often in arrears. The autocrat was the prisoner of the system of autocracy. His lamentable reputation in history derives less from what he did than from what he never tried to do. For him all evils were incurable.

The consequences of a *dilettante* on the throne were inevitable. 'There was the most intolerable incoherence in despotism,' declares Sorel, who always weighs his words, 'irresolution in omnipotence, anarchy in centralisation. All the powers were in conflict and each worked for itself. The Generals were paralysed by the fear of dismissal at any moment. There were party intrigues in the camps, where many of the officers owed their place to purchase or favour. The dikes were beginning to crumble.' The popularity of *Louis le Bienaimé* which followed his illness at Metz was as brief as a straw fire.

Judged by the low standards of his age Louis XV was not a bad man. His chief duty, as he saw it, was to preserve the system of autocracy unimpaired. A reference by an indiscreet courtier to the States-General provoked a sharp rebuke. 'Never say that again,' snapped the King. 'I am not cruel. But if my brother spoke like that I should not hesitate to sacrifice him to public order and the peace of the realm.' Convinced that his authority was from God, he regarded himself as master of the lives, fortunes and property of his subjects and above the reach of criticism. Most of the courtiers shared that conviction, which came to be challenged only by the bourgeoisie as the reign advanced. Lacking any profound sense of obligation to his subjects he felt he had done enough when he distributed bread after a bad harvest, money after a fire, pensions for elderly officers, and dowries for poor girls. Despite such occasional largesse, he was generally believed to care for little but his pleasures—not harsh but insensitive, not heartless but possessing an organ with a sluggish beat. He wished his subjects well but took no steps, either by innovation or renovation, to secure their welfare.

His second main task, as he conceived it, was the preservation of the Catholic faith from attacks by its enemies and the outward observance of his religious duties. Like his predecessor he said his prayers night and morning, heard mass every day, followed processions, and knelt in the road if the viaticum passed by. Like Louis XIV he detested Jansenists and Protestants. He spoke contemptuously of the *Philosophes*, whose writings he never read, as *ces gens-là*, though he reluctantly consented to appoint Voltaire a Gentleman of the Chamber and Historiographer and allowed him to stand for the Academy. Louis XIV had few intellectual interests and his successor fewer still. The ferment of ideas which made Paris 'le café de l'Europe', as the Abbé Galiani called it, was as remote from his field of vision as if it were located in another planet. The impression he produced was that of a spectator sitting at his ease in the royal box, not that of the conductor of the orchestra. He counted only in the distribution of offices and honours. Even here the field of choice was limited, for many of the higher posts at Court, in the administration, the Church, the magistracy and the army were hereditary. Owing to the absence of institutions in which the plight of the nation and the action or inaction of the Government could be discussed, public opinion found expression in anonymous pamphlets, broadsheets, and verses. 'Louis,' wrote a bitter

Parisian in 1749, 'you count the days by your evil deeds. If once we loved you it was because we were unaware of all your vices.' The King recognised that his stock was falling, but he made no effort to arrest the decline.

II

The failure of the monarch to play his allotted part was matched by the dearth of statesmen who understood the needs of France and possessed the courage to insist on drastic reform. The task of government was discharged by the Council, which consisted of about forty members, mainly heads of departments and Ministers without portfolio. In the absence of a titular *Premier Ministre* the Chancellor presided over meetings in the absence of the King. Though head of the judiciary, he possessed little power or patronage, and some of his work was discharged by the *Garde des Sceaux*. The most onerous post was that of Controller-General, but it was a thankless task to provide the money without supervising expenditure. Next in importance were the Ministers of Foreign Affairs, War, Marine, and the Royal Household. The Council was divided into five sections— home affairs, finance, commerce, justice, foreign affairs—but final decisions rested with the *Conseil d'État* or *Conseil du Roi*, the French equivalent of the British Cabinet. A seat on this body, whose decrees were laws, was a greater prize than the headship of a department, since it met two or three times a week in the presence of the King. In the middle years of the reign the leading figures were Orry, Controller-General, soon to be succeeded by Machault, Maurepas, Minister of Marine, and two elder states-men, Marshal Noailles and Cardinal de Tencin. The Duc de Saint-Florentin, Minister of the *Maison du Roi*, who served him for fifty years, was always at his side; Richelieu, First Gentleman of the Bedchamber, was never absent for long, and Bachelier, the chief valet, occupied a strategic position inferior to that of the Favourite alone.

Fleury was no eagle, but he was a better chief than the successors who divided his authority. The King hated them, declares d'Argenson, and treated them without consideration. 'Never was there such a bad team, more selfish and less resourceful. A revolution is inevitable, for the foundations are giving way. My readers may say that I run everyone down. Remember that in absolute monarchies Ministers are overburdened and are constantly obstructed by the Court, and thus no administration can be satisfactory.' D'Argenson was jealous and therefore unjust, for the team was well up to the average. For the first two years the King placed most confidence in the veteran Marshal Noailles. The most generally respected member was the learned and incorruptible Chancellor d'Aguesseau, one of the brightest legal luminaries of the *ancien régime*. After serving in the *Parlement* of Paris he had been appointed Chancellor under the Regency, was subsequently dismissed by Dubois and recalled by Fleury. He carried through some minor reforms of procedure but the codification of the law was beyond his strength.

The most important post was that of the Controller-General, for finance was the keystone to the whole structure; but it was one thing to proclaim a sound policy, another to overcome the stubborn resistance to reform. No Finance Minister in eighteenth-century France before Turgot brought to his office such zeal and such an opulent programme of overdue reforms as Machault, who succeeded Orry two years after Fleury's death. As an ex-Intendant he knew the problems of administration from inside and realised how much needed to be done. The War of the Austrian Succession was running its ruinous course and the need for more revenue was desperate. The *Parlement* of Paris grudgingly sanctioned a war tax of a *vingtième* but declined to register a permanent tax of the same amount on all classes, and the inroad on their traditional immunity from direct taxation was resisted by the clergy. The Minister also wished to close many convents, curtail the growth of new ones, ration legacies of land and money to the Church, develop internal trade, and foster agriculture. It was all in vain, for vested interests were too firmly entrenched. The clergy denounced his impiety, the grain speculators fought for their profits, and the King bowed to the storm by transferring him to the Ministry of Marine in 1754. Three years later his official career was terminated at the peremptory demand of Mme de Pompadour for personal reasons. With his fall went the last chance of financial reform during the reign of Louis XV.

The most colourful of the departmental Ministers was Maurepas, who had started his long career as Minister of the Royal Household at twenty-one, became Minister of Marine at twenty-six, and doyen of the Council at thirty-five with responsibility for the police at Paris and Versailles. He was a fluent talker, observes d'Argenson, but he treated trifles gravely and serious matters with levity. 'Satires and epigrams, in which he excelled, usurped the place of plans and policies. An *esprit fort*, he despised God, the King and royalty: fashion and frivolity were his deities. He found a thousand ridiculous imitators, promoted vice, oppressed virtue and good sense. This ensures admiration for his faults and follies, and consequently no administration has been worse than his. He laughs at the plight of the State, and has no remedies to suggest.' This spiteful portrait is too darkly tinted, but Maurepas may fairly be described as a light-weight.

Next in importance among the Ministers was Comte d'Argenson, younger brother of the diarist, who treats him with disdain for his alleged lack of principle. There may well have been an element of jealousy in this systematic denigration of a man whose ministerial career was so much longer and more successful than his own. Having graduated as an Intendant and a member of the Council of State, he was appointed in 1743 to the War Office, where he proved a good organiser and increased the number of bourgeois commissions. Trusted by the King, liked by the people, and on friendly terms with Mme de Pompadour, he held office till he was evicted after the Damiens incident. In 1744, to his intense delight, the diarist himself was appointed to succeed the feeble Amelot as Foreign Minister, after a long experience as Intendant and a member of the *Parlement* of Paris. His triumph was brief, for after a little more than two years he was dismissed on the ground of his intransigence in the closing phase of the War of the Austrian Succession. He never recovered from the blow, and his journal exudes the acidity in his soul. While certain Ministers and Court officials were unworthy of respect on account of evil living or gross incompetence, the higher civil servants who performed the routine work of the departments enjoyed a good reputation, but the absence of a firm hand at the helm was

G

sorely felt. 'C'est le vide qui règne,' was the bitter comment of d'Argenson, and for once he spoke the unvarnished truth.

III

Since neither the King nor his Ministers travelled about the country to see for themselves the resources and requirements of the provinces, the position of the Intendants was all the more vital. The '*Intendants de justice, police et finances, et commissaires départis dans les généralités du Royaume pour l'éxécution des ordres du Roi*' were instituted by Richelieu, abolished by the *Parlement* of Paris during the Fronde, and restored when the storm blew over. They were the eyes, ears and arms of the sovereign, the channels of communication between Versailles and the provinces, the executants of directives from the central government, collectors of statistics, sponsors of projects, petitioners for help in time of trouble. France, declared John Law, was governed by thirty Intendants. Most of them were middle-class lawyers whose paramount duty was to maintain the authority of the Crown against the nobility, the *Parlements* and the Estates. They gained knowledge and administrative experience which was of the highest value when, as was the case with Turgot and other leading statesmen, they were appointed Ministers. While the well-paid Governors divided their time between the discharge of ceremonial duties in their province and attendance at Court, the whole administrative responsibility rested on the Intendant, issuing *Ordonnances*, collecting the direct taxes, apportioning the *taille* between the parishes, fostering agriculture and commerce, organising the ballot for the militia, supervising the execution of public works authorised by the *Conseil d'État*, directing the hated *corvée*, relieving the poor, preserving order with power to hang criminals or send them to the galleys. Their most enduring achievement during the reign of Louis XV was the construction of excellent roads all over the country. They were the principal agents in the long process of administrative centralisation which began with Richelieu, and Napoleon's Prefects carried on their work.

While the influence of the Intendants steadily increased, the Provincial Estates, surviving from the Middle Ages, and consisting of three Orders, nobles, clergy, and commons, were lapsing into insignificance. Their task had been to raise local taxation and direct administration till Richelieu transferred their duties in the so-called *Pays d'Élection* to the Intendants throughout three-fourths of France. The remaining quarter, embracing the provinces called *Pays d'État*, retained their Estates, but it was only in Brittany and Languedoc that they exercised any administrative powers. They could neither make laws nor impose taxation nor borrow money without consent of the Crown. They could propose public works and execute them after obtaining permission, collect certain items of the revenue, and make grants to the Crown. Since they were not popularly elected, and included no spokesmen of the peasantry who formed the bulk of the population, they played a minor part in the life of the nation and were swept away at the Revolution.

In rural France there was no half-way house between the 40,000 villages and the Province—nothing corresponding to the modern *arrondissement* as a link between the Commune and the Department. The villages were not wholly without rights, for all who paid *taille* could attend the assembly which managed the common lands, kept roads and bridges, the church fabric and the parsonage in repair, elected the syndics and the collectors of the *taille*. But they were subject in every respect to the Intendant, who in turn had to secure the approval of the Council, and necessary tasks were often held up by bureaucratic delay. In this respect there was too much, not too little, centralisation. Every town possessed its charter and its General Assembly, which had once included all the citizens but had shrunk into narrow oligarchies with limited powers. The Mayor was appointed by the Crown, the finances were controlled by the Intendant, and proposals for public works were submitted through the Intendant for leisurely approval in Paris.

Passing from the sphere of central and local government to that of law we find a baffling confusion. There was nothing resembling our Common Law and our fundamental statutes. The power of the sovereign had slowly increased since the close of the Middle Ages and was vigorously championed by Crown lawyers, but a mosaic of jurisdictions—feudal, ecclesiastical, urban—survived. The most important were the thirteen *Parlements*, courts of appeal though themselves liable to be overruled by the Crown. Of these the *Parlement* of Paris was the oldest and much the most powerful, its regional authority extending far beyond the capital and including almost half the population of France. Its younger sisters were at Toulouse, Grenoble, Bordeaux, Dijon, Rouen, Aix, Rennes, Pau, Metz, Douai, Nancy, Besançon. Though primarily judicial, they claimed a share in the government, for the registration of the royal edicts which formed part of their duty seemed to them to imply the right to criticise or even to refuse proposals for legislation or taxation. Such challenges to the authority of the Crown could hardly be accepted, the sovereign often cancelling their decrees and removing cases from their jurisdiction. The first collision in the reign of Louis XV arose from the refusal of the Paris *Parlement* to register the anti-Jansenist decree of 1730. The request for an audience was met with an order for silent obedience. The Chancellor explained that the power of making and interpreting laws rested solely with the King, that the business of the *Parlement* was merely to see that the laws were obeyed, and that magistrates should set an example of obedience. Quarrels continued throughout the reign, coming to a head in the closing years of the reign before the *Parlements* were swept away by the Revolution. They had never been able to speak in the name of the nation, for they were staffed by the privileged classes. Standing midway between the Court and the people they commanded little confidence and respect in either camp. 'These great lawyers and the clergy are always at daggers drawn,' grumbled the King. 'I am sick of their quarrels, but the lawyers are the worst. At bottom the clergy are loyal to me, but the others want to treat me as a ward. The Regent made a great mistake in restoring to them the right of remonstrance. They will end by ruining the State.' That they were as stoutly opposed to the free discussion of political and religious issues as to the royal prerogative was illustrated by the decision to burn Voltaire's *Lettres Philosophiques sur les Anglais* in 1734. Nowhere in France was there to be found any institution standing for ordered liberty.

In addition to the *Parlements* about one hundred ordinary

courts dealt with local disputes and heard appeals from royal and feudal tribunals in cases where small sums were involved. Petty cases were taken in the courts of the *Bailliages* and *Sénéchaussées*, which also heard appeals from feudal courts. Louis XII, in need of money, had made judgeships purchasable, and Henri IV made them hereditary in return for a small annual payment called the *Paulette*. Finally there were a few special courts for the extensive Crown lands, and *Chambres Ardentes*—special commissions with summary jurisdiction—for such cases as corrupt financiers, smugglers, and heretics. The system of *épices*, virtually obligatory presents, the sum being calculated according to the length of the case, had taken root. Despite the commercialised element in the administration of justice the system worked fairly well, though against gross abuses there was no remedy.

Passing from national to private legal authorities we reach the maze of feudal jurisdictions, which played a decreasing part in the national life as the power of the Crown increased; for the major crimes, such as treason, false coining, homicide, highway robbery, had been gradually transferred to the State courts which also heard appeals from the feudal courts. In these private courts there were usages but no recognised system of jurisprudence. Roman law dominated in the south, customary or State law in the centre and north, and wide local variations rendered standardisation impossible. Cruel punishments were still inflicted, including torture to extract confessions and breaking on the wheel.

At the end of the long list of jurisdictions comes the royal prerogative of *lettres de cachet* which, by-passing the courts, required neither trial nor evidence nor limit of time for the sentence. Issued through the Minister of the *Maison du Roi* in the name of the King, few were for political offences or political reasons. Most were motived by family disputes, as in the case of the younger Mirabeau. Inmates of the Bastille were fairly well—sometimes extremely well—treated and in some cases were allowed to receive visitors. Yet, though the total number of victims was small, the danger of sudden arrest, without charge, trial or appeal, was never absent from the thoughts of writers whose political or religious utterances might give offence. For the abandonment of this extra-legal weapon in the royal armoury and for uniformity in the administration of justice France had to wait till the Revolution.

There was as little system in the finances as in the field of law: no budget was framed and the Government lived from hand to mouth. The Treasury, unable to meet the current demands of the departments, the salaries of the Court and public works such as roads, borrowed freely from the bourgeoisie and the interest was often in arrears. Not till the publication of Necker's celebrated *Compte Rendu* in 1781 was it possible to form a clear idea of the revenue and expenditure. The extensive *Domaine* was the private concern of the sovereign, at whose pleasure portions were sold or given away. The main item of expenditure was war and the services, and the principal source of revenue was the *taille*, from which the nobility, the clergy, the magistrates and the Court officials were exempt. Based mainly on land, the amount was fixed annually by the Government. There was also a capitation tax on every householder assessed on his estimated wealth, and a *vingtième*, a levy on all property, real and personal, first levied to meet the cost of the later wars of Louis XIV and revived by Machault. The Church, protesting that its immunity was part of the Catholic religion, substituted a *don gratuit* of varying dimensions at their quinquennial meeting. In addition to these direct taxes, revenue was derived from indirect taxes collected by the Farmers-General on such articles as alcohol, tobacco, playing cards, paper, jewellery, steel and iron, as well as from customs and excise, tolls on goods crossing the property of corporations and landowners. The *gabelle*, or salt tax, the *corvée* or forced labour for roads and public works, and the billeting of soldiers were particularly resented. It has been calculated that taxation, tithes and feudal dues took about four-fifths of the farmer's income. Local risings against the taxes were frequent and often cruelly suppressed.

The total sum collected from direct or indirect taxation was not excessive in proportion to the national resources, but hardship arose from the unequal distribution of the burden. The farming of indirect taxes to the highest bidder was described by Voltaire as organised robbery. The first Farmers-General were appointed in 1697 for six years, and the system continued till the Revolution. Though it was a convenience for the Government to hand over a mass of financial detail to private citizens, who occasionally made advances on loan to the Treasury, the large fortunes built up by the forty collectors and their assistants represented a serious loss to the State. The revenue steadily increased but expenditure outpaced it till half of it was allotted to the national debt. The Government was in chronic difficulty. Revenue was anticipated, the currency was debased, and loans were negotiated at high rates. So long as the financial exemptions of the privileged classes continued large deficits were unavoidable, and the growing burden of taxation inflamed the resentment of the *Tiers État*. Despite the grossly inequitable division of the national burden the nation as a whole steadily increased in wealth, though diffused prosperity had to wait for the sweeping reforms of the Revolution.

IV

The first of the privileged Estates was the Church, which possessed a revenue about half that of the Crown, derived partly from its own lands, partly from tithes. The prestige it had enjoyed throughout the seventeenth century had waned, and the Regulars—monks and nuns—had decreased in numbers. The quinquennial assembly, composed of representatives from the sixteen provincial assemblies, voted a gift to the Crown, which was supplemented in time of war by additional grants, but they were under no obligation to contribute. The wealth of the Church was very unevenly divided, rich sees, abbeys and sinecures contrasting sharply with the poverty of the village *curé*. Though the Crown was unable to levy taxation on the clergy, it exercised a larger measure of control than the Vatican. The Concordat of 1516 inaugurated the Gallican system. Confirmed and enlarged by the Four Articles of 1682, it proclaimed the right of the King to nominate to the Archbishoprics, Bishoprics and wealthy abbeys, subject to papal confirmation, and ecclesiastical decrees were invalid without the royal assent. The popularity of Febronianism in Germany and Austria emphasised the resolve of Catholic rulers to be masters in their own house. The higher dignitaries, many of whom held more than one post, were sometimes courtiers and men of the world, often non-resident, in a few cases dissolute or unbelievers. Most of the plums went to the nobility, the eldest son joining the army, the younger entering the Church. Yet the Church still presented an imposing façade and played a leading part in the life of the nation. There were 131 Archbishops and Bishops and 700 Abbés, some of whom lived like princes, above all the Rohans, hereditary Bishops of Strasbourg, the see, with a Cardinal's hat attached to it, passing from uncle to nephew for generations. The promotion of Dubois to the Sacred College was the grossest scandal since the death of Cardinal de Retz, and worldly Abbés, some of them laymen, enjoyed their revenues without performing any duties. No outstanding figure adorned the hierarchy after the death of Massillon in 1742 except Christophe de Beaumont, Archbishop of Paris for thirty-five years, sometimes described as the Athanasius of his century. The brightest ornaments were the Benedictines of St. Maur, whose heroic labours in the field of classical antiquity and ecclesiastical history shone like a beacon light in a dark world.

The Church in France was less ideologically homogeneous than in any Catholic country in Europe. The clergy were mainly Gallican in sentiment, while the Jesuits ardently championed the authority of the Pope. They had gained their power through the favour of Louis XIV who selected them for his confessors. 'Such fear of hell had been instilled into him,' wrote the Duchess of Orleans, 'that he believed that all who had not been instructed by the Jesuits were damned. To ruin anyone it was enough to say that he was a Huguenot or a Jansenist.' Next to their favour at Court the Order gained prestige by its excellent schools, which were attended not merely by the nobility but by well-to-do bourgeois like Voltaire and President Hénault. The Jansenists, on the other hand, sorely stricken by the destruction of Port Royal in 1709 and by the Bull '*Unigenitus*' in 1713, were discredited in 1729 by the hysterical scenes which followed the death of the Abbé Paris, a saintly parish priest and a notorious opponent of the Jesuits and the Bull '*Unigenitus*'. Devotees cut locks from his hair and carried away pieces of his clothes and fragments of his furniture as relics. During the funeral a woman threw herself on the coffin, crying aloud that her arm which had been withered for twenty-five years had recovered its power. Her story brought throngs to the grave and other cures followed. The excitement grew into mass hysteria, invalids being laid on the tombstone, the faithful writhing in convulsions and foaming at the mouth. The Day of Judgment, they believed, was at hand. At length Fleury intervened and the cemetery was closed.

The strength of the Jansenists had lain, not in their Augustinian theology which few could understand, but in the austerity of their lives. The good city of Paris, declared Barbier, was Jansenist from head to foot. Yet their stock fell steadily as the century advanced. The final blow was struck by a royal edict in 1730 making the Bull—already obligatory on the Church—binding on the whole people, and forbidding the printing and sale of Jansenist writings. When the *Parlement* of Paris refused the necessary registration Fleury overrode its opposition by a *lit de justice*. Certificates known as *billets de confession* to a *Unigenitus* priest were demanded from dying Jansenists before they were allowed to receive the last sacraments, and some priests required a *billet de confession* before they performed the marriage ceremony. Henceforth Jansenism survived only in a few convents and parsonages, and by the close of the reign it was little more than a memory. Never for a moment had there been a thought of leaving the Church. Their secretly printed organ *Nouvelles Ecclésiastiques*, though they were forbidden to read it under pain of excommunication, kept the members in touch. These fierce internal controversies discredited the Church and prepared the way for the reign of the *Philosophes*. Since the destruction of Jansenism, declares Lecky, all the independent characters and all the honest intellect of France seemed alienated from the Christian faith.

While the Jansenists gradually faded away, the Huguenots held their ground tenaciously against desperate odds. After the bloody suppression of the Camisards in the Cevennes Louis XIV boasted shortly before his death that the exercise of 'the so-called Reformed Religion' had ceased. But at this dark moment a new leader, Antoine Court, emerged, as dynamic as the guerrilla chief, Jean Cavalier, and proceeded to rebuild the shattered edifice from the foundations. Since not a single pastor remained, a candidate was sent to Zurich to be ordained and the new pastor then ordained Antoine Court. Places of worship being forbidden, prayer meetings were held in 'the desert'. When the movement began to spread through the south even secret religious gatherings were prohibited and new penalties were announced. After a price was set on the leader's head he fled to Lausanne, where he founded a seminary for the training of pastors of which he remained Director to the end of his life. Though deprived of all civil rights, threatened with long sentences to the galleys for attending public services, liable to execution on false charges like Jean Calas, who was broken on the wheel in Toulouse, their marriages unrecognised and their children regarded as bastards, the spirit of the Huguenots remained unbreakable. A few scattered congregations kept the flame alive till the Revolution restored their civil rights and enabled their numbers to increase; but nothing could make up for the ground lost by the revocation of the Edict of Nantes and the decades of savage persecution which followed.

The social stratification bequeathed by the Middle Ages lingered on till the eighteenth century, though the barriers were becoming less rigid. Within the ranks of the aristocracy disdain was felt by the old *Noblesse de l'Épée* for the parvenu *Noblesse de Robe*, mostly bourgeois who had climbed out of their class by purchasing offices carrying a patent of nobility and exemption from direct taxation. In the same way the nobles attached to the tinsel Court looked down on their impecunious colleagues who vegetated on their remote estates. Younger sons, unable to engage in commerce and industry, continued to find an outlet for their energies in the army and navy. The social influence and prestige of the *Noblesse* during the reign of Louis XV diminished as rapidly as their political status had waned in the era of Richelieu and the fiasco of the Fronde.

The *Tiers État*, consisting of lawyers and civil servants, financiers and contractors, men engaged in industry and commerce, with an ever-growing army of Intellectuals to voice their opinions and demands, looked to the future, not to the past. The increase in their numbers and their wealth had not been accompanied by a corresponding advance in political influence. That posts in the army, navy and diplomacy, and most of the higher appointments in the Church, were beyond their reach increased the sense of frustration and hostility to the *ancien régime* till their hour struck in 1789. While they were waiting for recognition of their rights the brightest intellects in the bourgeoisie, with Voltaire, Diderot and d'Alembert at their head, made Paris the Mecca of European culture. There was not a radical, much less a revolutionary, among them: all they asked was decent government and intellectual liberty.

The lowest of the classes was not recognised as an Estate. The peasants had shed various feudal burdens, and their condition was better than that of the tillers of the soil in most other continental countries, but their lot remained hard and at times almost unbearable. In so large a country, with great varieties of climate, soil and tenure, conditions varied considerably; but the *taille* and the tithe, the *corvée* and the *gabelle*, weighed heavily on all, and manorial rights were a nuisance when they were not a serious burden. Most were *métayers*, who paid their landlord a fixed share of the produce in place of rent. Many peasants saved enough to buy a little plot of land. The lowest section of the agricultural community was the landless labourers who worked for a pittance. The whole industry was hampered by the system of internal tolls which hindered profitable sales and economical purchases in neighbouring markets. The general level had risen since La Bruyère painted his macabre picture of creatures scarcely recognisable as human beings; but with the burden of taxation, the poor food, local famines, hovels for homes and lack of medical care, their lot was at best unenviable and at worst a national disgrace. The industrialisation inaugurated by Colbert had not developed fast enough to create an alternative market for their labour in the towns. The King pitied the sufferers but did not feel that it was his fault or responsibility. No eighteenth-century ruler or Minister dreamed of a Civil List which would have established the principle that the needs of the country came before the pageantry of the Court. 'You have seen nothing,' declared Chateaubriand, 'if you have not seen the pomp of Versailles.'

The army could always count on an unlimited supply of officers from the *Noblesse*, many of whom bought their commissions, but to obtain the rank and file was more difficult. The paucity of volunteers and the frequency of desertions necessitated the press gang and the enrolment of foreign mercenaries. The regulars numbered about 170,000, and a militia of about 60,000 conscripted for six years by ballot was almost entirely supplied by the peasantry on the basis of a quota for each district. The higher commands were usually allotted by Court favour. After the veterans of Louis XIV—Vendôme, Villeroi, Villars—had passed away, the ablest soldier of the reign was a foreigner, Marshal Saxe. The morale of the army declined, owing not merely to its defeats in the old and the new world, but to the lack of suitable officers and to the condition of the troops—badly fed, badly housed and stingily paid. No régime is secure unless it can rely on the troops. When the test came in 1789 the chief prop of the Monarchy collapsed and the army had to be rebuilt from its foundations on the principle that every private might carry a Field-Marshal's baton in his knapsack. From the laurels of Rocroy and Denain to the headlong rout of Rossbach was a lamentable decline. The navy had a better record, though it was more difficult for the Minister of Marine than for the Minister of War to obtain funds. While France had several potential enemies on land, England was her only potential rival at sea, and when the relations between the two countries were friendly, during the era of Walpole, Dubois, and Fleury, the fleet was let down. Since it was officered mainly by the *Noblesse*, promotion by merit was rare. Not till the emergence of Suffren could France boast of a great sea captain and meet the challenge of her northern neighbour on equal terms.

A hundred years ago Tocqueville analysed the administrative system and social relations in the most revealing work ever written on eighteenth-century France. The country, he explained, was subject to three governments: the King and his Ministers working through the Intendants, the feudal jurisdictions, and the provincial institutions. The central power was by far the strongest and its strength grew from year to year. The feudal authority was weak and waning rapidly. The provincial institutions were little more than picturesque survivals, ghosts of their former selves. Behind the façade of a dissolving aristocracy Tocqueville discerned a powerful central dynamo gradually extinguishing local authorities, privileged corporations and seigneurial rights. Though Louis XV was as weak as water, the machinery was being fashioned for more effective use when firmer hands assumed control.

The *ancien régime*, though inefficient and unpopular, was less oppressive in France than in many other continental states. Since feudalism as a system of government and aristocracy as a political force had disappeared, surviving privileges seemed the more odious because the structure of which they had formed part had crumbled away. Discontent rapidly increased, not because conditions became worse or the burden was intolerable but because a growing proportion of citizens grew less tolerant of abuses. The gravamen against Louis XV was not that he created a faulty machine but that he accepted its imperfections. France, he believed, was his domain, and he owed no account of his stewardship to his countrymen. Though he occasionally read in letters opened by the *cabinet noir* what his subjects said of him and his entourage, it never occurred to him that he must mend his ways. In 1743 it was still possible to save the Bourbon Monarchy, but he was not the man for such an exacting task.

5

THE FIRST THREE FAVOURITES

No one expected Louis XV to remain faithful to his plain and timid wife for very long or to rise above the low moral standard of the age. The profession of royalty combined the maximum of temptation with the maximum of opportunity. In a country where child marriages were the rule among the nobility, little was asked of a bride except to secure the succession of title and property by providing a legitimate heir. Having fulfilled that paramount duty, she felt no less entitled than her husband to consult her own tastes: if one or other partner made a fuss it was attributed to prudery or pedantry. That the sovereign had a right to the same privileges was taken as a matter of course. 'Of twenty gentlemen at court,' writes Barbier in his Journal, 'fifteen do not live with their wives and have mistresses. It is the same in Paris. So it is ridiculous to ask that the King, who is the master, should be worse off than his subjects and his royal predecessors.'

The matrimonial fortunes of the Bourbons were as chequered as those of the Valois Kings. Henry of Navarre, the founder and the most popular member of the dynasty, was notorious for his amours, and the story of his disguising himself in an effort to seduce the Princesse de Condé was known to everyone. That Louis XIII, the child of Henri IV and the fleshly Marie de Medicis, should be a model of continence seemed a miracle, all the more since for many years he lived apart from his Spanish Queen. That Louis XIV inherited the pathological sensuality of his grandfather was manifest before his marriage, and soon after a Dauphin was born to him at the age of twenty-three he deserted his wife for a succession of *maîtresses en titre*. While his son inherited his passions, his grandson, the Duc de Bourgogne, happily married to the Rose of Savoy, followed the precedent of Louis XIII. That the *liaisons* which play so large a part in the colourful story are not in all cases to be explained solely by the lusts of the flesh is as true of the mediocre Louis XV as of his majestic predecessor. Yet the differences were at least as great as the similarities. If the promotion of a woman to the coveted position of *maîtresse en titre* was not to impair the prestige of the Crown she must not attempt to interfere in the graver matters of State and the King must confine his favours to members of the aristocracy. It is because these conditions were observed by Louis XIV and ignored by his successor that in the former case the royal amours assumed no political significance, while in the latter they prepared the way for the downfall of the Monarchy.

Marie Leczinska provided France with an heir to the throne, but she could do little more to make her marriage a success. Lacking beauty, vivacity, and charm, she looked older than her years and quickly got on the nerves of the King. Amiable and tolerant though she was, her sterling qualities made no appeal to a young ruler whose distaste for work left far too much time on his hands. Her amateur efforts as a painter and musician failed to arouse his interest, and the serious literature she enjoyed meant nothing to a man who never cared about books. Hunting was a never-failing resource, but he liked to be entertained in the evenings by a bright and resourceful woman with whom he could feel at his ease. He was attracted to the middle-aged wife of the Comte de Toulouse, the latter a bastard of Louis XIV, who presided with womanly charm over a dignified little Court at Rambouillet, but it was a liking and nothing more. Still more to his taste in his lighter moments was Mlle de Charolais, sister of the Duc de Bourbon, a lively tomboy who boasted of lovers since her fifteenth year and would gladly have added him to the list. Lacking men friends he sought congenial female society.

Though d'Argenson entertained little respect for the idle King, he sympathised with his lack of domestic happiness. His unfriendly portrait of the Queen must be checked against that of the Duc de Luynes who knew her infinitely better, but it cannot be dismissed as mere gossip and malice. 'A Lady in Waiting,' he records in October, 1740, 'says the Queen is chiefly to blame for the King taking a mistress. She behaved like a prude, and no living creature has less *esprit*.' Some of her habits annoyed the King. One of her ladies held her hand and told stories to send her off, for she was a bad sleeper. She had so many clothes on the bed that her partner was almost suffocated. In the early days of marriage the King wished to play cards in her apartment and talk. 'Instead of petting him, she bored him with her talk. So he passed the evenings elsewhere, first with men, then with women like his cousin de Charolais and the Comtesse de Toulouse. He is very timid and wants people who put him at his ease.' His respect for the admonitions of his old preceptor had helped to keep him in the straight path, but soon after the birth of the Dauphin he began to go his own way. At a supper-party he raised his glass '*à l'inconnue*' and left the company guessing.

His first choice was Mme de Mailly, one of the *dames du palais* to the Queen. When the *liaison* began we cannot be sure, for in its early stages it was discreetly veiled, but the Duc de Luynes assigns it to 1733. Her father, the Marquis de Nesle, a dissolute gambler, set a bad example to his five daughters, at least three of whom captivated the King. Louise, the eldest, was married at sixteen to her cousin the Comte de Mailly, but the union was childless. She was nice-looking rather than pretty, reports d'Argenson, and very poor. 'She is good-natured, tractable and cheerful and by no means clever. Once her timidity was overcome she amused the King, and no affair has been conducted with more mystery or less scandal. She has become reserved and never puts herself forward. She seems out of touch with her family who are greedy for favours and fortune. Her ugliness scandalises foreigners who expect a King's mistress at any rate to have a pretty face.' She loved the King, testifies the Duchesse de Brancas, as the La Vallière loved Louis XIV; but it seemed to the courtiers as if there was something about her of the penitent.

The secret was fairly well kept till 1737, and in 1738, a year after the birth of Louise, the last of the princesses, she supped openly with the King at Compiègne. 'La chose est publique,' noted Barbier in his diary. 'The Queen is in a cruel position,' comments d'Argenson, 'having to retain her as a *dame du palais*. During her weeks of service she is very depressed. She knows Mme de Mailly is always on the watch to discover some new eccentricity with which to divert the King.' That the King ceased to live with his wife in 1738 was attributed to her refusal to receive him after a *fausse couche*, since she omitted to inform him of the doctor's warning that further miscarriages were to be feared. She was much too submissive to impose even a temporary blockade without the most cogent reasons, and after the painful birth of her youngest child she told her husband that she would gladly suffer as much again if she could give him a Duc d'Anjou. Yet the cessation of his visits was a relief, all the more since he sometimes arrived with his breath reeking of champagne. For the remainder of her life their contacts were brief and formal, without pretence of affection on either side. The vivacity of Mme de Mailly, which made up for her lack of beauty, formed a welcome contrast to the boring company of the Queen. The partnership brought more satisfaction to him than to her, since her happiness was overcast by the haunting fear that she might lose her place.

For the first and last time in the annals of the Court, the reigning favourite was displaced by a member of her family. Her younger sister, the Duchesse de Vintimille, more ambitious and uninhibited, a Montespan rather than a La Vallière, stormed her way into the citadel. Unhappily married, like most of the aristocracy, she felt no scruple in shaping her own career. 'She stinks like the devil,' commented her husband. She was a masculine type, large-limbed and ugly, but the King cared less for looks than for temperament. Tiring of the elder sister, he transferred his patronage to the new Favourite for whom he bought Choisy, a snug little hunting-box on the Seine, where he spent more time than at Versailles. Feeling less anxious than her elder sister about the tenure of her post, the new mistress took a bolder line with her lover, urging him to dismiss Fleury and interest himself in the army. Her triumph was brief, for she died in giving birth to the Marquis du Luc, commonly known as *le demi-Louis* from his likeness to his father. It was the first grief in the life of the monarch and the earliest of a series of moods of piety which

H

recurred at long intervals throughout his life. 'I do not regret my rheumatism,' he explained in a fervour of contrition, 'it is in expiation of my sins.' For some days he sat in silence, ate little, and occasionally left the table in tears. The penitential mood passed as quickly as the grief, for his emotions never caused lasting pain. For a brief space Mme de Mailly, who took care of her sister's child, recovered a measure of influence; but once again the King tired of her, and for the second time she was displaced by a sister, even more greedy and unscrupulous than Mme de Vintimille. When the King remarked 'j'aime ta soeur, tu m'ennuis', her fate was sealed. Turning her back for ever on the Court she paid her debts, donned a hair shirt, and devoted herself to good works in a conversion no less sincere than that of the La Vallière in the previous reign. 'Great news,' noted d'Argenson in his Journal in November, 1742. 'Mme de Mailly was dismissed and Mme de Tournelle taken, with a harshness unintelligible in a *Roi très Chrétien*.' The new Favourite demanded and secured the exile of the old to a distance of four leagues. Her nephew, the motherless Marquis du Luc, was to enter the army, become Maréchal de Camp, joined the Émigrés under Napoleon, and died on the eve of the Restoration. Though always more prone to blame than to praise, the diarist takes leave of Mme de Mailly in generous words. 'She has a good heart, is kind to her friends and relations, and has done no one any harm. She is regretted by everyone at Versailles.'

Mme de la Tournelle was a wealthy widow, the cleverest and the worst of the sisters. Cool and calculating, without morals or heart, she resolved to squeeze every ounce of profit out of her post. 'She was tall and majestic,' testifies the Duchesse de Brancas, 'with rather strong and regular features. Her large blue eyes had an enchanting look, and every movement breathed infinite grace.' She demanded and obtained recognition as *maîtresse en titre*, the title of Duchess, a house in Paris, jewels, a lavish monthly allowance, and the legitimisation of any children she might bear to the King. Her acknowledged model was Mme de Montespan. She was coached by her cousin, the Duc de Richelieu, whom she called her uncle, the champion rake of eighteenth-century France, who as First Gentleman of the Bedchamber had constant access to the King. Their correspondence, preserved among the Richelieu papers, records every move in the game to become the power behind the throne and reveals how insignificant a part was played by affection.

The new Favourite felt so sure of herself that she could afford to play pranks with her lover who called her *La Princesse*. 'I heard him scratching at my door,' she reported in November, 1742, 'but when he saw I did not get up he went away. He must get used to that.' When Richelieu advised her not to play with fire, she replied that he need not be alarmed. 'I am not surprised at your anger, dear uncle, for I expected it, but I think you are a little unreasonable. I can't admit that it was silly of me to decline a little visit. Calm yourself. All will go well.' The King's mood, as is the way with royal lovers, was as changeable as a weather-cock.

> I have told you, dear uncle [she wrote in May, 1743], how anxious I have felt about his cold attitude towards me recently. There were certainly some plots against me, and I hear Maurepas was the instigator. I have no proofs and the general friendliness I meet with makes me feel there is nothing to fear from the rest. If his super-ficial character had led to an estrangement I could have died of grief, but I should not have tried to get him back. You know him. His return has brought everyone to my side again. Though they did not exactly cut me it was easy to observe their constraint. The King said to me that I took no interest in public affairs since I never spoke of them. As you know, I conceal any desire or knowledge in order to encourage him to instruct me. He has spoken to me too often about my sisters' interference for me to wish to follow their example. We must go slow and give no ground for reproach. He is often fed up with work. The less I talk about events the more he likes to tell me, and then is the moment to act. I shall always unhesitatingly follow your advice and will do nothing without consulting you. Adieu, dear uncle. I am very happy. No one could be nicer to me than he, and I feel more attached to him every day.

Her ambition was gratified in the autumn with a title and an estate.

> Good news for you, dear uncle. The King has been so kind as to give me the duchy of Châteauroux. I am filled with gratitude. I learn that Mme de Maurepas is greatly upset by my dignity and envies me my *tabouret*.* Her husband, to please her, tried to postpone

* A footstool in the Grande Galerie.

this royal favour and to play me tricks. I close my eyes to these little intrigues so common in my position. The same persons who wanted to injure me are those who show me the greatest attentions. If I were to frown on them I should have to make faces on three-quarters of the people I meet.

The first qualification for her exacting profession was to have a thick skin.

The long-suffering Queen, who had tolerated the eldest of the three sisters, detested the arrogant woman who was forced on her as a Lady-in-Waiting, refused to speak to her, and sometimes pretended to go to sleep. Her disapproval was shared by Fleury, who begged his master to think of the prestige of France and appealed to his religious sentiments. It was all in vain, for the infatuated ruler had become her slave, and she was installed in the apartments previously occupied by her sisters. He loved her, testifies Choiseul, as much as he could love anybody. The last weak obstacle to her power was removed by the death of the Cardinal, and the coveted title of Duchesse de Châteauroux set the seal on her triumph. Furnished with a Household of her own and provided with a large estate, she became the Queen of France in all but name. Every step was discussed with Richelieu, who took counsel with Mme de Tencin, the heartless mother of d'Alembert and the most influential survivor of the dissipated circle of the Regent. The General Staff was completed by her brother Cardinal de Tencin, who was no better than the rest. It was a formidable coalition.

The Duchess was well aware of the unfitness of Louis XV for his exalted post at the height of the War of the Austrian Succession. 'The King came from a session of the *Conseil* very worried about all the plans for the next campaign,' she reported to Richelieu in November, 1743.

Some wish him to drop the Emperor [Charles VII, Elector of Bavaria], others to support his election. I begin to feel that everyone is too much on his own and that we need a stronger will than the King possesses. Your advice to me to speak more firmly may be sound enough and I shall follow it, but you know the tendency to let every Ministry go its own way. That is the routine which is difficult to change, and against prejudices the best arguments cannot prevail. Good intentions are not enough. As for myself I don't possess all the qualifications to strive for more power. I can see how many things are wrong but I don't know the answers. Certainly changes will be needed and you will suggest what course I should adopt. Cardinal de Tencin seems to be cultivating me, and I wonder what you think of it. His sister is a liability, for, clever though she is, she cannot hide her ambition. I have had several anonymous letters, doubtless from her, full of complaints of Maurepas. Her views vary with her interests.

The vast palace, as usual, hummed with intrigue.

The most formidable foe of the Favourite was Maurepas, the cleverest of the Ministers and most to the royal taste. It occurred to her and Richelieu that his influence might be diminished if the ruler could be induced to take a more active part in the task of government now that Fleury was gone, and to increase his popularity would be to enhance her prestige. In February, 1744, she informed Richelieu that he had decided to take part in the coming campaign.

He has just promised me, and I can assure you nothing can give me greater pleasure. You know how I love day-dreams, and at this moment my imagination depicts the most brilliant future. I see the King covered with glory, adored by his subjects and feared by his enemies. I believe the presence of the master will be worth another army. Marshal Noailles will remain in command with two forces, one under his orders, the other under the Comte de Saxe of whom high hopes are entertained. His Majesty will only have a small suite, which will be less expensive. You will agree with me that the finest *cortège* for a King of France is to march at the head of a victorious army. I hope success will make him realise how sincerely I cherish his glory. Hitherto the Cardinal has reigned in his stead: now it is time to show he can reign himself. I am not deceiving myself in attributing to him the necessary qualities, and my only fear is that he trusts too much in his Ministers. His judgment is better than theirs, I am sure, but he often defers to them. We must hope that he will have a will of his own, and I feel it will seldom be wrong. M. d'Argenson [Minister of War] has been to see me and talked of the coming campaign in a manner which shows that the King has given him no details, and I was careful not to hint that he was on the wrong track. He would be very annoyed if he knew that I have been told before him, as he is used to making his own proposals. The King should only announce his decision when the time for discussion is past.

The first half of 1744 was a happy time. Richelieu stood high in the royal favour, and the King sometimes added a few friendly words to the Favourite's bulletins to her uncle at the front. 'We had a gay time at Choisy and drank your health,' she reported. '*Le maître vous aime toujours*. You have no need of an advocate here, but if you had you know you could count on me.' A new distinction—and a fresh source of income—was added in April when she was appointed Superintendent of the Household of the Dauphine, though the princess had not yet arrived from Madrid. 'The whole of Versailles called on me,' she reported to Richelieu; 'tell me everything people are saying about my promotion.' She made up in will-power what she lacked in heart. 'You kill me,' exclaimed the indolent monarch, half in jest, half in earnest, when she implored him to bestir himself. 'All the better, Sire,' she rejoined, 'a King must wake up.' He could count on the gratitude of his subjects, for the troops were smarting under the defeat at Dettingen in the last campaign. The Queen's written request to accompany him was curtly declined by the most extravagant ruler in Europe on the ground of expense, and he left without saying good-bye. He would have been glad of the company of the Favourite, but he lacked the courage to take his mistress while leaving his wife at home. When he left for the Flanders front she felt as if the world had grown dark. 'How charming of you, dear uncle,' she wrote, 'to send me news of the King every day. I am dying of *ennui*. I no longer know Mme de La Tournelle nor Mme de Châteauroux. I am a stranger to myself. It is not an agreeable situation. How long this bad joke will last I do not know.' A week later she complained in similar terms to Marshal Noailles, the Commander-in-Chief. 'How happy you are, M. le Maréchal! You are with the King. How unhappy is your *Ritornelle*. She is separated from the King. You will see him all day, I perhaps only in five months. It is horrible, but you won't pity me; you have other things to think about and I don't expect it. I know your attachment to the King, so I don't worry about his safety.' When the Marshal sent her the news she longed to hear she replied: 'What you tell me about the King is enchanting but is no surprise. I was quite sure that as soon as he was known he would be adored: the two things are synonymous.' At this moment of watchful waiting she was flattered by a letter from Frederick the Great thanking her for her share in the making of an alliance between France and Prussia. 'The esteem I have always entertained for you is now reinforced by sentiments of gratitude. I feel sure that the King of France will never regret his action and that all the contracting parties will derive an equal advantage. *Madame, votre très affectionné ami, Frédéric.*'

An outburst to Richelieu dated June 3, headed 'burn this directly you have read it,' suggests that affection was not the sole motive for longing to join the King. Her wrath flamed up against Maurepas whom she held responsible for keeping her tethered at Versailles. She resolved to destroy him if she could, for a new danger had loomed up in her own family, where the rivalry of the sisters had become an established tradition.

As for Faquinet* I share your views and feel I shall only succeed with facts. But where am I to find them? Give me facts and I promise to turn them to good account. I hate him and he is the torment of my life. This is only for your ears. There is more talk than ever of Mme de Flavacourt† and they say she writes to the King. She is in high favour with the Queen, and has told her that she had no liking for the King but that the dread of banishment from the Court and a return to her husband would drive her to anything. I have not breathed a word to the King because I feel one gets nowhere with letters. When I come I will confront him with all I know to make him confess if there is any foundation. You will agree that what we know is enough to worry us. Tell me frankly. Does the King seem to think about me? Does he often talk of me? Does he miss seeing me? I am quite contented. He writes to me regularly in all confidence and friendship, but that is not everything. Perhaps a deep game is being played. Faquinet is moving heaven and earth. We must get rid of him. I don't despair of it, since I keep it always in mind and finally one succeeds. Give me the facts and I shall be in a strong position; but I must be on the spot. People say that Marshal Noailles does not want me to go, but the Duc d'Ayen [his son] seems to wish it. I don't understand it all. In truth, dear uncle, I was not made for this, and at times I feel terribly discouraged. If I didn't love the King so much I should be greatly tempted to quit. It is a continual turmoil and it upsets me more than you think. It is so repugnant to my character that

* Maurepas.   † Her sister.

I must be a great fool to get involved. But it is done and one must have patience. I feel it will all turn out as I wish.

When no summons arrived she resolved to wait no longer, convinced that her lover would be glad to have a decision taken out of his hands. Writing *en route* from Lille she declared that the latest news filled her with delight.

To take Ypres after a siege of nine days is a triumph for the King such as Louis XIV never achieved. Now he must keep it up, and I hope and expect he will. You know my inclination to see everything *couleur de rose* and my belief in my lucky star which will take the place of good Generals and Ministers. Mme de Modena is dying to see the King's entry into Ypres and asks me to get his leave. I have not done so because I am not sure if I ought to go myself: you will remember we agreed before you left that I should only appear if I were to be suitably received. I told her I would consult you. Tell me at once what you think, for there is not a moment to lose.

She was received with open arms, and after a brief stay at the front the lovers travelled slowly to Metz. It was the summit of her brief career, and even her enemies had little hope of engineering her fall.

The King had been subject to sudden illness since childhood, and a few days after his arrival his life was in danger. The Church assumed control, and the sufferer, thoroughly alarmed, whispered to his mistress: 'Perhaps we may have to part.' A little later he sent a message by the Bishop of Soissons, First Almoner, son of Marshal Berwick and grandson of James II, who had been chosen to accompany him to the front, ordering her and her sister Mme de Lauraguais to leave Metz. She had begged the Jesuit Confessor to avert a public dismissal if he could, but events moved too fast. The doctors, the clergy, the Royal Family and the King himself believed that the end was near, and Holy Communion could not be administered till the temptress had disappeared. After receiving Extreme Unction he obeyed the order of the Bishop to summon the officials of the Court and representative burgesses of Metz, and to announce to them that he asked pardon for his evil example and that the Duchesse de Châteauroux would lose her post in the Household of the Dauphine. 'The King displayed resignation, piety and humility,' records the Duc de Luynes in his diary; 'he embraced the Queen and begged her forgiveness for his misdeeds.' Only God had been offended, she replied; let him think only of God. The fearless Bishop, ignoring the danger to his career, ordered that the confession should be read from every pulpit.

The Favourite bowed to the storm and drove away, torn between despair and hope. Instead of returning to Paris she halted at Bar le Duc in order to keep an eye on Metz. Her only comfort was her conviction that if her royal lover survived he would want her back. Her changing moods are mirrored in the stream of letters to Richelieu, who warned her not to be too hopeful. 'That he should die is to me inconceivable,' she wrote in August.

The doctor is very hopeful. Of course he will think only of his soul when his head is weak; but when he feels a little better I wager he will think of me and finally ask his valets where I am. As they are on my side it will be all right. I am not a bit depressed if the King recovers as I expect. I shall not return to Paris. On thinking it over I shall be staying at Sainte-Ménehould with my sister, as the King did not say where I was to go. If he dies I shall make for Paris where we will have a talk. If I lose my post I don't care. What could they do to me? I shall stay in Paris with my friends, but I shall regret the King all my life, for I loved him to distraction, much more than I allowed to appear. While he is alive it is not for me to approach anyone, and I must bear my trials patiently. If he pulls through I shall be rewarded, and he will be all the more obliged to make public reparation. If he dies I will not degrade myself even for the kingdom of France. So far I have behaved with dignity and I shall carry on in the same manner. That is the only way to earn respect and to preserve the consideration I think I deserve. I believe he will welcome a visit from the Queen and will be very nice to her as he believes he owes her reparation for his misdoings. If he recovers, what joy it will be! I regard it as heaven's method of opening his eyes and punishing evildoers. If we come through you will agree that our star will carry us a very long way and nothing will be beyond our grasp.

Four days later she wrote from Sainte-Ménehould in good spirits.

To my intense delight I am convinced the King will recover. His devotion strikes me as excessive, though I am not surprised. Don't worry about my plan of remaining here. My letter was scarcely posted when I thought that it would look foolish, so we start tomorrow for Paris. It is all very terrible and makes me detest the world in which I have lived despite myself. Far from wishing to return to it as you imagine, I could not face it again. My sole ambition is reparation for the affront I have suffered. If you write by post just give me news of the King without comment. But I should like to know how Faquinet has been received. *Mon Dieu*, I give you my word that for me it is all over. I should be crazy to want to start again. You know how little I was dazzled by all the splendours. Now I must try to recover my peace of mind and not fall ill.

The King recovered almost as rapidly as he had collapsed, but his spirits were low as he pondered on what had occurred. The reconciliation with the Queen was only skin deep, and she was hurt by the refusal of her request to accompany him to Strasbourg when he was well enough to travel. Boredom weighed on him like a heavy pall, and nothing except the society of his mistress could restore sunshine to his heart. She understood him so well that she read his heart like an open book. She hoped he would travel alone, as that would eliminate the Queen and then, on his return home, he would resume his usual life. 'I feel certain that is how he feels. The first time he sees his *aides de camp* he will be a bit embarrassed, but everything possible must be done to put him at his ease.' News that he had been ordered a second Communion gave her a fright. 'I have drafted a little letter,' she confided to Richelieu, 'and I am waiting for the moment to send it—telling him all that has happened since he fell ill. But I must choose the moment, for one cannot risk a *faux pas*. He continues to feel bored which I fear retards his convalescence, but he has the power to put things straight. I tell you we shall come through all right. It will be a happy moment and I should like to be there. Burn all my letters.' A day or two later she reported her arrival in Paris. 'If he is not as ill as I believe and not worse than you say, they will frighten him to death. *Mon Dieu!* I am only worrying about him. Nothing can make up for my humiliations which struck me to the heart. As I was about to enter my carriage I met d'Argenson who cut me with an air of contempt. Everyone avoided me and seemed to hold me responsible for what goes on. But my own troubles are nothing. It is his condition which worries me. In friendship's name send me news, give me some hope, dear uncle, I no longer live, and I need you to restore me to life. Comfort the most unfortunate of women.'

Ten days later her drooping spirits had revived.

He is out of danger and I feel easier. Since his illness I have lived in the midst of convulsions and tears. He will never know how I have wept. It was not my past glory that I regretted, it was for himself. I only saw his good qualities, what he has done for me, and I was really inconsolable about him. He has not yet mentioned my name. No doubt he will listen to his *entourage*. He is weak, and I can only expect to be forgotten. Dear uncle, do not leave him. I need not beg you to bear my interests in mind. You know they are your own as well and those of good servants of the King. People are saying he has promised to be completely reconciled to the Queen, as everybody desires. You will know how far that is true. He can never have anything more than a regard for her, and his heart will always belong to another. If, however, that came to pass, the priests would have a good time and all the follies of the last reign would return. I am isolated and I cannot concentrate. Sometimes I want to remain as I am, aloof from the whirlpool; sometimes I wish to be drawn in again to prove I love him for himself. I should like to revenge myself on the people who, thinking I was finished, tried to humiliate me, and in so doing I should serve the state. I open my heart to you. Nothing is yet settled. As you say, the main thing is to avert the triumph of the hostile cabal. You were quite right not to leave Metz when you were pressed to do so: you would have been lost. You showed great courage in resisting the designs of your enemies. If you find favourable opportunities, keep me in mind.

A fortnight later the Duchess wrote in better spirits.

Calm yourself, dear uncle, good times are at hand. We have had some hard trials but they are over. I cannot think of the King as a *dévot*, but I can imagine him *honnête homme* and a good friend. Whatever his reflections, I think they will all be to my advantage. He is absolutely sure of me and he is convinced I love him for himself. I have felt I loved him desperately, but it is important that he knows it, and I hope his illness has not affected his memory. No one has known his heart till now except myself, and I assure you it is a good heart, very good, quite capable of feeling. He will be pious but not a bigot. I love him a hundred times more. I will be his friend and henceforth I shall be beyond the range of attack. All the wiles of the Faquinet during his illness will only render my position happier and more stable. I shall not have to fear either change or illness or the devil himself, and our life will be a delight. Try to believe what I say. It is not all a dream: you will see it come true. It is based on my knowledge of the man, and I know every corner of his heart, with all that is fair and good in it.

The last item in this unique correspondence reported the King's visit to the capital on November 13.

I cannot describe the enthusiasm of the good Parisians. Unjust as they are to myself, I can't help loving them for their love for the King. They call him *Louis le Bienaimé*, and this cancels out all their injustices to me. You don't know what it meant to me to be so near and not to get the slightest notice from him. My grief is indescribable. I do not venture to appear. People are so cruel that whatever I did would be regarded as a crime. Moreover I have given up hope. Far from wishing to demand the exile of certain people as a condition of my return, I am ready to respond to a simple command from the master. But tell me, do you think he loves me still? You hint that I cannot count on my return. Perhaps he thinks there is too much to efface. He doesn't know it is all forgotten. I couldn't resist the temptation to see him. I was condemned to seclusion and grief at a moment of universal rejoicing. I wanted at any rate to see the show, taking care not to be recognised. I saw him pass, looking happy and touched—so he is capable of tender feeling. I fixed my eyes on him—and—such is my power of imagination—I believe he cast me a glance and sought to recognise me. His carriage passed at so slow a pace that there was time to study him closely. I can't express my feelings. I was in the big crowd, and at certain moments I blamed myself for a man for whose sake I had been cruelly treated. Yet, carried away by the delighted acclamations of the spectators, I had no longer the strength to think of myself. Only a single voice, quite close to me, recalled my misfortune by a very offensive phrase.* No doubt, dear uncle, you will blame me, but the temptation was too strong to resist. Since then I am more agitated than ever. I contrast my present position with my past. I have never counted very much on my friends, but I am grieved to see how many of them have fallen away. I believe that sooner or later some misfortune will come my way, or that I

* According to Soulavie, who edited Richelieu's papers, the words were *Voilà son putain*.

shall be the victim of false accusations. I have presentiments from which I cannot escape.

When all seemed lost the wheel of fortune took a violent turn. Back at Versailles and completely restored in health the King retained his self-confidence and resolved once more to do whatever he liked. 'What have I done to be loved like this?' he exclaimed again and again when he witnessed the rejoicings at his recovery. Now was the time to show his gratitude in some practical way, but the opportunity was missed. After an interval he invited the Favourite to return. She would come incognito, she replied, until her enemies were dismissed, and would then resume her old position of authority. Though he was as easy-going as the Duchess was vindictive, he resented the conduct of the group who had manœuvred him into a spectacular confession of his sins. The Bishop of Soissons was ordered to remain within his diocese, and the Duc de Châtillon, whom he believed to have estranged the Dauphin, was banished from the Court. Though she failed in her supreme ambition, the disgrace of Maurepas, he was humiliated by being chosen to convey the invitation to her and her sister to resume their functions at Court.

At this triumphant hour the Favourite was struck down and passed away at the age of twenty-seven. Though she attributed the violence of her sufferings to foul play and Richelieu regarded Maurepas as the villain of the piece, peritonitis rather than poison appears to have been the cause. All Paris rejoiced, testifies the Duc de Croy. She was bled nine times. During the eleven days of her agony, lucid intervals alternating with delirium, she was visited by her two surviving sisters and made her confession to a Jesuit, who declared that he had known few women so resigned to death. The King sent for news twice a day. Her biographers, the de Goncourt brothers, believe that he temporarily filled the void with the fourth sister, the Duchesse de Lauraguais. Be that as it may, the reign of the de Nesle sisters which had lasted for more than ten years was over. The latest and ablest of them had enhanced the status of *maîtresse en titre*, transforming her from a royal plaything into an institution of State, and from the hour of her death the choice of her successor became the main topic of conversation in the vast whispering gallery of the Palace of Versailles.

6

THE ROYAL FAMILY

I

SINCE the Royal Family lived in a glass house and the swarm of courtiers had little to do except to play cards, gossip and intrigue, we can visualise all its members and their relations to one another. Louis XV liked to regard himself as a family man, and there is general agreement that he felt a mild affection for his daughters though not for his wife or son. It is equally clear that, with the exception of the Duchess of Parma, none of them played a significant part in his life. Though by instinct a kindly person, he was too self-centred and too superficial to break his heart about their feelings or their fate. Not one of them meant so much to him as his five successive *maîtresses en titre*, the Mailly sisters, the Pompadour, and the du Barry. His moments of unclouded happiness were few, for at heart he was a lonely man.

The most devastating analysis of his character was attempted by Choiseul, after nearly twelve years of almost daily contact as his chief Minister. Smarting under his dismissal at the instigation of Mme du Barry, he produces a caricature. Princes, he bitterly declared in his Memoirs, were by nature baser than other men, and of all the princes in Europe the Bourbons were the most contemptible.

A man without heart or brains, loving mischief as children love to hurt animals, with all the faults of the meanest soul, he lacked the capacity owing to his age to exhibit his vices as often as his nature desired. Like Nero he would have been enchanted to watch Paris burning from Bellevue, though he would not have had the courage to order it. He would have liked above all to witness the executions at the Place de Grève, but he lacked the courage to attend. If one had wished to give him the pleasure of having someone broken on the wheel in the little marble court at Versailles, I feel sure he would leave the bed of his mistress to watch the details of the execution from a corner of the window. He made up for it as much as he could by eager attendance at burials. He was constantly talking about them and about illnesses and operations. He showed satisfaction at the death of people he knew, and if they recovered he foretold that it would not be for long. What he most enjoyed in the hunt, I feel, was the destruction of life. With such a temperament it was astonishing that he did not love war; but his cowardly fear of death was even stronger than his taste for the suffering and death of others.

His evil nature is partly due to his poverty in ideas. His torpid soul can only be stirred by disgusting spectacles. But his taste for evil also derives from his natural malignity which leads him to inflict suffering when he sees the chance, and never leads him to do good, whatever the opportunity. I do not believe that anyone ever noted a generous sentiment. If he can be said to possess a virtue, it is that of being fairly generous in money matters. He is usually thought to be a good father, but nothing is further from the truth. He cannot abide his son, who does not conceal his contempt. He cares nothing for his grandchildren, preferring the Dauphin just because he is awkward and unlikely to become the hope of the nation. His vanity is inconceivable but he cannot give it scope, for he is rightly aware of his incapacity. Though jealous of his authority he is weakly submissive to his Ministers. He displays the most repulsive indifference to every sort of business and all kinds of people. His vanity makes him think it is enough to maintain his authority that from time to time he dismisses Ministers in whom he has shown the fullest confidence by always following their advice. He only retains M. de Saint-Florentin, Minister of the Household, because he feels himself his superior in talents and is aware of his unceasing rogueries and dissolute life. *Mauvais sujets* can rely on his favour, since he shares their failings and hopes they will provide some excuse for his own. He regards the publicity of his amours as a demonstration of his authority. He considers the opposition to the object of his fancy as a lack of respect for himself. He feels that everyone should bow down to his mistress because he honours her with his favour. Occasionally fear leads to an appear-

ance of remorse, but he detests people who appear to disapprove
him. His character resembled soft wax on which the most diverse
objects leave their trace. His spoiling as child and heir made him
feel that he belonged to a different species. One day when talking
of our pleasures and of the offence to religion they involved, he told
me I should be damned. I protested that the verdict was too
severe; yet it made me tremble for him, since by his own confession
he seemed to have offended the Deity even more than myself,
thereby causing a greater scandal. He replied that our positions
were very different. He was the Lord's Anointed and God would
not allow him to be damned if, as was his mission, he sustained the
Catholic religion in his kingdom. As an emanation of God he
could indulge his failings without crime or remorse.

Another fallen Minister, though less shrill in tone, echoes the
complaint of weakness and ingratitude. D'Argenson's Journal
in the years following his dismissal from the Foreign Office is a
stream of denunciation. 'He liked to see everything through my
eyes,' he notes in July, 1747, 'approved everything and let me
act as I liked. All went well till malignity gradually did its work.'
The villain of the piece was not the King but the Minister of War.

My brother had evicted me from all the posts I had won by hard
work and merit, pursuing me with cowardly treachery and con-
cealing his hatred behind a veil of geniality. Now I am out of
everything and have lost all consideration. The Master was persuaded that I was not up to my job, whereas I made all the decisions
and everything went according to programme. Our monarch [he
notes in November, 1752] is a gentle but timid bird. He dislikes
working with the Ministers as the finances are so bad; and their
fear of him creates his fear of them. So they shirk decisions, leaving
everything to him, and he fears to make mistakes as much as to be
deceived in business affairs. My brother fosters his failings for his
own advantage and never remonstrates—a courtier and flatterer,
never the Minister. The King was good and just [added the diarist
in 1754] but he dreaded a row in the Council.

While d'Argenson is much less venomous than Choiseul, they
agree as to his unfitness for his post.

A far more favourable picture of 'mon bon maître' is painted
by the Duc de Croy, who did not know him so well. Though
the King possessed a good heart and a good brain, he had two
major faults—timidity and sensuality.

He loved his family and his grandchildren. At the age of sixty he
was the handsomest man at Court. He was gay, polite, gentle,
friendly though dignified, a good talker with a retentive memory.
He was too inclined to follow the advice of his Ministers and
mistresses. Possessing a thousand good qualities he lacked the
resolution to turn them to account. Though he devoted much time
to his pleasures, he did a good deal of work. Yet his Ministers
easily influenced him and he left almost everything to their judgment. Since there was no First Minister, each was supreme in his
own department. He took some pains but perhaps not enough.
It was easy to gain his confidence, and his mistresses won it quicker
than the rest. Since he was very fond of Mme de Pompadour
scarcely any favour was given except through her influence. Yet in
great affairs it is uncertain if he told her everything, as he was
temperamentally reserved. I incline to think he was more a lover
than a friend. As for the state of the kingdom I think he was aware
of it—perhaps rather its best side—and regretted it, being by nature
kindly and made to be loved. There was more firmness in him than
was generally believed. He had some excellent qualities, far more
good than bad. He never lied and possessed good judgment. He
was gentle and an excellent father and relative. He was well informed in the sciences, especially astronomy, physics, chemistry
and botany, but with the greatest modesty. In general his modesty
went too far and became a vice. Always seeing more correctly than
the others, he always thought he was wrong. I often heard him
say, 'I should have thought so and so' [and he was right], 'but the
others say the contrary, so I am mistaken. It is not for me to
decide.' He surrendered rather than claimed his rights. He never
willingly said anything malicious or harsh. He preferred talking of
gloomy things. If he was not particularly clever, he had excellent
commonsense. He was extremely brave, though too modest. He
could have been a great general if he had wished, but he did not
love war. He only lacked the courage to take his own line and he
always, through modesty, adopted the advice of others while he
saw better than they. Louis XIV was too proud, Louis XV too
modest. His sole vice was women, but he thought that if he
repented at death and received the sacraments, it was a trifle.

A somewhat similar portrait of a well-meaning *roi fainéant* is
provided by the Comte de Cheverny, the Introducer of Ambassadors. 'He spoke of affairs as if someone else was on the throne.
That was due to his faulty education, for he was the best of men
whatever malevolent tongues may say, and I loved him passion-

I

ately. He never spoke about politics and took little interest in
the sciences, so the talk was always of the hunt of the day or the
morrow.' He had little love for dogs, but he possessed a spaniel
which accepted caresses from no one but himself. 'He was all
the more pleased because he knew that this animal was perhaps
the only creature to love him for himself, and he never had
another.' This picture of intellectual *incuria* is confirmed by the
testimony of Cardinal de Tencin, a prominent member of the
Council when Fleury left the scene.

> I think [wrote his sister to Richelieu in 1743] that Mme de la Tour-
> nelle [Duchesse de Châteauroux] should be asked to try to rouse
> the King from his torpor in regard to public affairs. My brother's
> efforts have been of no avail: it was like talking to the rocks. I
> cannot conceive how a man can wish to be nothing when he is
> capable of being something. What happens in the kingdom appears
> no concern of his. In the Council he displays complete indifference
> and accepts everything that is suggested, his apathy leading him to
> follow the line of least resistance.

He had no sense of money, gambled recklessly at cards, and
would have resented an attempt to curb his extravagance had any
Minister dared to apply the brake. No one has ventured to
compute the fantastic cost of the Households of the members of
the Royal Family, each one of whom was served by a horde of
functionaries with very little to do, including doctors, chaplains,
musicians, readers, valets, cooks and coachmen. Pensions were
flung to all and sundry who possessed sufficiently influential
friends at Court. The number of royal residences steadily
increased, and gambling debts—his own and those of his entourage—piled up. 'The poor King is betrayed and religion every
day more discredited,' reported the Papal Nuncio in 1753, 'to
the universal scandal and grief of the good folk of whom there
are some in this sink of iniquity.'

II

The estimates of Marie Leczinska, 'la bonne reine', differ less
than those of Louis XV, since every witness stresses both her

virtues and her lack of personality. 'Simple, smiling, touching, almost saintly,' is the verdict of Sainte-Beuve. She did nothing but good, testifies the Duc de Croy. Even the sour d'Argenson is fairer to her than to most members of the Court.

She sets a good example in fecundity, piety, sweetness of temper, humanity. Lacking charm and coquetry, her only hold on her husband is his need of heirs. She is neither hated nor loved. There is nothing individual in what she says or pretends to feel. She often fails to understand, is charitable from bigotry, *dévote* in a superstitious way. Yet she is not without intelligence. Critics of the King or the Ministers rally round her, and without wishing it she leads a party. The Dauphin and Mesdames have the confidence in her of ill-trained children. Though she is respected, she is full of religious superstitions, led astray, like most of our foreign women, by the priests.

It was a consolation to her that her piety was transmitted to her son. Without political influence, modest, patient, affectionate, generous in thought and deed but timid and colourless, she had critics in plenty but not an enemy in the world. She had far more heart than the King and delighted in her little circle. 'Without my friends,' she exclaimed, 'the world would be a wilderness for me.'

We come closest to Marie Leczinska in the 130 letters from her adored and adoring father published in 1901 covering the last twelve years of his life. Their delight in each other's company struck every observer on his frequent visits to Versailles, and the correspondence reveals a tenderness rare in princely records of the eighteenth century. The letters scarcely allude to the events of the day: the main themes are the doings of the Royal Family, reports and inquiries about health, and above all ceaseless expressions of a father's love. 'Ma chère et unique petite Marie, vous êtes un autre moi-même, je ne vis que par vous.' He was proud of her position as Queen of France and saluted her as the guardian angel of the kingdom. He was the happier of the two both by temperament and circumstance, for he was master of his own time, entertained on a substantial income from Louis XV, and left the burdens of government to an energetic French Intendant. Father and daughter alike detested the ecclesiastical policy of Choiseul, and to both of them the *Parlement* was an abomination.

'The more I think of the horror of the measures against the poor
Jesuits,' wrote old Stanislas in 1762, 'the less do I believe it can
happen.' Happily both passed away before the suppression of
the Order by the Pope himself. The heart of Marie Leczinska
was interred at Nancy beside that of her father in accordance
with her wish.

We come almost equally near to the Queen in the voluminous
diary of the Duc de Luynes which records the doings of one of
the dullest little circles in Europe, but also one of the few where
the Ten Commandments were treated with respect. Though
holding no post in her Household he belonged to her entourage
owing to the appointment of his wife as *dame d'honneur* in 1735.
The Duchess was worthy of him and of the unchanging affection
of her mistress, who supped with her almost every evening and
wrote to her when they were parted. The Duke's brother,
Cardinal de Luynes, was no less *persona grata* and was a regular
member of the little group—*mes honnêtes gens*—whose devotion
rendered life bearable. The atmosphere made no appeal to the
young, and when her daughters looked in they did not stay long.
'I frequented the Duchesse de Luynes,' records the Comte de
Cheverny. 'The Queen forbade all etiquette. All the old ladies
of the palace were there. *C'était fort triste.*' When the era of
child-bearing was over her chief occupation was good works,
the provision of clothes, food and money for the poor, exceeding
her income and incurring debts which on three occasions had to
be met by the King. Her *lecteur* Moncrif read to her the lives of
the saints, Joinville's biography of St. Louis, the letters of Mme
de Sévigné and other books. She painted and played a little but
possessed small artistic talent. In the sphere of public affairs her
chief interests were the cause of Poland, for which she could do
nothing, and the authority of the Church. She reverenced
Christophe de Beaumont, *notre saint Archévêque*, and the Jesuits
had no warmer friend. Emboldened by the knowledge that the
attack on the Order was distasteful to the King and was passion-
ately resented by the Dauphin, she for once appealed to Choiseul,
with whom her relations were on a footing of polite neutrality,
to stay his hand. *'Il faudrait un miracle. Faites ce miracle et vous
serez mon saint.'* The appeal was in vain, for the Minister had
secured the assent of the King.

The liveliest *habitué* of the little circle was President Hénault, a rich, kindly epicurean, who combined his duties as President of the First Chamber of the Paris *Parlement* with the delights of literature and society. Member of the Académie Française, author of the *Abrégé Chronologique de l'histoire de France*, the first widely read summary of the fortunes of the French people—described by Voltaire as the most useful of books by the most amiable of men—he was a welcome guest in every salon in Paris. His aim was to make life pleasant for himself and his friends by good cheer, worth-while talk and faithful friendships, and Grimm saluted him as one of the happiest men of the time. His *liaison de convenance* with Mme du Deffand was no bar to the favour of the pious Queen, who appointed him in 1753 Superintendent of her Household with an apartment at Versailles. 'He is most attractive and accomplished in every way,' noted the Duc de Luynes in his diary, 'gentle, clever, agreeable. The Queen has taken to him. Every day after dinner she sends for him and they talk for an hour or more. Her virtue and genuine piety place her beyond the range of scandal. She likes conversation and clever people. She has read widely and is well informed; evil is something she cannot even imagine.' His merits and even his failings were an asset to society, wrote Mme du Deffand, who knew him better than anyone. 'His vanity inspires an extreme desire to please, and his easy-going nature enables him to get on with all sorts of people. Everything combines to make him the most attractive of men. He is exempt from the passions which chiefly affect our peace of mind: ambition, self-seeking, envy, are unknown to him. His passions are mild, his humour gay and unruffled. To much intelligence he adds all the graces, facility, and tact imaginable. He is the best company in the world. His wit is lively and it does not wound.' His dinners were famous, not only for the company but for the fare, for he was reputed to have the best cook in the capital.

Since the Queen's allowance was irregularly paid and her charities exceeded her means, Hénault's advice was often in demand. 'I have halved my stakes,' she wrote to him; 'you know I buy nothing for myself.' Her affection for 'mon cher Président' was revealed by her interest in his soul. 'Have confidence in God and you will be happy.' While detesting the *Philosophes* she

never regarded him as one of the tribe, friendly to them though
he was, and she always hoped for his conversion. 'My prayers
are worth little, but I offer them for you. I assure you I love you
with all my heart.' The friendship of the pious Queen and the
worldly magistrate does honour to both. Many of her letters to
him survive, mainly about family matters and health—colds,
rheumatism, indigestion. 'J'ai des vapeurs à mourir.' The name
of the King is rarely mentioned, for he had ceased to count in
her life. Occasionally a deeper note is struck. 'I spent yesterday
with the Carmelites at Compiègne and found an atmosphere of
blissful peace.' Though made for the simple joys of family life,
she would have been equally happy as a nun.

In one of the most elaborate portraits in his Memoirs President
Hénault celebrates Marie Leczinska as one of the greatest of
French queens.

> She lives by rule. The morning is occupied by her prayers, her
> books of devotion, a visit to the King, then a time of relaxation,
> usually painting, though she never took lessons. She gave me three
> of her pictures. At midday she is dressed, then mass, then dinner.
> I have often seen a dozen ladies there, and she talks to them all about
> their own affairs. After dinner I follow her to her apartments,
> where she is no longer the Queen. She works at her tapestry and
> talks about what she has read. Sometimes she plays on the guitar
> or the harpsichord, laughing at her mistakes. She dismisses me at
> three. Then comes her time for reading, mostly books on history
> in French, Polish, German and Italian. Her Household reassembles
> about six for cards. After supper she goes to the Duchesse de
> Luynes about eleven, where there are at most five or six people,
> and retires at half-past twelve. Conversation which avoids scandal,
> Court intrigues and politics might seem difficult to sustain, but it
> rarely flags and is usually quite lively. She welcomes differences
> of opinion and hates flattery. No one enjoys jokes more and she
> has a ready laugh. Her irony is gentle. Her allowance of ninety-six
> thousand francs goes in charities, and I have often blamed the
> Duchesse de Villars, her *dame d'atours*, for letting her beggar herself.
> Yet this Princess, so good, so simple, so gentle, so affable, can
> assume an air of dignity which inspires respect. In passing from
> one room to another she becomes the Queen again, and preserves
> in the Court that sense of grandeur associated with Louis XV. Her
> letters reveal nobility of soul and gaiety of spirit. She never inter-
> venes in affairs, so the King always grants her requests. Her strict-

ness in religious matters is of importance in our century. She pardons everything, and excuses everything except what might hurt. If this is the language of friendship it is also the testimony of a man of the world who observed her at close range over many years and knew that she would never read what he wrote.

When her beloved *dame d'honneur* the Duchesse de Luynes passed away in 1763, the post was filled by the Comtesse de Noailles, niece of President Hénault. Though no one could replace the most intimate of her friends, the Queen recognised the sterling qualities which soon earned her affection. 'I am not difficult to live with,' she exclaimed. It was an abiding grief that the only person to whom her loving nature made no appeal was the King. Her life began in exile and poverty and ended in sorrow. She disliked Choiseul for his immorality and his hostility to the Jesuits, and the loss of her father was a crushing blow. Six of her ten children predeceased her. When the Dauphin, her favourite, passed away in the prime of life, she wrote, 'I am and always shall be sad. My only consolation is to reflect that those I mourn would not wish to return to this vale of tears. It is no fun being Queen.' Though the King mellowed a little in her closing days, she was glad to go in 1768 at the age of sixty-five. In one respect she was *felix opportunitate mortis*, for she was spared the horror of the installation of Mme du Barry as *maîtresse en titre* in the following year.

III

The Dauphin, like his grandfather, is one of the riddles of French history. Would he have been a great monarch if he had lived? Did he possess the strength of character to force through reforms which might have averted the Revolution, or would he have confined his efforts to the defence of the Church? There was no Saint-Simon to sing his praises or to lament at his funeral that they were burying the hopes of France. Though less of a personality than the Duc de Bourgogne, he was at any rate a better man than his father, as the latter grudgingly recognised. 'My son is lazy, hasty, and changeable,' declared the King. 'He cares nothing for hunting, women, or good living. But he loves what is right, is truly virtuous, and is not lacking in intelligence.' He certainly would not have been content with the *rôle* of a *roi fainéant*. While Michelet dismisses him as a corpulent bigot his biographer Emmanuel de Broglie salutes him as a noble and tragic figure.

The birth of the Dauphin—the only surviving son in a family of ten—was hailed with delight, for no one wanted to see a Duke of Orleans on the throne. The lad was entrusted to the faithful old Duchesse de Ventadour who had mothered his father. In childhood he closely resembled the Duc de Bourgogne—vivacious, precocious, self-willed, hating contradiction. In his seventh year he was transferred to the Duc de Châtillon, an excellent choice, and began to appear at public ceremonies. His religious instruction was assigned to the Bishop of Mirepoix, who made him *dévot* and helped to teach him self-control. 'The Dauphin is terribly and increasingly violent, though only in his eleventh year,' noted d'Argenson in 1740. 'He strikes his attendants, including the Bishop of Mirepoix. Two members of his circle tell me he is the worst-hearted child they ever knew, without attachment to his servants and enjoying their misfortunes, proud, bold, obstinate. He cares little for his parents. Here are perils for France.' When the Duc de Châtillon remonstrated, the lad replied: 'I disavow in advance all the follies I may commit; think at such moments it is the wind blowing.' 'The wind blows pretty strong,' commented his tutor. 'Yes, sir, and thunder is not far away.' Outbursts were followed by penitence and apologies, and his Governor tolerated them as growing pains. 'A boiling vivacity and a precocious sense of his destiny are the cause of his faults, but his heart is too good to cause apprehension. His ill-humour is over in a moment; the next minute he comes and confesses his error.' In the sphere of religious instruction the Bishop had an easier task, for the lad displayed a fervent piety from his early years. He was adored by his Polish grandfather who held him spellbound by stories of the adventures of his early life. 'How should a ruler make his people happy?' asked the lad. 'Love them,' replied old Stanislas; 'that should teach you more than all the pundits.'

The problems of childhood were less formidable than those

of adolescence, when the Dauphin's nature underwent a curious change. With diminishing vitality he became reserved, preferring solitude and avoiding fêtes. The transformation may have been partly due to the physiological causes which were to make him stout and lethargic, but a growing sense of responsibility played its part. To the question what he had most enjoyed on his first visit to Paris at the age of fourteen he replied, 'To have such a reception.' His mother witnessed the ripening of his character with delight. 'I have only one son, but heaven has pleased to make him wise and virtuous beyond my expectations.' Another factor was the increasing awareness of his father's shame. While still in his teens his outspoken criticisms of the King incurred the gentle rebuke of the patient Queen. Though the *dévots* at the licentious Court were always a small minority, they rejoiced at the prospect, however remote, of their standard-bearer on the throne who dismissed Voltaire with the words 'Cet homme mérite les derniers supplices.' Others shared Barbier's conviction that a *dévot* ruler was the worst misfortune which could happen to a State.

Eager to do his duty in every sphere, the fourteen-year-old Dauphin begged to accompany his father to the front in the campaign of 1744. 'I praise your desire to follow me at the head of my armies,' replied the King, 'but your person is too precious to expose yourself before the succession is assured by your marriage. When you have children, I promise never to go to the front without you, but I hope that time will never come. As I only make war to ensure a solid and lasting peace, if God blesses my good intentions I will sacrifice everything to secure it for the remainder of my reign. It is good that you should share these sentiments and regard yourself as the father rather than the master of the peoples who will one day be your subjects.'

The first serious friction occurred when the King lay for a few days between life and death at Metz. Defying his father's instruction to come no nearer than Châlons, the Dauphin followed the advice of his Governor the Duc de Châtillon to proceed to Metz. When a rumour reached him *en route* that the end had come, he exclaimed: 'What a misfortune for the poor kingdom! My God, have pity on me.' Annoyed by his disobedience the royal sufferer received him coldly, ordered him to leave, and exiled the Duc de Châtillon to his estates. The Dauphin thought he was already Mayor of the Palace, complained the ailing King.

At the age of sixteen, following the precedent of Louis XIII and Louis XIV, the Dauphin was married to a Spanish cousin. The event was celebrated by costly fêtes at Paris and Versailles, and the bride won the heart of her husband though to others she seemed stiff and lacking in charm. How deeply he grew to love her was shown by his grief when she died a year later in giving birth to a girl, herself fated to an early death. His loss at the moment when he tasted real happiness for the first time confirmed the tendency to solitude, piety, and study. The Spanish princess, who remains a rather shadowy figure, was quickly forgotten by everyone except her husband. All thoughts turned to a successor, for France cried aloud for an heir. His own preference was for a sister of the deceased, but the choice of the King fell on a Saxon princess. The details were settled by d'Argenson, whose brief tenure of the Foreign Office ended with this event. 'Who would have believed,' he notes in his Journal, 'that owing to the cabal at Court I should receive my *congé* on the same day that the marriage was celebrated at Dresden? They were jealous of my power.' It was some consolation that the match which he had helped to arrange proved a success, not merely in securing the succession but in bringing a measure of happiness to the bridegroom.

The Dauphin's second marriage was welcomed by everyone except the Queen, for Maria Josepha, a girl of fifteen, was a daughter of Augustus of Saxony who sat on the throne of Poland once occupied by Stanislas. That, however, was an old story, and compensation had been found in the Duchy of Lorraine. To prepare her for her task her uncle Marshal Saxe sent her mother a letter and advice. The King, he declared, was fond of his family; she must regard him as her refuge and her father and tell him everything, though with everyone else she should be on her guard. In that case he would advise her. The Queen, he added, was kind. The Dauphin had plenty of brains, more than was generally believed. The ladies of the Court were clever enough but ill-natured. Saxe did not add that the marriage was not the wish of the Dauphin, who was too broken-hearted to smile. The French Ambassador at Dresden reported that the bride was not a beauty. She asked for a portrait of the Dauphin and a history of France, and was supplied with President Hénault's *Abrégé Chronologique*. When Richelieu was dispatched as special envoy to fetch her, he reported that her French was bad and that she was not pretty, but that she was none the less charming. At Versailles she pleased everyone except her husband, who could not restrain his tears: shy and reserved, she could do little to break the ice and wisely played for time. 'The Dauphin says he does not love her like his first wife who was more mature and intelligent,' noted d'Argenson. 'She is only a pretty child, with grace and vivacity, but she talks little and her French is bad. The Saxons are less intelligent than the Spaniards.'

'All this caused me mortal pain,' reported the bride. 'I tried to prove my wish to please him by blind obedience to his slightest wish, but there were few opportunities as he hardly spent a moment alone with me. Mme Henriette witnessed my pain and described it to him. Then he took pity on me and treated me a little better, and finally he was friendly and kind.' 'He is very fond of the Dauphine,' records d'Argenson in October 1747. 'She does not domineer over him like his first wife and has entirely adapted herself to his wishes. The King and Mesdames love her tenderly. She has overcome the disapproval of the Queen who long pretended to hate in her the fortunate rival of her father. We are impatiently awaiting an heir.' She understood her husband's grief and respected his loyalty to the memory of his first wife, and he was touched by her quiet sympathy. Thus the barriers were slowly lowered and two estimable human beings gradually found their way to each other's hearts. The process was assisted by his favourite sister Henriette, whose early death was a blow to them both. 'I loved her from the first,' confided the Dauphine to her mother, 'and I owe her the happiness of my life, for the Dauphin's friendship for me is entirely her doing. For I must confess that when I arrived he held me in aversion. He had been prejudiced and regarded me as a child.' Neither of them wore their heart on their sleeve and their virtues required time to appreciate.

The Dauphine, testifies the Duc de Croy, had a good figure and a good complexion; her eyes were charming when animated, but her nose and teeth were bad. 'On the whole her face, though not pretty, is extremely attractive. She possessed plenty of intelligence and was eager to please.' Less flattering is the testimony of Cheverny, who described her as the most jealous of women, cross to her household and little liked. Luynes, the most reliable of witnesses, agrees that she lacked the gift of friendliness and that she had occasional bouts of ill-temper, though they were brief. Possessing no popular gifts, the Dauphin and Dauphine earned more respect than affection and were voted very dull by most of the courtiers. 'They cared to see no one,' noted d'Argenson; 'in their dark room lit with only a single candle they liked to play quadrille and say with pleasure *nous sommes morts*.' Nothing interested them, added Luynes, not hunting, not cards, not plays, only music.' His indifference was attributed to his *embonpoint*. 'Have I not a well-nourished son?' observed the King to the Saxon Minister with a note of disapproval in his voice. Though it may have indisposed him to physical exertion, it had no inhibiting effect on his mind, which was as active as that of his grandfather the Duc de Bourgogne. When the King, Queen, and Dauphin attended a thanksgiving service at Notre Dame on his recovery from smallpox in 1752 there was no applause. The Dauphin breathed bigotry, declares d'Argenson, the sour anti-clerical. 'In Catholic countries princes receive a purely clerical education and are surrounded by priests who advocate the interests of the Church rather than the love of God and make princes superstitious and intolerant. In everything he desires the exact contrary of his father. He is a bigot, which the King is not. He loves priests and bishops, since the King maltreats them. With such tastes it is a gloomy prospect when he comes to the throne, and he has made himself detested by the people. Our citizens dread his accession as a calamity, and the contrast makes them appreciate his father.' Yet even the disgruntled diarist admitted the possession of certain virtues. 'The Dauphin is a unique mixture of good and bad qualities,' he notes in 1753: 'bigotry, not religion; good-hearted and inhuman; intelligence and stupidity, childishness and prudence.'

During the trying early years of marriage the Dauphine found consolation in the steady affection of the Royal Family. The King took to her from the first and his liking was returned. During his absence at the front she wrote him affectionate little

notes. 'I embrace you, dear Papa, with all my heart. Be assured
of my extreme tenderness.' The King loved her as much as his
own children, perhaps more, reported her uncle Marshal Saxe to
her father. In her eagerness to give France an heir after a mis-
carriage she journeyed to Forges, following the precedent of
Anne of Austria, since the waters were believed to promote
fertility. The family began with a daughter in 1750, and when
the Duc de Bourgogne appeared in 1751 there was a thanksgiving
service at Notre Dame; but Barbier noted that no one cried
Vive le Roi and officials had to order the crowd to cheer. Though
the King was only forty-one his subjects were already looking
forward to a worthier successor. Instead of public festivities
the Dauphin proposed a dowry for six hundred girls, telling the
King that he would regret so much money wasted on fireworks.
He refrained from journeys which involved enormous expense.
His own allowance was so small that at times he borrowed in his
eagerness to help suffering and need. His rare visits to Paris
revealed the discontent of the people. On one occasion when he
and his wife were on their way to Notre Dame a large crowd of
women stopped their carriage on a bridge, crying 'Give us bread,
we are dying of hunger.' The Dauphine trembled and the
Dauphin threw them the contents of his purse. 'We don't want
your money, Monseigneur,' was the response; 'we want bread.
We love you. Get rid of that woman who is ruining the country.'
Though that was beyond his power his desire to evict the
Pompadour was as strong as theirs. The kindly Queen suggested
a rather less chilling attitude towards the Favourite.

THE DAUPHIN: The mere thought of that association revolts me.
THE QUEEN: Do you think it revolts me any less? One must
    master oneself for the glory of God.
THE DAUPHIN: If I were master I would make an example
    which for centuries would frighten off those who are
    tempted to corrupt the virtue of Kings.

When forced to sit next to her in a carriage he turned his head
away and uttered no word.

Was the leader of the *dévots* himself immaculate? 'It is said
that the Dauphin is trying to take a mistress despite his bigotry,'
comments d'Argenson in September, 1753. He was not so

austere as was generally believed since he tried to seduce two ladies, testifies Cheverny, who adds that the Dauphine was very jealous. An undated letter reveals her distress without mentioning names. 'I have long known of his bad conduct and of the morning visits he receives. It is scandalous and I am very upset. But I shall receive him tomorrow as usual for one must dissimulate.' A recently discovered document* records the execution on June 25, 1794, of Auguste Dadonville, born October 2, 1758. Among the reasons which brought him to the scaffold was his admission that his father was the Dauphin, who met his mother Mme Dadonville in the atelier of the painter Fredon. Though the declaration may not be conclusive, it is all the evidence we possess. The Dauphine's troubles ended during her husband's serious illness when she braved the perils of smallpox and nursed him with loving care. The crisis brought them closer than they had ever been, and her devotion increased her popularity. Her sympathy on the death of his dearly loved daughter by the first marriage made the partnership still more harmonious. Though Marie Josepha lacked the vivacity and radiance of the Rose of Savoy, her solid qualities commanded respect.

When Luynes complained that the Dauphin cared for nothing but music he did him an injustice, for he was a lover of books and the arts. Like most eighteenth-century princes he read Hume's *History of England* in a translation, studied Montesquieu and admired Bolingbroke's ideal of a Patriot King. Like his grandfather he prepared himself for his calling by study and recorded his conclusions in memoranda some of which are still preserved. A Christian should not have a mistress and a King should not have Favourites. His duty was to sacrifice his interests and his pleasures, to forget himself, to dedicate himself wholly to his people. He should combine the vigilance of a pastor with the tenderness of a father. France had possessed many sovereigns worthy to rule and not a single tyrant. No Empire had received from heaven so many blessings as France, and they would continue so long as her rulers rendered their people happy. Like all the best princes in the eighteenth century he accepted the ideal of Enlightened Autocracy: constitutional monarchy as practised in England made no appeal to him. He was deeply distressed

* Printed in Vrignault, *Les Enfants de Louis XV: Descendance Illégitime,* 1955.

by the state of France, and the most urgent task was to grapple
with the financial chaos. He approved Machault's attempts to
include Church property in the *vingtième* and regretted the decision
of the Church to confine itself to a voluntary gift.

The Dauphin's brief taste of authority while the King was
immobilised by the attack of Damiens impressed observers with
his ability and his loyalty to his father. He had been too young
to show his mettle during the King's grave illness at Metz, but
now he was twenty-eight. 'My son, I leave you a very troubled
country,' whispered the King on what he believed might be his
death-bed. 'I hope you will govern better than I.' The interregnum increased not only his self-assurance but his disapproval
of the attempts of the *Parlement* to diminish the authority of the
Crown. A letter to his father on its attempts to make capital out
of the Damiens incident reveals his authoritarian attitude. 'They
think themselves the only good citizens. Despite your benevo-
lence they make you out a tyrant. To yield is to encourage fresh
demands and to make the people believe they are in the right.
In my opinion unwavering firmness is the only means to preserve
your life and authority. Leniency now would perhaps bring a
deceptive calm for a few days, but it would cost you dear in the
long run, for they would strike again at the first opportunity.'
On the King's recovery the Dauphin left the stage, but his
stock had risen. There were few whose conversation was so
agreeable, testifies President Hénault. 'He is exceptionally well
informed: public law, history, *belles-lettres*—he is familiar with
them all, getting the heart out of every book. He possesses an
admirable memory, good judgment and a keen sense of humour
like the Queen, and is never afraid to talk freely. He revealed
his intelligence, insight and above all his eminent wisdom when
the King bade him take his place in the Council after the Damiens
affair. The Ministers could not stop talking of him and left every
meeting filled with admiration.' Mme de Pompadour paid her
chief enemy a high compliment. 'The Dauphin has a good heart,
and he is perhaps the only heir who would shed tears if his
father died.' Like Louis XIV, Frederick William I and Frederick
the Great of Prussia, George II, George III and Catherine the
Great, Louis XV excluded his heir from all share of power
though he was henceforth permitted to attend meetings of the

Council. The only eighteenth-century condominium was that of Maria Theresa and Joseph II.

The closing phase of the brief lives of the Dauphin and the Dauphine was clouded with private sorrows and public anxiety. He disliked the Austrian alliance, and the Prussian invasion of Saxony in 1756, which involved the flight of the Elector to Warsaw and the surrender of his troops, was a blow to her pride. When she heard of her mother's death a few months later she exclaimed 'Happy woman!' The death of their precocious eldest son was a further trial. 'Political and religious affairs are equally bad,' wrote the Dauphin to the Bishop of Verdun in 1762. 'Authority halved, America lost, a ruinous and hopeless war: these indicate the pattern of the remainder of my life—repulsed, fettered, humiliated. I live for my children, who are my sole consolation.'

When the rout at Rossbach in 1757 struck France like a blow in the face, the heir begged his father to appoint him Commander-in-Chief. He would do nothing without the advice of the Generals, and would be there merely to encourage the troops and to show that princes were not indifferent to the fortunes of France. 'Every Frenchman would become invincible at the spectacle of your only son at their head.' 'Your letter,' replied the King, 'has touched me to tears. One must not be carried away by misfortune. Only great evils require great remedies. This is only a scuffle. I am delighted to find in you the sentiments of our fathers, but it is not yet time for us to part.' Forbidden to serve at the front he agreed with Bernis that France ought to make peace and regretted his dismissal. He disliked his successor Choiseul as the friend of the Pompadour and the *Philosophes*, and the new Minister strove to prevent him from exerting any influence. The Treaty of Paris seemed to him an unparalleled humiliation.

No sooner was the disastrous Seven Years War at an end than a fresh trial for the Dauphine occurred. The death of her father Augustus III in 1763 produced the usual struggle for the succession. It was natural for Maria Josepha, with her strong family sense, to wish a third member of her house elected to the Polish throne. Her candidate was her favourite brother Prince Xavier who had commanded a Saxon corps in French pay and had long aspired to wear a crown, but she could do nothing for him. The Empress Catherine put forward her discarded lover Stanislas Poniatowski whose candidature was supported by the King of Prussia as the price of a *rapprochement* with Russia. Louis XV had done his best for Stanislas Leczinski thirty years earlier and was not disposed to try again.

It plunges me in the bitterest grief [wrote the Dauphine to her brother], destroying not my hopes, for I never had any, but my desires. But in fairness to France I must say that it is not ill-will but impotence. Our misfortunes have reached a point which it is difficult to imagine, and we are more to be pitied for our inability to help you than you for lack of help. And your sister, here in the middle of it all, is more to be pitied than anyone, with her heart torn and pierced, to see her brother whom she loves so tenderly bereft of all hope of the Polish crown and France unable to secure it for him. I could fill a volume with my sad reflections, but remember that I love you, that I am Saxon and French, and you will readily guess what I suffer. The Dauphin is equally grieved, for you know he has long wished to see you on the Polish throne.

While the loss of the Polish prize by her family was the sharpest grief of the Dauphine's closing years, the hardest blow the Dauphin had to bear was the overthrow of the Jesuits. Since the King took little part in the struggle, the Order centred its last hopes on the heir. Cheverny recalls a conversation with Choiseul which made such an impression on him that he vouches for every word. The Dauphin sent for the Minister before a meeting of the Council in 1764 after the *Parlement* had confirmed the decree of dissolution.

DAUPHIN: I take the greatest interest in this matter.

CHOISEUL: My conclusions, Sir, are all against the Society.

DAUPHIN: I warn you I shall oppose you with all my power.

CHOISEUL: Monsieur will sacrifice to them the most important interests?

DAUPHIN: Yes, Sir, and I would give half my kingdom to preserve them in case of need.

CHOISEUL: Quoi, Monsieur, the heir thus exposes his prejudices. I venture to tell you, even at the risk of deserving your wrath and risking my head, here are the proofs. I submit to your excellent judgment, I appeal to your virtues,

K

your prudence, your honour. The opposition of a subject
to the heir proves my conviction that the decree of the
Parlement must be confirmed. M. le Dauphin would sacrifice
half his kingdom to preserve a Society which has been and is
the misfortune of France. Nothing will turn me from my
duty.

The Dauphin continued to fight in the Council, declaring that
in honour and conscience he could not extinguish a society so
useful for the preservation of religion and the education of youth,
but he received no support.

The Dauphin, like his grandfather, was snatched away before
he had his chance. 'The poor Dauphin is dying,' reported
Horace Walpole on a visit to France in October, 1765. 'He is a
spectre and cannot live three months. His wife is a devoted
nurse, and he tells her: "How I love you."' To the Queen's
assurance that he would recover he replied that he had no desire
to live. Even the cynical Richelieu was impressed by his resignation. 'I should never have believed, Sire,' observed the Duke
of Orleans to the King, 'that one could be so peaceful and serene
at the gates of death.' 'That is how it ought to be,' rejoined the
King, 'if, like my son, one's whole life was without reproach.'
'He would have been a great man,' comments the Duc de Croy,
'and it was cruel that he had to die.' It was the greatest loss since
Henri IV, declared Horace Walpole, but there was far less
mourning than for the pupil of Fénelon. At Versailles the end
of the long illness, which had held up the festivities of the bored
courtiers, was hailed with relief in certain quarters, and Horace
Walpole reported the satisfaction of the *Philosophes* that the nightmare of a *dévot* ruler and the return of Jesuit influence was
removed. Quesnay, the King's doctor, knew too much about his
master's ways to admire him, but he preferred his easy-going
régime to any possible alternative. When the elder Mirabeau
visited the chief of the Physiocrats in his room in the palace the
following conversation took place.

MIRABEAU: The King does not look well.
QUESNAY: That is bad news. It would be a great loss.
MIRABEAU: I too love the King, but I never saw you so worked
up.

QUESNAY: I am thinking of what would follow.

MIRABEAU: But the Dauphin is virtuous.

QUESNAY: So he is, and he has good intentions and is intelligent. But the bigots would rule him, for they are his oracles. The Jesuits would govern the state as at the close of the reign of Louis XIV, and the *Parlements* would be no better treated than my friends the *Philosophes*. The times of John Hus and Jerome of Prague would return.

'It is a terrible blow for me and the whole kingdom,' wrote the King to his grandson the Duke of Parma. 'I cannot get used to having no son. It is impossible for me ever to have a greater loss.' Yet there may also have been a certain feeling of relief. The succession was assured and the austerity of his heir had been a perpetual rebuke. The King had always preferred the Dauphine to his son, and now was the time to show his affection. 'Without his kindness I could not have borne it,' she wrote; 'it is my only support.' She did not have to bear it long, for two years later she followed him to the grave. Her eldest son had died at the age of eleven, a second son only lived for three months, but three more sons—who were to become Louis XVI, Louis XVIII, and Charles X—assured the succession. Two princesses, Clotilde, destined to marry into the House of Savoy, and Elizabeth, destined to a crown of thorns, completed the family. Maria Josepha had fulfilled her mission.

IV

The relations of Louis XV with his six daughters were far more satisfactory than with his wife and son. They never tried to interfere in matters of State, and though they frowned on his mistresses they never formed a cabal. Two of them, Sophie and Victoire, were so colourless that they played no part in his life, but the other four possessed plenty of spirit. His favourites, the twins Louise Elizabeth and Henriette, died before him and were sincerely mourned. All six were more attached to their indulgent father than to the Queen who was inclined to scold them about trifles.

The death of Henriette, the more lovable of the twins, was deeply felt by her father. At her funeral shouts of rebuke reached the King's ears. 'That comes from offending God and making his people miserable; God takes his beloved daughter.' Her sister Louise Elizabeth—Babette—was dispatched to Madrid at the age of twelve to marry Don Philip, a younger son of the King of Spain, and became Duchess of Parma when the Duchy was allotted to her husband as a result of the War of the Austrian Succession. Since the little principality, which she described as 'this hole of Parma', failed to satisfy her ambitions and her marriage was unhappy, she always pined for Versailles. After the birth of a son, afterwards Duke of Parma, and a daughter, later the ugly wife of Charles IV immortalised by Goya, she was allowed by her husband to spend a year in France. Arriving in August, 1752, she was affectionately welcomed by her father, saddened by the recent loss of Henriette. A second visit, soon after the Damiens incident, lasted two years, after which she died of smallpox in 1760. Her son Ferdinand, who numbered Condillac and Mably among his teachers, succeeded his father in 1765 and—aided by his able French Premier Dutillot—ranks among the minor Enlightened Autocrats of the eighteenth century. Like other French and Spanish Bourbons he expelled the Jesuits, abolished the Inquisition, and closed redundant monasteries. He married Amelia, the least attractive of the daughters of Maria Theresa. Louis XV extended his affection for Babette to her son. His letters to his grandson, published in 1938, deal mainly with health, hunting, and the weather, and reveal a grandfatherly interest but little deep feeling. 'I promise to aid you with advice,' he wrote on the death of his son-in-law. But the young prince felt quite capable of ruling his little duchy without guidance from Versailles.

On the death of Henriette and the Duchess of Parma, Adelaide took the lead among the princesses, not merely by seniority but by force of character. Temperamental, haughty, brusque, rather masculine, full of energy and ambition, she inspired little affection throughout her life. There was talk of a marriage to the Prince de Conti or to Prince Xavier, brother of the Dauphine, but like her three younger sisters she was fated to die an old maid. She possessed intellectual and musical tastes, learning English and

Italian, the latter from Goldoni. The catalogue of her library contained five thousand titles. Alone of the four princesses she was the subject of unfriendly gossip. Victoire was pretty, gracious and well liked, Sophie ugly, timid, and tongue-tied. The versatile Beaumarchais, who started his brilliant career as a watchmaker and had won some celebrity as an amateur harpist, taught the girls music and organised weekly concerts in their apartments sometimes patronised by the King and Queen. Despite such distractions it was a monotonous and trivial life. Mme Campan, who became *lectrice* to the princesses after the death of their mother in 1768, describes the dreary routine. 'The King saw little of his family. Every morning he visited Mme Adelaide, often drinking his coffee which he had made himself. She rang her bell to summon Victoire, who rang for Sophie, who in turn notified Louise whose apartments were furthest away. The latter, who was misshapen and extremely small, had to hurry and sometimes only arrived just in time to embrace her father before he was off to the hunt. Every evening at six Mesdames interrupted my reading to join the princes in what was called *le débotter du roi*. The King kissed them on the forehead, and the visit was often so short that the reading was resumed after a quarter of an hour.' He had pet names for them all—Loque, Coche, Graille, Chiffe—but there was little warmth on either side. His heart was elsewhere.

When one of Marie Leczinska's *dames du palais* became a Carmelite, the Queen and her daughters drove to a Paris convent for the ceremony. Deeply moved, Adelaide begged leave to follow her example. 'Wait till you are twenty-five or a widow,' replied her father. It was only a fleeting whim, for she was not made for austerity. The impression on Louise, the youngest of the princesses, aged sixteen, was more enduring. 'During the ceremony,' she wrote later, 'I resolved to ask God every day to let me break the ties which held me back. I should never forget what I owe to her for her example. I should never have thought of consecrating myself to God, for, though young, I was inclined to love the world.' She had to wait seventeen years till her dream came true. Mme Campan, her *lectrice*, read to her five hours a day till her voice became husky. The princess prepared a glass of *eau sucrée*, explaining that she wished to finish the

course she had planned. She never told her mother, fearing that
she would oppose it on the ground of her weak health, but on
her death the time had come to act. Life at Versailles was a
spiritual vacuum. Her resolve was strengthened when Mme du
Barry was installed as *maîtresse en titre*, for now her thoughts
turned to the salvation of her father's soul. She selected a convent
at St. Denis noted for its strictness, for she had already practised
secret austerities. 'Myself a Carmelite and the King converted,
what happiness! God can and will do it, my saintly mother, if
you ask Him. He would do it for me if I possessed all the faith
I desire.' She confided her plan to the Archbishop of Paris,
whom she begged to inform the King. Her father took a fortnight for reflection, during which she anxiously awaited his
decision. 'When he hears of my resolve, will he consent, and
can he witness its fulfilment without turning to God?' The
reply, when it came, showed Louis XV at his best. 'If it is for
God alone I cannot oppose His will nor your determination.
God will give you the strength to support your new condition,
since, the decision once made, there is no turning back. I embrace you with all my heart, dear daughter, and I give you my
blessing.'

When the King told her sisters, Adelaide hotly resented being
kept in the dark and Victoire shed silent tears. When asked by
her *lectrice* Mme Campan whether she would follow Louise, the
latter replied, 'I shall never have the courage, for I am too fond
of the pleasures of life.' On entering the convent on April 11,
1770, at the age of thirty-three, Louise dispatched letters to her
three sisters. 'My grief equals my surprise,' was Adelaide's
affectionate reply, 'but you are happy and that is enough for me,
dear heart. You know my needs, which are more pressing than
ever.' 'I forgive you with all my heart for not telling me,' wrote
Sophie. 'Your sacrifice is fine because it is your own choice.
Be assured I shall love you all my life and will visit you when
you give me leave.' Victoire was too upset to write direct.
'It is only with God's help that I can bear this separation,' she
confided to the Prioress. 'I feel I must tell you that Louise has a
weak chest and often spits blood.' 'I have obeyed your wishes,'
wrote the King, 'though in many matters I am your superior.
Now you must obey the Superior of your community. She

would be wise to show you some consideration at first so that you can go forward to your goal. Be assured of my friendship, dear Louise, or Saint Thérèse de Saint Augustin.'

Her first visitors were her sisters, who wept as they embraced the novice. 'You have no need to weep for me,' said Louise, who retained her composure, 'unless you envy my perfect happiness.' Other visitors followed—nephews and nieces and the new Dauphine on arriving in France *en route* from Compiègne to Versailles. To another welcome visitor, her late *lectrice* Mme Campan, she apologised for having driven her so hard. 'I over-worked your young lungs, but I knew I should be able to read only books of edification here, so I wanted to finish the historians who interested me.' The moralists, she added, were right when they declared that happiness was not to be found in palaces. The most regular of her visitors was the King, usually about once a month. On the first occasion he was very depressed on arrival, but he cheered up when he found her so happy. Some-times he appeared in state, with an army of cooks, more often privately, but always bringing food for himself and his suite.

THE KING: I don't know how you can be happy in such a
    hard life.
LOUISE: I could not be happier. My life is certainly austere,
    but the thought that I am here for the salvation of those I
    love is my consolation.

For the ceremony of the clothing (*vêture*) the Pope dispatched a Nuncio and Bishops attended at the command of the King. During the ceremony Louise was perfectly serene. She took her vows a year later, and in due course became Mistress of the Novices and Prioress. Despite the meagre diet she astonished her family by growing stout. The peace that passes understanding was hers at last. Her strategic position as a saintly Carmelite enabled her to exert an influence on her father of which she had never dreamed. That he had supported the campaign against the Jesuits with reluctance and largely owing to the necessity of retaining the confidence of Spain was known to his family no less than to his Ministers; and when Clement XIV astonished the world by suppressing the Order in 1773 Louise, in collaboration with the Archbishop of Paris, strove eagerly for its restoration.

Their appeals were in vain, since the Pope declined to retrace his steps. She was more successful in obtaining financial support for the Carmelites of St. Denis, but her request for aid for poor Carmelites in other parts of France fell on deaf ears. After seventeen years of tranquil happiness within the convent walls, she passed away on the eve of the Revolution which destroyed the world she had known and left. If zeal for the Church and a sacrifice of position such as no French princess had ever made deserve official recognition, her Beatification can have been no surprise to those who had known and loved her in her later years.

7

MME DE POMPADOUR

FRANCE had received the news of the illness of Louis XV at Metz in 1744 with consternation, and his rapid recovery was greeted with delight. The popularity he had enjoyed as a child had waned, but the thought of his loss stirred what was left of monarchical sentiment into new life. Little though he deserved the title he was hailed as *Louis le Bienaimé*. Half the reign was over and there was still plenty of time to amend. It is the measure of his unworthiness that, while his countrymen were ready to pardon his failings, he made no effort to respond to their trust. No one has dared to argue that Louis XV, unlike his unhappy successor, was more sinned against than sinning. The era of harlotocracy, to employ Carlyle's drastic expression, had begun, and it was to continue till the end, naked and unashamed.

On the death of the Duchesse de Châteauroux at the close of 1744 a scramble began for the succession to the most coveted and lucrative post in France. The King's choice was expected to fall on the Duchesse de Lauraguais, the fourth of the de Nesle sisters, but why should he not look beyond the world of the aristocracy? He had never known much of the Parisians at first hand, but he learned a good deal of gossip from his valets and from sampling the correspondence of his subjects opened in the post. Many members of the professional classes had made money and were discriminating patrons of art. The *Tiers État* was on the up-grade socially long before it began to count in politics or the services, and there were few doors which beauty and money could not unlock. Since the succession was assured and he had finally parted company with the Queen, there seemed nothing to prevent him from consulting his own wishes. We shall never understand the character and conduct of Louis XIV and Louis XV if we interpret them as the mere slaves of passion. They were sufficiently human to crave for congenial feminine companionship and to rejoice when it was found. No eighteenth-century ruler except Frederick the Great was content without the warmth of family life or some makeshift equivalent.

The fame of Jeanne Antoinette Poisson had reached Versailles some time before she crossed the threshold. Mme de Mailly had been captivated by the playing of the harpsichord by a certain Mme d'Étioles at a friend's house in Paris, and President Hénault had sung her praises. 'I met one of the prettiest women I ever saw,' he reported to Mme du Deffand in 1742. 'She sings with gaiety and perfect taste, knows a hundred songs, and acts in comedy at Étioles in a theatre up to the standard of the Opera. She has a lovely complexion, chestnut hair, wonderful eyes and teeth, a fascinating smile, dimples, animation, and a perfect figure.' Cultivated and well-to-do, she was one of the most attractive young women among the higher bourgeoisie of the capital. She had risen above the level of her family, for one of the most fastidious of women was the child of rather coarse parents. Her father, the son of a peasant, had worked his way up as an agent of the Paris brothers, influential army contractors and bankers in the Regency era, but when their accounts were said to be irregular he was involved in their temporary disgrace and a commission declared him a debtor to the Treasury. Since he could not pay, his goods were seized and he was condemned to death. He fled abroad and was only allowed to return after eight years, when he was cleared of the charges. Meanwhile his wife, a woman of good looks, courage and resource, had to fend for herself and her family. After one or more *liaisons* her material problem was solved by a stable association with Le Normant de Tournehem, a rich Farmer-General and a friend of the Paris brothers. He gave her daughter the best available education, which included playing the clavichord, singing, acting, engraving, dancing, and riding. At the wish of her exiled father she was sent to a convent school for a year at the age of eight.

The most memorable experience of her childhood was a visit at the age of nine to a fortune-teller who pronounced her *morceau de roi*. The oracular utterance was stamped on the memory of her mother and was registered in the pet name Reinette. Her mother's lover found her a husband at the age of twenty in his nephew Le Normant Seigneur d'Étioles, to whom he promised a handsome dowry for the bride and his fortune when he died. It was an excellent match from a material standpoint, and he proved a decent and affectionate partner. The two families—the Poisson parents and the young couple—lived with their benefactor de Tournehem in his spacious Paris home and at the Château d'Étioles near Choisy, the King's favourite hunting-box in the forest of Sénart not far from Versailles. While her husband's family had contacts with rich business circles, the gifted hostess attracted leading Intellectuals, among them Voltaire, Montesquieu, Fontenelle, Crébillon and Maupertuis, was received by Mme Geoffrin, and was a guest at President Hénault's elegant supper-parties. When news of her salon and of her acting in a theatre built by her for amateur theatricals began to reach Versailles, the Duchesse de Châteauroux scented a rival. That Mme d'Étioles was determined to shine on a larger stage was proved by placing herself, beautifully attired and driving her own phaeton, in the King's path when he hunted from the Château de Choisy. When he inquired her name and sent presents of game the first milestone was passed on the road to fortune. The reigning mistress ordered the audacious competitor not to appear at the hunts, and when the Duchesse de Chevreuse spoke to the King of 'la petite Étioles', the Châteauroux stamped hard on her foot. By one of the accidents which deflect the course of history, the sudden death of the reigning mistress left the field open to whoever possessed the wit and the will to seize the glittering prize.

Her hour struck during the celebrations of the marriage of the Dauphin to his cousin, a sister of the Spanish princess who had been betrothed for a brief space twenty years earlier to Louis XV. The sumptuous masked ball at Versailles was open to anyone suitably attired, and among the throng which surged into the brilliantly lighted rooms was Mme d'Étioles, dressed as Diana. When all were assembled and the other members of the Royal

Family had made their appearance, the King entered the Galerie des Glaces and was observed in animated conversation with the newcomer. They met again by arrangement a few days later at the ball given by the Paris municipality at the Hôtel de Ville. The King, accompanied by the Duc d'Ayen, arrived about midnight after meeting the Dauphin who had left the party and was on his way back to Versailles. After looking in at the Opera, where another ball was in progress, he dismissed his carriage, drove incognito to the Hôtel de Ville, supped with Mme d'Étioles and, accompanied by the Duc d'Ayen, drove her to her Paris home. Reaching Versailles at 9 a.m. he went to Mass as usual and then to bed. 'Il a jeté le mouchoir,' cried the onlookers. Soon afterwards she was installed in the room which had been occupied by Mme de Mailly, connected with the King's apartments by a private staircase. When her husband, returning from a business journey, heard the news he begged her to return; but such a trifle as a bleeding heart could not be allowed to interfere with the royal command, and Mme d'Étioles parted from the father of her children without a pang. They never met again. Ambition had triumphed, and at this stage the scheming woman entertained as little affection for her second partner as for the first. That she never felt the slightest twinge of remorse was hardly surprising in an age when marriage in the higher circles was rarely a union of hearts. If any further excuse for her adultery was required, she could claim that her qualifications for the post were unique. She was coached in Court etiquette by her old friend Abbé de Bernis and the Marquis de Gontaut, an intimate of the King, and Collin, a capable young lawyer, was engaged as her secretary and factotum. A deed of separation from her husband was obligingly provided by the *Parlement* of Paris. The summer passed quietly at Étioles while she waited for her official inauguration as *maîtresse du roi*.

During the interval the King went to the front and received his baptism of fire at the battle of Fontenoy. His stock, which had risen during his illness at Metz and had fallen after his recovery, rose again when he shared the perils of his troops. He was greeted with loud cries of *Vive le Roi*, testifies Valfons in his Memoirs, and when he was urged to withdraw from the zone of fire he refused. 'Sire,' exclaimed Richelieu, a brave soldier

as well as a courtier and a rake, 'your presence alone can restore
the situation and gain the day.' The sixteen-year-old Dauphin,
who had accompanied his father, displayed equal courage, and
begged to be allowed to charge at the head of the cavalry. 'I am
too young to be known to the nation,' he argued, 'but I naturally
wish to imitate my father's subjects.' His life was too valuable
to be risked, for he was the only surviving son. It was the
culminating moment in the brilliant career of Marshal Saxe, but
a high price had to be paid in French blood. As the King surveyed the dead and dying men on the battlefield he remarked to
the Dauphin that he now saw what a military victory involved.
No King of France was less a lover of war.

Louis XV wrote to the new Favourite every day during his
absence at the front, and his return was the signal for the official
presentation. The ceremony took place on September 15, 1745,
and the Princesse de Conti consented to be her sponsor in return
for payment of her debts. 'Mme de Pompadour was presented
to the King at six o'clock,' records the Duc de Luynes in his
journal. 'There was a crowd in the ante-chamber but only a
few in the King's cabinet. The conversation was very brief and
extremely embarrassing on both sides. A similar crowd had
gathered for the presentation to the Queen and all Paris wondered
what she would say. It was expected that she would merely make
some remark about her dress, the usual topic among ladies when
they have nothing to say. But the Queen, aware that Paris had
planned the conversation in advance, felt bound for that very
reason to talk of something else.' She mentioned a mutual
friend, adding that it had been a pleasure to make her acquaintance. 'I do not know if Mme de Pompadour heard her,' records
the Duc de Luynes, 'for she speaks rather low; but she seized
the opportunity to assure her of her respect and her desire to
please her. The Queen seemed well satisfied with these words.'
After the callous indifference of the de Nesle sisters it was a relief
to receive a little consideration: since the King must have a
mistress, better a refined and well-mannered specimen than a
virago. The blow was further cushioned by the payment of
debts incurred by the Queen's abounding charities. Unlike his
gentle mother, the austere Dauphin frowned on the rising sun,
and confined the conversation to a few words about her dress.

In a poem entitled *La Bataille de Fontenoy*, which enjoyed prodigious popularity, Voltaire saluted the victory of his old friend.

> *Sincère et tendre Pompadour,*
> *Car je peux vous donner d'avance*
> *Un nom qui rime avec l'amour*
> *Et qui sera bientôt le plus beau nom de France.*

The France of the easy-going, colourless, mediocre Fleury had melted into the pageant of the Pompadour.

Six weeks after the presentation the Duc de Luynes recorded that she had made an excellent start. 'Everyone seems to think she is extremely polite. Not only is she not ill-natured and never speaks evil of anybody, but she forbids such talk in her presence. She is bright and talkative. Far removed up to now from arrogance, she frequently mentions her relatives, even when the King is there, perhaps, indeed, rather too frequently.' That he spent most of the day in her apartments told its own tale. Such was the beginning of every *liaison*, but how long would it last? Neither friend nor foe would have dared to predict that the royal favour would continue till the day of her death nearly twenty years later.

The Court, as usual on such occasions, was sharply divided, her critics, among them Richelieu, Maurepas and the d'Argenson brothers, complaining of her bourgeois birth, her champions, including Marshal Saxe whom she called *Mon Maréchal*, stressing her unquestionable charms. The former disability was dealt with when the King, reviving a lapsed title, named her the Marquise de Pompadour and henceforth referred to her in conversation as *la Marquise*. Richelieu, formerly the champion of the Nesle sisters, disapproved the choice of a Favourite over whom he possessed no influence but quickly realised the futility of opposition. She responded by informing him that the King was very satisfied with him, as was the whole public. A far more dangerous foe was Maurepas who, believing himself securely anchored in the King's favour, scarcely troubled to conceal his disdain. Yet in everything except birth she towered above her predecessors, and no impartial observer could contest her intelligence or deny her charms. 'In her grace, the lightness of her figure, the beauty of her hair, she resembled a nymph,' wrote the Comte de Valfons. 'To so many natural advantages were added every accomplishment. She was a good musician with a sympathetic voice, excelling in declamation, and she varied the King's pleasures by performances in which she played the leading part. Mistress of the King and of the universe, she was surrounded at her toilette like a queen.' 'Everyone found her extremely polite,' records Luynes, 'with never a harsh word for anyone.' Happy in her success, she desired to use her influence for the benefit of her friends. 'If I can be of use to you,' she remarked to Valfons, 'let me know.' Only once did he take advantage of her offer, and she kept her word. Throughout life she delighted to oblige her *protégés*, subject to the condition that no act or word should endanger her position or interfere with her plans. Among her earliest beneficiaries was Voltaire, a frequent visitor to Étioles, for whom, despite the King's dislike, she procured well-paid sinecures as *Gentilhomme de la Chambre*, Historiographer of France, and election to the Académie Française. Her earliest victim was Orry, the Finance Minister, who was dismissed at the wish of the Paris brothers, old friends of her family.

The most engaging feature of her character was her loyalty to her parents. Her mother lived just long enough to rejoice in the fulfilment of the fortune-teller's prediction. Her father survived for another decade, and though his coarse ways debarred him from the royal table at Versailles, he was received when the Court was in residence elsewhere. His debts were paid, and he was ennobled and presented with a large estate. Her few surviving letters reveal genuine affection. 'Do not worry about my health,' she wrote in 1750; 'it is very good. Nothing will upset it, for my principle is to do my best and not to trouble about gossip for which I have given no cause. I have nothing to reproach myself with, so I am serene.' Two years later she reported that the King had made her a duchess, and added, 'Good night, I am overwhelmed by visits and letters—another sixty to write.' Having lost her son in infancy, her affection was centred on her daughter. 'Alexandrine is growing ugly,' she confided to her father; 'provided she is not repulsive I shall be content. I do not wish her transcendent beauty, which merely incurs the enmity of all the women who, with their friends, make up two-thirds of the population.' From time to time she had to tell him that his requests were impossible, for there were limits to her influence and her income. 'I am much less wealthy than I used to be in Paris,' she explained. 'What I possess was given me without asking. The expenses for my houses have been a great worry. I never desired great wealth, and I defy fortune to make me unhappy. Only my resilience carries me through, and the public does me justice.'

The best specimen of the Poisson family was her brother, who deserved her affectionate efforts on his behalf. Since his understanding of the arts equalled her own, she procured his appointment as Superintendent of Buildings and packed him off to Italy to widen his experience. 'I recommend above all the greatest politeness and discretion,' she wrote to him *en route*; 'in society be amiable to everyone. If you confine your favours to persons you esteem you will be detested by almost the whole of mankind. Do not think that because I am young I cannot give you good advice. After four and a half years here I know more than a woman of forty. Though I thought I loved you dearly I never imagined your departure could cause me such grief.' She delighted in the reports of his reception by the King of Sardinia and other princes. Everyone liked him at home and abroad. Though the King gave him the title of Marquis de Marigny and called him *petit frère*, his head was never turned. The only friction between brother and sister arose from her fruitless efforts to arrange a brilliant marriage.

> I do not wonder at the consideration paid to me in France [she wrote], where everyone has or may have need of my services, but I am surprised it extends as far as Rome. Despite this satisfaction my head is not turned. Except for the happiness of being loved by a person one loves, a solitary and retired life is preferable. The older I am, the more philosophic I become. The happiness of the King's company makes up for everything; but the rest is a tissue of wickedness and platitudes, in fact, of all the miseries to which we poor human beings are heirs. It makes one think, especially some one born as reflective as myself. Everywhere you will find falsity and all the vices. Yet life in solitude would be dull, so we must put up with people's faults and pretend not to see them.

On his return from Italy her brother won golden opinions in the discharge of his official duties, and aroused none of the jealous hostility which plagued his sister till the day of her death. He

MADAME DE POMPADOUR
(*Rothschild Collection*)

was a frequent guest of the King, not merely out of compliment
to the Favourite but owing to his sterling qualities. Her plan
to marry her daughter to a son of the King and Mme de Vintimille
found no favour, and the problem was solved by her death at
the age of ten.

Mme de Pompadour impressed foreign visitors with her com-
petence for her task. 'After paying my respects to all the Royal
Family,' reported the Prince de Ligne, whose acquaintance with
the Courts of Europe was unsurpassed, 'I was taken to a sort of
second Queen who had the air of being the first.' Her serenity
and poise rested not only on her confidence in her abilities but
on the conviction that the King was her trusty friend. That they
felt a genuine affection for each other was the impression of those
who saw them together. Spending most of his time in her
company he seemed happier than ever before. A pleasant picture
of his first *petit souper* is painted by the Duc de Croy, at that time
a young Colonel who was always a welcome figure at Court in
the intervals of his campaigns.

> The dining-room was charming, the supper most agreeable and
> unconstrained. We were waited on by two or three valets who
> retired after serving us. Freedom and good manners prevailed.
> The King was gay and uninhibited, though always with an air of
> distinction. He did not seem in the least timid, talking much and
> well and obviously enjoying himself. He appeared very much in
> love with Mme de Pompadour, and without false shame. He struck
> me as very well informed about little things, without committing
> himself in important affairs. Discretion was his second nature,
> though people think he tells the Marquise almost everything. We
> were eighteen at table, among them Marshal Saxe, whom the King
> seemed greatly to like and esteem. We were two hours at table,
> quite at our ease and without any excess. Then coffee and cards
> till one in the morning.

Two years later, at the second marriage of the Dauphin, the same
witness describes the King as madly in love.

Mme de Pompadour honestly strove to win the toleration if
not the approval of Marie Leczinska, and dreaded the loss of her
favour. 'I have just spoken to the Queen, Madame,' wrote the
Duchesse de Luynes in February, 1746, 'and begged her to tell
me if she had anything against you. She replied in the friendliest

L

tone that there was nothing, that she greatly appreciated your attention on all occasions, and that she wished me to tell you so.'

> For the last three days I have been deeply grieved, as you will readily believe, knowing as you do my attachment to the Queen. Terrible charges have been made to M. and Mme la Dauphine who kindly allowed me to prove their falsity. I was told that the Queen had been turned against me. Imagine my despair, I, who would give my life for her, whose favours I value more and more. Of course, the kinder she is to me, the greater the jealousy of the monsters and the more horrible their charges, unless she is good enough to be on her guard against them and to inform me of their nature. It will be easy to justify myself—my conscience is at ease. I hope, Madame, that your friendship and still more your knowledge of my character will guarantee my statements. I shall have wearied you with this long story, but my heart is so full that I could not hide my feelings. You know my sentiments for you, Madame, which will only end with my life.

While caring nothing for the chase and the card-table, the King's principal pastimes, Mme de Pompadour shared his mania for building and landscape gardening. The first purchase was Crécy, a small house quickly transformed into a large one, with a sufficient number of neighbouring properties to enable the King to hunt. Choisy, built for Mme de Vintimille and subsequently occupied by Mme de Châteauroux, was enlarged by Gabriel, the King's favourite architect, and newly decorated. Even more exquisite was Bellevue, the only large house built for Mme de Pompadour, beautifully situated on the Seine near Saint Cloud, which she sold to the King in 1757 as a country residence for his unmarried daughters. While building and landscape gardening fascinated them both, interior decoration was mainly her sphere, since the King cared more for his houses than for their contents. She became the most generous and discriminating patroness of the arts that France has ever possessed, and not even her harshest critics deny her exquisite taste. Small residences were constructed for her close to the vast palaces at Fontainebleau and Compiègne. In the capital she bought and enlarged the Hôtel d'Evreux, now the Élysée Palace, but rarely used it and bequeathed it to the King. At Versailles she possessed a house connected by a corridor with the palace. To a fine mansion on the Loire she made only two visits and bequeathed it to her brother. The *École Militaire* for the sons of officers was her own idea, and Gabriel was entrusted with the design. She died too soon to witness the completion of his masterpiece the Petit Trianon.

A second unfailing delight was the theatre. While performances by professionals had long been a pastime of the Court, Mme de Pompadour introduced amateur theatricals. A special administrative department under the control of Richelieu, entitled *Les Menus Plaisirs*, commanded ample funds and provided weekly performances, while births and weddings in the Royal Family were celebrated by balls and fireworks; but there was room for something more intimate. The initiative was warmly welcomed at Court, where sufficient dramatic and musical talent existed to provide first-rate performances after repeated rehearsals. A miniature *Théâtre des Petits Cabinets*, with seats for fourteen spectators, was constructed in the palace with decorations by Boucher. Rules drawn up by the Favourite explained that it was not a school and that beginners should not apply. The first season, lasting from January to April, 1747, included *Tartuffe*, and invitations to the performances were eagerly sought. A cherished ambition was realised when, through the friendly medium of the Duchesse de Luynes, the Queen was induced to witness the performance of a light comedy chosen by the King. The popularity of the new venture led to the demand for a larger theatre in the palace, with forty seats. The enterprise lasted for five years, during which 122 performances were given of 61 plays, operas and ballets. When operas were staged, the amateur orchestra was reinforced from the ranks of the King's musicians. Life at Versailles during the early years of the Pompadour régime was a perpetual carnival. Enraptured by her manifold accomplishments the King exclaimed 'You are the most charming woman in France.'

France was at her feet, but was it not too good to last? Having climbed to a giddy height she saw yawning precipices on either side of the path. Her fate depended on two uncertain factors— the continued fidelity and the physical survival of the King. He had evicted his first mistress and at Metz he had gazed with terror into the jaws of death. At any moment a thunderbolt might fall from a cloudless sky and strike her down. The first great alarm is vividly described in the Memoirs of Mme du Hausset, her confidential maid who knew all her secrets. One night the King was taken ill in her bed and the faithful attendant was hastily called. 'Come here, the King is dying.' Happily the royal sufferer was able to give orders. 'Fetch Quesnay and say your mistress is ill.' Quesnay, the King's doctor, also doctor and friend of the Favourite, thoroughly understood the strength and weakness of his master's constitution. By the time he arrived the crisis, probably due to overeating and indigestion, was over. He fetched a drug, remarking, 'At sixty this would be serious.' After three cups of tea the King was able to return to his room leaning on Quesnay's arm. As it occurred at night and the doctor was too loyal to give his master away, no one knew of the incident. In the morning he sent a note to Mme de Pompadour by Quesnay himself. 'My dear friend must have had a great fright, but I am very well as the doctor will confirm.' Mme du Hausset was equally incapable of betraying her mistress. 'The King and I have such confidence in you,' remarked the Favourite, 'that we regard you as a cat or a dog and talk as if you were not there.' She sat in a little ante-room where she heard everything unless the conversation was in low tones. After this alarming experience the King gave her 4,000 francs and made her a present every New Year's day, while her mistress presented her with a clock and a portrait of the King on a snuff-box.

Louis XV, perhaps with a subconscious memory of the wholesale casualties in the Royal Family in his childhood, was morbidly attracted by the topic of death, despite his brooding fears for his own soul. Mme du Hausset reports that he frequently talked of it, rarely laughed, and was often in low spirits. One day he proposed to read a sermon by Bourdaloue to Mme de Pompadour, and when she tried to turn the subject he remarked: 'Then I will go on with it in my own room.' Nothing could be more terrifying to a royal mistress than an attack of piety, however brief it might be; self-indulgence might easily lead to satiety, and satiety to contrition. The transition from Mme de Montespan to Mme de Maintenon remained a vivid memory for the older members of the Court. Temperamentally inclined to pessimism, Louis XV had little expectation of improvement in the health of the State, and he never expected a new broom to sweep clean. 'Like the rest of them,' he would say, 'he promised grand things, none of which will ever come off. He does not know this country. He will see.' He had equally little belief in his courtiers and his Generals with the shining exception of Marshal Saxe. Aware of his own unworthiness he demanded little from his subjects. Such a ruler, lacking ideas and ideals, could do nothing for France.

The gnawing uncertainty about her future was the price which every Favourite had to pay, and Mme de Pompadour never felt wholly at peace with herself. Four years after her promotion she confided her troubles to a friend. 'The life I lead is terrible: scarcely a minute to myself, constant journeyings, inescapable duties. It is impossible to breathe. Pity me, do not blame me.' Such moods of depression arose partly from physical causes, for her health had never been good. She was a bad sleeper, and she suffered from chronic fatigue which she strove to conceal from the King. She had to be *toujours en vedette*, for her lover had to be conquered anew from day to day. Like Louis XIV he would have resented any interference with his plans, such as moving from place to place on a particular day or her inability to appear at a festivity to which he was looking forward. Without being entirely heartless he was as inconsiderate as most pampered autocrats. As her power grew from year to year the daily round became ever more exacting, particularly after her miscarriages, and the strain almost too grievous to be borne. The combination of physical exhaustion with mental anxiety continued to wear her out. She knew that she had to fight to keep her footing, for there was no halting place between the Capitol and the Tarpeian rock. When she told her father that a good conscience rendered her immune against the shafts of her enemies she was deceiving herself, for no human being—let alone such a bundle of nerves— could remain indifferent to the storm of abuse, including threats of assassination, which beat upon her head. 'I pity you sincerely, Madame,' remarked Mme du Hausset, 'though everyone else envies you.' 'My life,' was the reply, 'is a perpetual conflict.'

Mme de Pompadour was *persona gratissima* with the artists and the *Philosophes*: with the former in gratitude for her lavish patronage and prompt payment of their bills, with the latter because, in the words of d'Alembert after her death, 'At the bottom of her heart she was one of us.' In Boucher's celebrated portrait of 1758 she holds an open book in her hand. While the King performed his religious duties with mechanicaɪ regularity, she had no taste for piety. She was denounced as the patron of the *libres penseurs* by Christophe de Beaumont, Archbishop of Paris, and her friendship with the leaders of the Enlightenment was notorious. Voltaire was at her feet and dedicated *Tancrède* to her. Montesquieu persuaded her to suppress a reply to his *Esprit des Lois.* Marmontel appeared at her Sunday toilette, and she aided his candidature for the Académie Française. Crébillon, old and poor, received a pension and a lodging in the Louvre, and was honoured by an *édition de luxe* of his tragedies. She secured a pension for d'Alembert and the withdrawal of the veto on the *Encyclopédie.* When the conversation at supper one night turned on gunpowder and other inventions, she remarked that the *Encyclopédie*, which would provide the answer to such questions, was forbidden. The King ordered a copy to be brought from his library and the desired information was supplied. That he had no use for the brilliant writers who adorned the salons of Paris was an abiding regret to the child of the Enlightenment. The catalogue of her library, sold after her death, listed over three thousand items, mainly concerned with French literature and history. The State china factory was moved from distant Vincennes to Sèvres, close to Bellevue, where she could foster its progress and encourage the sales.

The enemies of the Favourite within and without the palace were legion. The *Poissonades* found a ready sale in the capital and specimens penetrated the walls of Versailles. Convinced that Maurepas was the master strategist behind the campaign and himself the author of some of the most malicious satires, she resolved to destroy the offender who mimicked her talk and her bourgeois ways. Since he could neither be won by flattery nor silenced by threats, her only resource was a direct appeal to the King. She tested her influence one day when he was working with the King by requesting the cancellation of a *lettre de cachet.* All orders, rejoined Maurepas, must be in the name of the King. 'Faites ce que demande Madame,' ordained the ruler. She denounced him to the King as 'fripon et menteur, le président de la fabrique,' and even pretended to believe that he planned to poison her. Though the King liked him and enjoyed his witty talk, her importunity prevailed. 'I no longer require your services. Retire to Bourges and do not reply.' 'Honnête homme,' comments the Duc de Croy, who adds that his fall was widely deplored. The Minister took his sentence calmly and had to wait twenty-five years till a new King recalled him to office.

Henceforth the Favourite reigned without a rival. She spoke of *Nous*, and the only chair in her boudoir was her own. When Richelieu returned after the War of the Austrian Succession with the title of Marshal and began his term as First Gentleman of the Chamber, he was expected in some quarters to attack her, but he found her too strongly entrenched. The King's reply to attacks on the lady of his choice was to bestow on her the title of Duchess, the highest at his disposal. Her only ally in the Ministry was Machault, the Finance Minister, who controlled her income and paid her debts till his ambiguous attitude during the Damiens crisis led to a break. Only a woman of unquestionable ability and infinite resource could have held her own against the fickleness of the King, the frowns of his children, and the ceaseless machinations of her enemies. The fall of Maurepas brought no cessation to the stream of *Poissonades* against 'Daughter of a leech, yourself a leech.' Though the crescendo of denunciation rose to a roar when food was scarce in Paris and bread was dear, she never seriously concerned herself with the reaction of the people to the lavish expenditure associated with her name.

The voluminous journal of d'Argenson mirrors the moods of the Royal Family, the courtiers and the author as envious eyes watched the ascent of Mme de Pompadour to the position of uncrowned Queen of France and waited eagerly for her fall. She had so many powerful enemies and the King was regarded as so incurably fickle that no one predicted an indefinite continuance of her sway. As a hostile observer he is as little to be trusted as Saint-Simon in his scorn for Mme de Maintenon, but his impressions over many years are more revealing than the anaemic entries of Luynes. Two years after her rise her enemies were confidently expecting a collapse. 'The Royal Family begins to conspire,' he recorded cheerfully in February, 1747. 'At the last hunt she was in the carriage of the Dauphin, the Dauphine and Mesdames, who had agreed not to talk to her whatever she said. She was furious. Thus the storm gathers.' A week later he thought it was about to break. 'Keen observers feel sure she will soon be dismissed. The cause will be the feeling of disgrace to see the King in fetters and his favour so misplaced. The Royal Family will manage it. Today the Dauphin and Mesdames, by the Queen's orders, begin the attack by contempt and scarcely speaking to her. They plan amusements for the King to induce him by cards and suppers to live in his family of whom he is very fond, particularly of the new Dauphine.' 'The Dauphin's rudeness, apathy, and hatred of the mistress grows,' noted the diarist on March 13; 'when he sees her his anger redoubles, and the Queen spurs him on.' When the Dauphin and the Pompadour put forward rival candidates for a post, the Dauphin won. The Court buzzed with speculation, for she had few friends. 'Everyone says she will soon have to go,' wrote the diarist on April 30; 'there are the same pointers as there were with Mme de Mailly. The King has had no relations with her for months. She is depressed, loses flesh, and has become odious. She employs the time that is left to her to extort all possible favours for herself, her family and her friends, and we witness unworthy sights.' A week later he was still more confident. 'I hear the King has taken a great dislike to her, and there is talk of other ladies.'

A year later, in March, 1748, there is the same hostility, the same wishful thinking, the same illusion about the sentiments of the King. 'She sells everything, even regiments. The King is increasingly governed by her. People ask what can be done under a master who neither thinks nor feels.' Seeing her at Mass he found her greatly changed, looking unhealthy and exhausted. 'She cannot stand up to the life she leads—late hours, spectacles, always thinking how to amuse the King.' His hopes rose ever higher. 'There is more talk than ever that the King will dismiss her,' he noted in September, 1748. 'For eight months he has not touched her. Her resources for prolonging the spell—the comedy, ballets, dancing, music—are exhausted. Several courtiers begin to turn their back on her. Perhaps the King at last knows and feels the disgrace of her charms. He reads in the secrets of the post what people say about him. One hopes he will not abandon his pleasures with the aid of bigotry at the expense of reason. His temperament is believed to be greatly diminished by having begun too young, but he will always need some female society. There is talk of two great ladies of the Court. Let the new Sultana live with him like a respected friend.' A year later, in August, 1749, d'Argenson records that she has become a skeleton. 'The lower part of the face is yellow and dried up; as for her throat, there is none. Yet the King by force of habit treats her carnally better than ever. Several courtiers saw him the other day caress her cynically behind a screen.' He showed how much he thought of her—and how little of her enemies—when he took her to Havre in 1749 for an inspection of the fleet. In October, 1751, the diarist reluctantly admitted that she was the First Minister, and in May, 1753, that she was more powerful than ever.

A far more sympathetic portrait is painted in the voluminous journal of the Duc de Croy, a respected courtier and soldier, who first saw her shortly after her début at Versailles. She was at her toilette. No one could be prettier. She was full of engaging talents. The King was quite right to love her best, for she was most amiable. In a delightful phrase he describes their relationship as *un scandale de convenance*. 'She was on excellent terms with the Queen, as she had urged the King to treat her with great consideration. She was always at her card parties, behaving with much grace and propriety. From time to time, like every one else, I went to her toilette. She arranged everything very well and was informed about everything. Marshal Saxe, who seemed very attached to her, was often there.' Like most other people, the Duc de Croy pestered her with requests for posts for his friends, usually in vain, for even the Favourite could not always work miracles.

Though journals are far better testimony than memoirs compiled long after the period they describe, the latter often record enduring impressions. Duport, Comte de Cheverny, was appointed at the age of twenty to the post of *Introducteur des Ambassadeurs*, serving for six months every year. Writing after her death he pays her what many Frenchmen regarded as the highest of compliments: 'Every man would have wished to make her his mistress. She was tall. Her eyes had a fire, intelligence and brilliance that I never saw in another woman. She puts the prettiest of them into the shade. At Compiègne the Ambassadors, except the Nuncio, after being presented to the Royal Family, went to her reception. Nobody understood so well how to treat everyone in a fitting manner. To avoid etiquette she received at her toilette. The arts, the talents, the sciences, paid her homage. The talk was gay and natural though not profound. Her conversation was adapted to each of her visitors.' Voltaire, the most accomplished flatterer in Europe, her favourite author and friend, saluted her with the words: 'Vous réunissez tous les arts, tous les goûts, tous les talents de plaire.' The most convincing confirmation of the compliment was provided by the painters who conveyed something of her matchless elegance and charm. Socially it was the most brilliant period of the reign. People grumbled about hardships, commented Barbier in 1745, but they always found money for their pleasures and fêtes.

The deepest cause of her anxieties, as she sorrowfully confessed, was her temperament, and she found it increasingly difficult to respond to her lover's demands. When Mme du Hausset remonstrated with her on her heating diet, she explained that she feared she might cease to be attractive to the King. In her extremity she turned to Dr. Quesnay who experimented with stimulating drugs. When aphrodisiacs proved of no avail, her royal lover, as she had resigned herself to expect, looked elsewhere for a warmer response. Physical relations ceased in the early fifties, probably in 1751. The greatest and most unprecedented of her triumphs was that in losing the lover she retained the friend.

It was at this turning-point in her career that what her biographers describe as her conversion took place. To the patron of the *Philosophes* who had never displayed the slightest interest in religion the ending of the *liaison* offered a welcome opportunity of putting herself right with the *dévots* at Court. It would be no less incorrect to attribute the change exclusively to a spiritual urge than to dismiss it as merely the result of calculation. No doubt her motives were mixed. How far she shared the King's belief in the doctrine of eternal punishment for earthly sins we cannot tell; but she may well have agreed with many another sceptic that if a risk of hell fire existed, and if it could be met by certain ecclesiastical precautions, it would be folly not to play for safety. An old and cherished ambition was realised when the cessation of her *liaison* with the King enabled her to be added to the *dames du palais* to the Queen in 1756. 'There is universal disapproval of her promotion,' wrote her enemy d'Argenson.

> It is hoped that the King, learning of this public outcry, will dismiss her. People complain of her ranking with the great nobility. The Queen's ladies are planning to inform her that they cannot retain their posts. Everyone blames the King. Why, it is asked, did he demand this sacrifice of the Queen? Yet, so far, there is no change in his attitude to his *bonne amie*. He cannot drop her, and perhaps he prides himself on treating her with even more favour as his reply to criticisms, since he is proud of his autocratic power. She is pretending to lead him back to religion by her example as she sees him attracted to other beauties. Till recently she posed as an *esprit fort*, but since the latest visit to Fontainebleau she has begun to talk of revealed religion and to fear the divine judgments.

She accompanied the Queen to daily mass, read books of devotion and prayed in Paris at her daughter's tomb. At the wish of the Jesuit Père de Sacy, whom she called her confessor, she dispatched a penitent letter to her husband proposing that she should return to him; if not, would he approve her appointment as a *dame du palais*? His reply to the first question, as she hoped and expected, was No, for he was living happily with a mistress; to the second, Yes. The advice of Père de Sacy to leave Versailles was not pressed, for she knew that with Louis XV out of sight was out of mind. What the Jesuits were reluctant to sanction was granted by a more accommodating Abbé, and she proceeded to partake of the Sacraments. Three years later, in 1749, she dispatched a letter to the Pope, drafted by Choiseul, complaining that his Jesuit confessor refused the King access to the Sacraments so long as she remained at Court. Only sentiments of gratitude and the purest friendship, she explained, united them. To the demand for her dismissal the King had replied that he needed her for his happiness and his work and that she alone dared to tell him the truth. The Favourite meant much more to him than the Sacraments. 'Her system, which I have noted for years,' commented the Duc de Croy, 'was to gain possession of his mind and, like Mme de Maintenon, to end up by becoming *dévote* with him.'

After the Jesuit attack had been repulsed a storm blew up in another quarter. When the King's passion cooled and the private staircase to her apartments was blocked up, her enemies looked round for a rival in the hope of evicting her from the Court. They found what they needed in the newly married Comtesse de Choiseul-Beaupré, and in 1752, during the usual autumn sojourn of the Court at Fontainebleau, victory seemed within their grasp. The decisive moment arrived when her backers were assembled in the apartment of the younger d'Argenson, Minister of War. The door opened and the young Countess, breathless and dishevelled, rushed in. 'It's all over,' she exclaimed. 'I am loved. She will be dismissed. He has given me his word.' D'Argenson's joy was shared by his mistress, the Comtesse d'Estrades, cousin by marriage and former friend of Mme de Pompadour who had brought her to Court; but Dr. Quesnay, who moved from palace to palace with the King, sat silent. 'It will not affect you,' remarked the Minister; 'we hope you will stay on.' 'I have been attached to Mme de Pompadour in prosperity,' he rejoined tartly, 'and I shall remain so in her disgrace.' When he left the room Mme d'Estrades exclaimed: 'I know him, he won't give us away.' With the ball at her feet the new Favourite committed an error in tactics which ruined the campaign. She sought the aid of Choiseul, a cousin of her husband, whom she thought likely to take her side, since he was no friend of the Pompadour. When the King learned that she had betrayed the secret of his letters the scales fell from his eyes; the delinquent was banished from Court and died in childbirth. The result of the plot, of which the frail beauty was the instrument rather than the author, was to strengthen the position of Mme de Pompadour whose gratitude to Choiseul for his timely intervention transformed an enemy into a friend for life.

The first grave crisis in her fortunes had been overcome and the threatening clouds rolled away, though further and less formidable attempts at her overthrow were to be made. Despite her fading physical charms she was the uncrowned Queen of France. 'More than ever is she the First Minister,' admitted d'Argenson ruefully in December, 1756. 'She dominates the King as strong personalities dominate weak ones.' Richelieu, who detested her, thought her too formidable to attack. She was born for the place, testifies the Duc de Croy. At first she tried to please everyone, but when she felt more secure and learned the

secrets of the palace she became less considerate though always
remaining polite. Like all the other young men, whether soldiers
or civilians, he paid court to her because it was the only way to
rise. His reward was an invitation to her weekly supper. Part
of her strength lay in the knowledge that she would always stand
by her friends. It was equally well understood that she would
not lift a finger for anyone who challenged her position or
opposed the wishes of the King. Why, asked the President de
Mesnieres, one of the luminaries of the *Parlement*, had his son
been refused a post? 'Because you furnished the *Parlement* with
arguments,' was the reply. Though the result of two long conversations was negative, the lawyer was impressed by the ability
and eloquence with which she championed the right of the King
to do whatever he wished. In addition to her charms and taste
she had plenty of brains, and she stands out as the only Intellectual
among the mistresses of the Kings of France.

The main result of the breaking of intimate ties was the
establishment of a private brothel for the use of the King. 'How
is it that at sixty-five you have the same desires as at twenty-
five?' he asked Richelieu, a notorious expert in the arts of love.
'Sire,' was the reply, 'I frequently change the object. Novelty
produces the desired result.' The King followed his advice, and
during the long interregnum between the fourth and the fifth
maîtresse en titre he purchased some small houses in the name of a
Paris bailiff in a quiet part of Versailles known as the *Parc aux
Cerfs*—as great a scandal in the annals of the Bourbons as the
mignons of Henri III in the record of the Valois. 'There were
two or three occupants at the same time,' testifies Valfons, 'who
had no communications with each other. Each had her own little
house, a chambermaid, a cook, a laquais, and a *gouvernante* in
charge. They had a box with a grille at the *Comédie*, which they
frequented in turn and where I often saw them. They received
no one, but they were allowed any teachers they wished.' The
establishment was managed and the girls were chosen by the
chief valet Lebel, the unofficial Minister of the King's pleasures,
who kept in touch with brothels in Paris. He was just the man
for the task for he had a mistress of his own, and Cheverny
describes one of his supper parties where two women of easy
virtue were present and a good deal of horseplay occurred. The

King's visits were incognito, and some of the inmates were told that their patron was a wealthy Polish nobleman. 'The King has a little girl of fourteen as concubine,' wrote d'Argenson in his journal on December 10, 1752; 'he likes young girls as he is afraid of syphilis.' 'He is more than ever sunk in fleeting amours,' he added on April 18, 1754; 'he has several little *grisettes* at the same time.' Mme de Pompadour resigned herself to the shameful expedient, remarking to Mme du Hausset, 'All these little uneducated girls will never take him from me.'

We have little information as to how many occupants there were, what were their names, how many children were born, and what became of them and their offspring. Only two come alive. 'La belle Morphise,' a girl in her fifteenth year, named Murphy, daughter of a Paris cobbler of Irish descent, passed several years in the *Parc aux Cerfs* and is believed to have had two or three children. When the King was shown her miniature at the age of fourteen he exclaimed: 'I cannot imagine such a beautiful child. This portrait can only be an ideal.' When she obeyed his summons he took her on his knees, gave her a house, and occasionally received her at the palace. The Maréchale d'Estrées encouraged her to seek the position of *maîtresse en titre*, and in May, 1753, d'Argenson noted that such was the general expectation. Finally her pretensions were her undoing and she was married off with a large dowry.

A larger share in the King's heart was claimed by Mlle de Romans, daughter of a provincial lawyer, who objected to being immured in the *Parc aux Cerfs* and was provided with a residence at Passy, where she tried without much success to arouse his interest in her coming child. 'I noticed, *ma grande*,' he wrote in an autograph letter, 'that you had something on your mind when you left yesterday, though I could not guess what it was. I do not desire our child to be registered under my name, but that does not mean that I may not recognise it in a few years if I feel so inclined. I wish him (or her) to be called Louis (or Louise) Aimé, son (or daughter) of Louis the King, or of Louis Bourbon, whichever you prefer. I also wish the foster parents to be poor people or domestics. *Je vous baise et embrasse bien tendrement, ma grande amie.*' The boy, baptised Bourbon, son of Charles de Bourbon, Captain of Cavalry, was recognised in 1762, the only bastard of Louis XV to receive this distinction. Not one of them was legitimised. Mme du Hausset describes an incognito excursion with her mistress to the Champs Elysées, where they found the proud mother with the child at her breast. Some courtiers predicted that he would become a new Duc de Maine, and on the death of Mme de Pompadour his mother importuned the King for the vacant place of Favourite. She pressed too hard, was dismissed, separated from her child, and forgotten. The boy was kindly treated by Louis XVI and Mesdames, was named Abbé de Bourbon, and died of smallpox in 1787.

Another competitor for the royal favour, the Marquise de Coislin, a cousin of the de Nesle sisters, seemed dangerous enough to alarm Mme de Pompadour in 1755, but she quickly offended the King by her greedy demands. Mlle Romans was succeeded in 1762 by Mlle Tiercelin, a girl in her sixteenth year, who bore the King a son in 1764, and was exiled in 1766 with payment of her debts. The child, later known as Abbé le Duc, was rescued from the guillotine by the revolution of Thermidor, received a pension from Napoleon and later from the restored monarchy, and lived till 1837. The Comtesse d'Esparbès, friend of Mme de Pompadour and mistress of young Lauzun, Choiseul's nephew, and the Duchesse de Gramont, Choiseul's sister, were also candidates for the royal favour, but none of them fulfilled the conditions exacted by the King. The houses in the *Parc aux Cerfs* were sold in 1771 when the charms of Mme du Barry supplied his requirements for the remainder of his life. In *Les Enfants de Louis XV*, Vrignault, the most recent inquirer into an unsavoury subject, lists eleven certainties among the royal bastards, five probables, and four possibles. The latest biographer of the Comte de Narbonne, Émile Dard, has little doubt about the paternity of the future Minister of War under Louis XVI, friend of Napoleon and Ambassador, for his god-parents were the Dauphin and the Duchess of Parma, and he was brought up at the Court under the special care of Mme Adelaide. Whatever the exact figures there were enough of them to dishonour *le Roi très Chrétien* who, like other monarchs, lived in a glass house.

8

THE UNCROWNED QUEEN

I

SINCE the death of Cardinal Fleury in 1743 there had been no First Minister, and the King lacked the nerve to take the reins into his own hands. He felt the need of a trusted adviser, but in whom could he confide? In home affairs it seemed possible to muddle along, but on a wider stage far-reaching decisions were sometimes unavoidable. He was always far more interested in foreign affairs, and he honestly desired to maintain the proud position of France as a Great Power. Like Fleury he had reluctantly joined in the War of the Austrian Succession, but there was so little to show for eight years of bloodshed and expenditure that he welcomed the cessation of hostilities in 1748 on terms widely deplored as inglorious if not actually humiliating. Never thirsting for military glory, he desired the remainder of his reign to be an era of unbroken peace. France was founding an empire in India and the New World, and she coveted nothing nearer home.

The avoidance of war depends less on the wishes of peace-loving rulers or satisfied states than on the ambitions and vendettas of their neighbours. Though Maria Theresa had almost beggared herself in the attempt to recover Silesia, she was determined to try again as soon as she recovered her breath. Even then, it was clear, the task would be beyond her strength unless she secured a powerful ally who could be trusted to persevere to the end. Though England had close ties with Hanover, she was less interested in the Continent than in colonisation; Russia was chiefly concerned with Eastern Europe; Spain had almost ceased to count, and hostility to the House of Hapsburg had been an axiom of French policy since Francis I. So bleak was the prospect as viewed from Vienna that a radical reorientation appeared the only alternative to leaving the jewel of Silesia in the possession of 'the wicked man'.

No one regarded the Treaty of Aix-la-Chapelle as anything better than a truce, and on the return of peace the Empress asked each of her counsellors for his advice on the desirability of a new course. While most of them, including the Emperor, continued to distrust France and had no change to propose, Kaunitz, the youngest and cleverest of the team, pleaded for a *volte-face*. Prussia, he argued, was the principal enemy and Silesia must be recovered; but this was clearly unattainable without the aid of France, since England could provide little help on the Continent. Maria Theresa, whose thoughts had been travelling in the same direction, declared herself fully converted, and her weak-willed husband followed suit. 'People believe I think of nothing but Silesia,' she remarked to the French Ambassador. 'I assure you that at present I do not give it a thought. Of course I regret it, and if the situation improves my attitude might change; but I repeat that at the moment I am not thinking about the subject.' The Ambassador reported to Paris that she was, so to speak, throwing herself at the head of His Majesty and that it might be dangerous to ignore her advances.

In the following year, 1750, Kaunitz was dispatched to Paris as Ambassador to foster the *détente* initiated at Vienna. No more suitable appointment could have been made. A born diplomat no less than a *grand seigneur*, he entertained lavishly, cultivating financiers and *Philosophes* as zealously as the official world.

The King and Mme de Pompadour and his entourage are very friendly [he reported]. That does not mean very much, but these personal contacts may prove extremely useful in certain circumstances. I have had a long talk with Mme de Pompadour and told her a lot of things which I hope she will pass on to the King. She assured me of his affection for the Empress, and not merely at the present moment: even during the war he had always entertained

M

sentiments of friendship and high esteem. We agreed that if they could meet the most complete and enduring confidence would be established.

Kauntiz was far too clever to hustle the timid King. The first task was to dispel enmity and suspicion, the second to loosen the ties which bound France to Prussia. Not a word was breathed of the ultimate design to enlist the support of France for an onslaught against the robber in Berlin.

When Kaunitz had sown the seed of reconciliation he was recalled to Vienna to assist the Empress as her Chancellor in shaping Austrian policy, and he stood loyally at her side to the day of her death. Nothing more could be achieved at Versailles so long as the Prussian alliance was regarded as the corner-stone of French policy, and no change could be expected unless substantial advantages were offered. The two projects nearest the heart of Louis XV were the placing of the Prince de Conti on the Polish throne at the next vacancy—a closely guarded secret discovered by Austria through some unknown channel—and the exchange of his son-in-law's little Duchy of Parma for the glittering prize of the Austrian Netherlands. Here at any rate were bargaining counters, and in the summer of 1755 the Empress and Kaunitz decided to try their luck. Seven years had elapsed since the close of the War of the Austrian Succession, and the army had been thoroughly overhauled: the time had come to think of revenge and of fashioning a coalition for that formidable enterprise. Their trump card was the discovery that the Prussian ruler was negotiating with England behind the back of his French ally. Since France could hardly be expected to promise to join in an attack on her only covenanted friend, her benevolent neutrality was obviously the first goal.

How was the approach to Louis XV to be made without informing the Austrophobe Ministers? After considering and rejecting the Prince de Conti as an intermediary, as she would have preferred, the Empress and Kaunitz decided to seek the aid of the Favourite, who enjoyed far more influence with the King. 'Madame,' he wrote, 'I have often desired to recall myself to your memory. Now is the time, and I believe you will not be displeased. Count Stahremberg has some matters of the gravest significance to propose to the King which can only be discussed through the channel of someone whom he honours with his entire confidence. Our proposals would not cause you to regret your trouble in requesting him to select a negotiator.' After reading the letter handed to her by the Ambassador Mme de Pompadour advised the King to select her old friend and *protégé*, Abbé de Bernis, for whom she had procured a pension and a room in the Tuileries. Starting as a writer of light verse which found many admirers and secured his election to the Academy, he entered on a new career when he was appointed in 1751 to the Embassy in Venice, where his social success won him the confidence of his chiefs. He was about to leave for a higher post in Madrid when a heavier burden was laid on his shoulders. The idea of a *rapprochement* with the hereditary Hapsburg foe alarmed him as much as it would have alarmed any other of the King's advisers. He explained to the Favourite that it would be unpopular in France, that it might involve war with Prussia, that competent French Generals were lacking, that the finances were unsound, and that Austria's sincerity was in doubt. During the conversation the King entered and asked Bernis what he thought of the letter from Vienna. He repeated his objections and the King exclaimed in a rather injured tone: 'Like the rest of them you are an enemy of the Queen of Hungary. So we must tell Stahremberg we cannot listen.' Since the expression on the King's face clearly indicated his own predilections Bernis suggested non-committal discussions.

The Ambassador was invited to Babiole, a little summerhouse in the gardens of Bellevue, where he found Bernis and the Favourite awaiting him. He proceeded to read a memorandum of the Austrian proposals, glancing up after each article to observe the effect. The most surprising item was the statement that Prussia was negotiating with England, the hereditary enemy of France. After a further meeting the Ambassador was informed that France could not break with her ally without definite proof of disloyalty. Meanwhile she would be prepared for a joint undertaking that any breach of the Treaty of Aix-la-Chapelle would meet with resistance by Austria and France. With this declaration, which threatened no one, other states might associate themselves. At a later stage the proposed exchange of the Duchy of Parma for the Austrian Netherlands might be discussed as a first step towards a solid and perhaps eternal alliance. Disappointed though she was by this cautious response, the Empress and Kaunitz accepted the principle of a purely defensive treaty, though this would rule out an Austrian attack on Prussia. The obligation to resist aggression was to be confined to the Continent, which would leave England free to attack France at sea or overseas. So far the negotiations had been kept secret even from Rouillé the Foreign Minister, but at this stage Bernis, who held no office, declined to carry the burden of work and responsibility alone. The King grudgingly consented to associate the Ministers of Foreign Affairs, Finance, the Navy and the Royal Household, but not d'Argenson, Minister of War, whom he regarded as too Austrophobe. Though secret meetings between Bernis and Stahremberg continued in the Luxembourg, no further progress was made. It suited both parties to mark time, each of them waiting for proof of Prussian duplicity. It was decided in Paris to send a special envoy to elicit from Frederick himself what he had up his sleeve.

On the eve of the arrival of the Duc de Nivernais in Berlin Prussia signed the Convention of Westminster on January 16, 1756, pledging the signatories to resist attacks on German territory from any quarter, by which they had Hanover and Silesia chiefly in view. When the envoy expressed his surprise at the *fait accompli*, Frederick explained that he had been strongly pressed by England and was alarmed by the massing of Russian forces on his frontier. Since France had no desire to attack Hanover, how could such a pact threaten her interests? The treaty was welcomed in Vienna as calculated to destroy the Franco-Prussian partnership and to increase the attraction of Austria's offer of friendship. 'Great news for Austria!' exclaimed Kaunitz: 'the French Government must have lost all feeling if it does not in its secret heart cherish thoughts of revenge.' The Prussian Ambassador in Paris reported the surprise and consternation of the French Government which had ignored Austrian hints of Frederick's disloyalty. This unexpected shift of the wind removed the hesitations of Versailles, and Prussia was informed that the alliance could not be renewed unless the Convention of Westminster was dropped.

Deserted by her Prussian ally and with a colonial conflict with

England on her hands, France saw no alternative to the alliance
which she had declined in the previous autumn. Bernis still
shrank from a possible or even probable involvement in Maria
Theresa's vendetta against Frederick, but the alternative of isola-
tion appeared even more dangerous. 'Some people have said
that the union of France and Austria was a monstrosity,' wrote
Voltaire in his *Siècle de Louis XV*; 'since it was necessary it was
also natural.' Though the Duc de Broglie, the leading expert on
the diplomacy of Louis XV, agrees with him, other historians
deplore the decision which involved France in the humiliations
of the Seven Years War. Incensed by what was regarded as the
perfidy of Prussia, the French Government proposed to resume
negotiations on the basis of the Austrian proposals of the previous
autumn—the dropping of the Prussian alliance and financial aid
for the coalition to secure the reconquest of Silesia, in return for
territory in the Austrian Netherlands for the King's son-in-law
who would surrender the Duchy of Parma. No reference was
made to the candidature of the Prince de Conti for the Polish
throne which had figured in the earlier exchanges. Despite his
resentment of Frederick's action, Louis XV declined to supply
French troops, not from any tenderness for Frederick, whom he
had always disliked as an *esprit fort*, but because the total ruin of
Prussia might leave Austria in a position of undue predominance.
Though the Balance of Power was less talked about in the
eighteenth than in the nineteenth century, it was never out of the
mind of statesmen and diplomatists.

After prolonged negotiations conducted by Bernis, Rouillé,
and Stahremberg, a neutrality convention and a defensive treaty
were signed on May 1, 1756. Each party promised to furnish
either 24,000 men or a subsidy in the event of the possessions of
the other being attacked, and France undertook to exclude the
Austrian Netherlands from the strategy of her quarrel with
England. The agreement was welcomed in France as assuring
that Austria would not again be a foe in an Anglo-French conflict.
The share of the Favourite in the *renversement des alliances* was
small, for Louis XV needed no prompting when the link with
Prussia was snapped, but it was not entirely negligible. 'We owe
everything to her,' wrote the Austrian Ambassador to his chief,
'and it is to her that we must look for everything in future. She

likes recognition and deserves it. I shall keep in close touch with her.' Acting on this advice Kaunitz addressed her in flattering terms.

> It is entirely owing to your zeal and wisdom, and I must thank you for having been my guide. I must add that their Imperial Majesties do you full justice and entertain for you all the sentiments you could desire. The achievement seems to me to merit the approval of all impartial people and of posterity. But what remains to be done is too important for you to withhold your collaboration, to leave the task unfinished, and not to render you for ever dear to your country. I feel certain that you will continue to devote your attention to this weighty affair. I believe success to be assured, and no one will feel greater pleasure than myself in the fame and satisfaction you will derive from your services.

That the Austrian Chancellor intended these fulsome compliments for other eyes we cannot doubt, for to flatter the Favourite was to delight the King.

Mme de Pompadour reciprocated with a present of her portrait by La Tour. When the Ambassador supped with her they drank to the health of the Empress, and she was never to waver in fair weather or foul. Contrary to a widespread belief, Maria Theresa never wrote to her, but she forwarded a miniature framed in brilliants. The Favourite expressed her gratitude in exuberant letters to the Empress and Kaunitz drafted with the approval of Choiseul and the King.

The sudden invasion of Saxony by Prussia in August, 1756, provoked by the discovery of aggressive intentions in St. Petersburg and Vienna, was angrily resented at Versailles as an attack on the native land of the Dauphine which had no share in the anti-Prussian coalition. Locked in a colonial conflict in two continents France could not provide unlimited support to Austria and Saxony, but the token force of 24,000 promised by the Treaty of Versailles was exceeded. Bernis continued to handle foreign affairs and was saluted by the War Minister d'Argenson with the fatuous compliment: *Vous remplacerez Richelieu.* Anyone less like the Iron Cardinal would have been impossible to discover.

II

At the opening of 1757, when the thoughts of the Government were concentrated on the Seven Years War, the position of the Favourite was threatened, not by the appeal of another pretty face but by the knife of an assassin. Louis XV had long believed that he was destined to the fate of Henri IV, and it now seemed as if his dark premonition was to prove correct. We can follow every phase of the Damiens incident in the sober journal of the Duc de Luynes.

> Today [runs the entry of January 6], after dinner, the King returned from Trianon to see Mme Victoire who was not very well. Having given orders to drive back to Trianon at 5.30, he came downstairs at 6, the Dauphin at his side, the Duc d'Ayen behind him, and four other attendants close at hand. He had reached the bottom step when he felt a blow on his right side and exclaimed, 'I have been struck.' There stood a man of about forty-five, in brown clothes. One of the guards knocked his hat off, another seized him. When the King put his hand to the wound between the fourth and fifth rib it was covered with blood. 'I am wounded, and that is my assailant,' he exclaimed. 'Keep hold of him but don't kill him. Why do they want to kill me? I have harmed no one.'

Though bleeding freely he walked upstairs without support. The first surgeon was summoned and discovered that the wound —about four inches long—was not deep, for the knife was small and the victim was in his thick winter clothes. Obeying the first maxim of eighteenth-century medicine the doctors bled him. Though the first night was disturbed he was never in the slightest danger. The doctor declared that an ordinary mortal would have been allowed up in his dressing-gown on the following day, and that convalescence was only a matter of two or three days. The Queen had merely been told that he was ill, and when she reached the bedside he greeted her with the alarming words ' Je suis assassiné'. Convinced that he was in mortal peril he asked for Extreme Unction, and a priest spent part of the first night at his bedside in earnest conversation and fervent prayer. He said he forgave his assailant and would take no part in deciding his punishment.

The King named the Dauphin as his lieutenant, empowering

him to summon the Council and to preside. 'I leave you a troubled kingdom,' he remarked; 'I hope you will govern better than I.' Henceforth the heir, who had long been present at the *Conseil des Dépêches* without being permitted to express an opinion, was allowed to speak. His tactful conduct during these hectic days earned general respect, for he showed no indecent haste to seize the reins. Even d'Argenson admitted that he presided at the Council with an intelligence, dignity and even eloquence one did not expect. 'So now he is associated with the Government, but do not let us expect too much, for he is surrounded by wretched bigots. We shall see if his influence leads to a religious pacification or to even more odious measures against the Magistrates. He is very unpopular. He is bigoted, ruled by intriguing bigots, hard, inhuman, caring nothing for pleasure, obstinate, with only half the brains of the King.' D'Argenson's anti-clericalism, we must remember, rendered him unjust to anyone who passed for a *dévot*. Every day the Dauphin reported the deliberations of the Council to his father and asked for orders. In the words of Bernis no one could have shown more prudence and filial respect. When he asked the patient on the morning after the attack if he was suffering, the King replied: 'I should suffer much more if it had happened to you.' The two men, so different in character, only came close to one another when one of them was ill. Prayers were ordered in the churches, and the Duc de Luynes pronounced the affection and anxiety of the people to be as great as during the critical illness at Metz thirteen years earlier. 'At bottom,' commented d'Argenson in his Journal, 'the King is loved by his subjects and everyone is touched.' The crime was the talk of Europe, and Choiseul, French Ambassador in Rome, described long afterwards the consternation it aroused.

The servant who dressed me to visit the Pope wetted me with his tears so that he could not see what he was doing. Nothing was more touching than this universal grief. I have since often thought of my impression when I saw the man who caused it and realised that if half his subjects, those in closest contact with him, myself in particular, were to perish, our loss would not affect him in the least. I have learned that one loves one's master, above all Louis XV, when one forms an image of him and does not see him in the flesh.

It was the last occasion on which his subjects cared whether he lived or died.

For eight days the King lay silent and depressed behind the curtains of his bed. 'The first time we saw him,' testifies the Comte de Cheverny, the *Introducteur d'Ambassadeurs*, 'this handsome man looked at us with such sadness, as if to say: Look at your King whom a wretch wished to assassinate and who is the most unhappy man in his kingdom.' On the fourth day he felt well enough to receive the diplomatic corps, though not a word was uttered on either side. Meanwhile the usual attempts were made with the aid of torture to extract information from the assassin, formerly an employé in a Jesuit college in Paris. Though he occasionally spoke of 'nous' he refused to divulge any names, and it was generally believed that there were no accomplices. His assertion that he had not desired to kill was treated with contempt.

No member of the Royal Family had such cause for anxiety as Mme de Pompadour whose whole future was at stake. On his first visit after the incident Bernis found her in despair.

> She threw herself into my arms with cries and sobs which would have touched even her enemies, if courtiers were ever touched. I urged her to be prepared for anything and to submit to Providence. As the friend of the King, no longer his mistress for several years, she must await his orders to leave, since the possessor of state secrets and letters of the King could not be a purely private person. I promised to keep her informed and to divide my time between my duty to the state and the claims of friendship.

Bernis passed the night in attendance on the King, slipping away at frequent intervals to report. His picture of emotional collapse is confirmed by Mme du Hausset, who records that people called to see how she looked and that she did nothing but weep and faint. It was in vain that Dr. Quesnay assured her that the royal victim was not in the slightest danger, and that he could go to a ball if he were not a King. Death was by no means the only peril; for might not the ominous silence from the sick-bed portend that his thoughts were turning to piety as they had done at Metz? That he was spending a good deal of his time with priests was a bad sign, and her arch-enemy the Dauphin was frequently at his side.

The reassuring bulletins from the sick-room increased the probability that the dreaded decree of banishment would never come, and the Favourite believed that the King would never act unless he finally despaired of his life. After all, why should she be dismissed? At Metz Mme de Châteauroux was the *maîtresse en titre*, a post which in 1757 had long been vacant. In the words of Bernis, she was the custodian of all the secrets of his soul and knew all his affairs—no longer a mistress to expel but an irreplaceable friend. Though the King knew that Bernis was her intimate friend her name never passed his lips. For eleven days not a word reached her, and the palace buzzed with rumours of her fall. The worst symptom was that her *protégé* Machault, formerly Controller-General and now Minister of Marine, kept away. 'Et c'est là un ami,' she bitterly exclaimed. When he came at last he declared—without authorisation—that it was the King's wish that she should leave Versailles. After he left she poured out her heart to Bernis, the most faithful of her friends. 'I must leave, my dear Abbé,' she exclaimed in tears, and gave orders to prepare her house in Paris and to bring her carriages to the door. At this moment the Maréchale de Mirepoix was announced.

MME DE MIREPOIX: What are all these boxes for? Your staff say you are off.

MME DE POMPADOUR: Alas! dear friend, it is the master's will, M. Machault told me.

MME DE MIREPOIX: What did he think?

MME DE POMPADOUR: That I should go at once.

MME DE MIREPOIX: He wants to be the boss. He is betraying you. *Qui quitte la partie la perd.*

The Favourite took the advice to remain, knowing that the King was improving every day. Remembering how he had recalled Mme de Châteauroux after her eviction from Metz, she feverishly awaited a message from the master of her fate.

An equally painful interview took place with Comte d'Argenson, Minister of War, an open enemy, whom she asked to call.

MME DE POMPADOUR: You know that since the unhappy event I neither live nor breathe in peace. I am always begging for news and am awakened ten times in the night to hear it.

When such a precious life is at stake nothing can be over-looked. I take every precaution prompted by my love for my master. You see my reward. Every morning for the last fortnight my servants find horrible notes on my terrace. I have stationed a watch, but no one has been caught. The King is always questioning me about them. He likes to know everything and has threatened me with his anger if I hide anything. So I am forced to tell him the truth. He has read many of these notes and is annoyed. He should not see these abominations. He cannot sleep. Continue to watch over his safety, but do not speak to him about this any further.

D'ARGENSON: No one is more anxious to do so than myself. Please beg the King not to question me further.

MME DE POMPADOUR (icily): I understand. You prefer to see him unhappy though you pose as the good servant. But, Sir, these notes are most extraordinary. It is very strange that Berryer, who controls the police, fails to find any of them, and that your few servants, who are not looking for them, always discover them.

It was not very difficult for the Minister to guess that his fate was sealed if the King were again to smile on the Marquise.

On the eleventh day the agonising ordeal ended with a happy visit from the King. Having fully recovered his health he left his apartments without a word to anyone, and when he returned he was smiling and resilient. With his easy-going nature he would have been content to see the familiar faces around him as if nothing had happened, but he had to reckon with a woman's tears. The Favourite, like Mme de Châteauroux before her, was determined on revenge. After the prolonged strain her nerves were once again out of control and she even lashed out at the faithful Bernis. 'You *are* clever. By showing me equivocal marks of attachment you discovered the secret of enchanting the Royal Family.' The storm was soon over and she tried to repair her mistake, but for the Ministers of War and Marine who had been long in the King's service there was no more mercy than there had been shown to Maurepas. They had dug their own graves. A curt written intimation informed d'Argenson that his services were no longer required and that he must leave for his estate in Touraine within forty-eight hours. He declined his wife's offer to accompany him, preferring the company of his mistress Mme d'Estrades, formerly a bosom friend of the Favourite. Kindly and helpful though she was by nature, Mme de Pompadour struck without mercy, for the royal favour was for her the breath of life. 'Someone has abused the King's confidence,' exclaimed the fallen Minister pale as death, to Valfons, who describes the scene. 'You know my respect for the King. How many vigils have I dedicated to his glory. Can he ever forget Metz where, when he was believed to be dead and was abandoned by all, I warmed him in my arms and never quitted him for a moment? It is not his will or his heart which sends me into exile but that wretched woman who has been up to mischief.' Machault, on the other hand, was dismissed in flattering terms which revealed the extreme reluctance of his master. 'Though assured of your probity, circumstances compel me to ask for your resignation as Minister of Marine. You may rely on my protection and friendship and you can ask favours for your children. You will retain your salary and honours.' 'They forced me to dismiss him, a man after my own heart,' wrote the King to the Duchess of Parma, 'I shall never console myself.' Neither Minister returned to office. If the disgrace of Maurepas in 1749 had been a warning to foes of the Favourite, the simultaneous eviction of d'Argenson and Machault taught its lesson so clearly that her supremacy was never openly challenged again.

III

The Favourite emerged from the Damiens episode stronger than ever, and her influence on the conduct of the Seven Years War, above all in nominations, was unconcealed. Her friend and *protégé*, Bernis, now the leading figure on the political stage, was admitted to the Council and was appointed Foreign Minister in June, 1757, after long performing the duties of the office. The death of Marshal Saxe in 1750 left France with third-rate Generals, and the disasters of the Seven Years War sharply contrasted with the victories of the conflict which ended in 1748. In view of her hold on the King and her ardent advocacy of the Austrian alliance, it was inevitable that Mme de Pompadour should be held in large measure responsible when French arms were disgraced. After long negotiations the Second Treaty of Versailles, signed on May 1, 1757, enlarged the agreement of May, 1756, and completed the *renversement des alliances*. In addition to the 24,000 French soldiers promised by the First Treaty of Versailles, France now undertook to provide 10,000 German troops for Austria, equip 105,000 French troops, contribute 12 million florins annually, and continue the struggle till Silesia was reconquered. In return she was to receive certain towns on the frontier of the Low Countries. That there would be no prizes for either side, Austria failing to regain Silesia and France forfeiting her most valuable colonies, could not be foreseen.

The rout at Rossbach, the most humiliating disaster in the history of the French army, reduced the Favourite to tears, for the defeated commander Soubise was her only friend in the higher ranks of the services after the death of Marshal Saxe. When he was ordered to join his forces to those of Richelieu, Bernis' approval of the plan aroused her wrath. The interests of Soubise, replied Bernis, were less dear to him than those of the State. Henceforth the relations of the Favourite and Bernis cooled, and his defeatism annoyed the King. While Kaunitz strove to counteract his gloom by flattering the Favourite, Bernis argued that France would lose more than she was likely to gain by continuing the war. Her real enemy was not Prussia, so recently an ally, but England who was threatening French possessions in India and Canada. Feeling himself unequal to the task of waging a war without a belief in victory, he sought counsel from his old friend Choiseul, French Ambassador in Vienna. 'My supposed quarrel with Mme de Pompadour is the talk of Paris,' he wrote on March 31, 1758, 'but as I love her with all my heart and abhor ingratitude, we shall always be intimate friends. When we disagree we shall argue, for I never abandon what I believe to be the truth; but you may be sure we shall never quarrel.' The King, he added, was the best master in the world, but he did not know how to say ' Je le veux' when he thought it would cause pain.

Bernis' letters to Choiseul during the summer of 1758 are one long cry of distress. 'We have no Ministers,' he complained, 'and I include myself. We have touched bottom.' The war was unpopular, the French Generals were failures, the finances were chaotic, economies were impracticable, the navy was in decay, the subsidies to Austria were in arrears.

> I die ten times a day. Unless we make peace we shall perish in dishonour. You are my best friend in the world, and you might be the King's most useful servant. I warn you solemnly that if we do not make peace this winter the state is doomed. The nation is in despair. Our navy is lost, we have no more sailors, no army, no Generals. I do not wish to desert Austria, but the machine will collapse and the allies will fall away when our subsidies cease.

The more Bernis thought about it, the more convinced he became that the burden was beyond his strength and that Choiseul was the only man for the task. Meanwhile he proposed that Committees of Ministers should help him draft proposals for submission to the Council where the King was accustomed to preside. Among their suggestions was that the Council should investigate the expenditure of the Court and the Departments of State with a view to economies. The new system was abandoned on the fall of Bernis, its author, after a trial of six months, for as usual vested interests proved too strong.

On September 12, 1758, Bernis explained his views to the Favourite. Choiseul, he argued, should be appointed his successor since he enjoyed the confidence of Vienna and would bring fresh energy to the campaign. 'I will look after the Sorbonne and the *Parlement*, and will work with him in political affairs. Then no one will fear that I covet the post of First Minister, and you will have two friends united at your side.' Bernis' idea of a condominium was fantastic, for reasons of health if for nothing else.

> I warn you and beg you tell the King that I cannot answer for my work. My head is always confused, and it has been a martyrdom for a year. If he wishes to keep me he must give me relief. I do not want to propose anything you dislike, but I defy you to fill my place with anyone but Choiseul. He alone grasps the whole system and enjoys the confidence of Vienna. If the King does not agree, someone else must be found with whom I can work. If I can have

some respite my health will be restored; today it is terrible, and I have lost my sleep.

A week later the picture is even darker.

My health is worse than ever from colic, insomnia, overwork, anxiety. It grieves me to distress you, but you would never forgive me for deceiving you and the King. A better administration is the only remedy for the evils of the state. Peace is essential, however difficult to secure. I do my best to persuade our allies. How can we hope for military successes? We shall always have the same Generals, and the King of Prussia will always beat us at the game of war.

A memorandum requested by Mme de Pompadour for the eyes of the King may be described as Bernis' political testament.

Choiseul is prepared to take office if he is allowed to retire after the war and if he and I collaborate. I cannot break the treaties I made. He is the only man for the Foreign Office. Soldier and politician, he knows Vienna, is a great worker, is resourceful, and has much better nerves than I. I must quit the Foreign Office, and if it is felt that my absolute retirement would not harm the state I should like to be released. Be assured I shall never forget your friendship or my obligations. Pardon me all the torments I have caused you for the welfare of the state. There is still time to remedy the evil. I adore the King: his glory is dearer to me than life. No thought of ambition poisons my zeal for his service. I have everything, but I lack the happiness of seeing him respected by his enemies and his allies. With courage to remedy abuses the situation could be restored. Next to the King no one has a greater interest in it than you, and no one, by character and sentiments, is more fitted to collaborate in such a blessing. The confidence in you provides the means.

On October 6 Bernis sent in his resignation. 'I am sorry that your health prevents you from continuing your labours,' replied the King.

No one desires peace more than myself, but I want a solid and honourable settlement. I am ready to sacrifice all my interests but not those of my allies. Do not let us act precipitately. The campaign is nearly over. Let us wait till the crisis comes. Perhaps time may bring us happier occasions not involving a total loss or the disgraceful abandoning of our allies. On the return of peace retrenchments of all sorts must be made, especially in the services, which are impossible during a war like this. Let us be content to diminish abuses and expenditure without throwing everything overboard. I consent with regret to you transferring foreign affairs to the Duc de Choiseul, whom I think the only fit person just now since I do not wish to change my policy. Inform him that I have accepted your proposal, and let him tell the Empress and agree with her whom she would like as his successor.

Next day, October 10, Bernis joyfully reported to Mme de Pompadour the arrival of the coveted red hat from Rome, adding, 'I owe it to you, as I owe you everything.' The King had shown real joy at his promotion, he reported to Choiseul, saying that he had never made such a fine Cardinal.

> He approves you as my successor. In your first six months you can do whatever you think desirable, as is the right of newcomers. I am yours, body and soul. There will be no jealousy between us. I will co-operate in all your wishes. I believe our friendship will be useful to the King and the state. We will discuss matters, perhaps argue, and finally agree—two heads under one hat. You must explain to the Court at Vienna the advantage to it of this arrangement.

Bernis was counting his chickens before they were hatched, for the Cardinal's hat, so far from assuring him the continuance of the royal favour, was a solatium for his approaching fall. Everyone except himself knew that his idea of a condominium was impracticable. Responsibility could not be divided, his health was broken, and he differed from his appointed successor on the vital issue of making peace. While he desired to end the·war on almost any terms, the King, the Favourite and Choiseul were resolved to persevere. A letter of October 14 to Mme de Pompadour is the first indication that his plan of remaining as an *Éminence Grise* might not be adopted.

> Neither you nor the King have told me whether I am to remain in the Council. If so, the idea must be removed that I have lost the confidence of my master, otherwise it would be better to retire altogether. I possess the confidence of the *Parlement* and half the clergy. Thus I can maintain the kingdom in peace, but for that my credit must be preserved and I must be able to live decently at Court. The favours the King showered on me have almost all been

determined by the needs of the public service. I have ruined my
health and incurred debts. I support the whole of my family, which
is poor. My hat is due to the late Pope for my services at Venice.
Neither the King, you and I ever thought of it. My favours were
not bought by servility. I felt I must put the facts before you.
I covet your esteem as much as your friendship, and the least
insinuation from you upsets me because I think I deserve your
respect.

Next day Bernis reported to the King.

I have sent your letter to me to Choiseul. It is more desirable than
ever that the Court of Vienna should feel the necessity of restoring
peace to Europe: its courage and its hatred of the King of Prussia
blind it. It does not sufficiently appreciate that its ally risks the
loss of all its colonies in order to satisfy the vengeance of the
Empress. I continue to believe, Sire, that the greatest *coup d'état*
would be to make peace this winter and to secure the assent of our
allies. Where are we to find the men and money to continue the
struggle?

Choiseul, he hoped, might take the same view.

The King would like to make peace [he wrote on October 19], but
he is not pessimistic. Yet the finances are in disorder, public spirit
is lacking, zeal is gone. I see no means of preserving the state
except by peace and economy. For internal affairs Mme de Pompadour needs a friend in whom she feels entire confidence, and he can
only be you. We are not being governed, and we can only be
governed by her influence. You alone, in guiding her, can guide
the King. Thus your prompt return is indispensable. If you can
make peace, it will be the greatest service; if not, try to diminish
the burden.

However desirable it might be for France to quit before disaster
overtook her, the intransigence of Vienna rendered it impossible,
and Bernis felt the ground slipping away under his feet.

I feel I have lost some of your confidence, without which I cannot
be of service to the King [he wrote to the Favourite on November
14]. I have called to the Council all your friends. I have been
accused of ambition and ingratitude towards you. I have sacrificed
myself in favour of your friends, exhausted my health, poisoned
my life with worry. Recall the time when you ceased to show me
the letters of M. de Stainville. I have always shown you his. From

N

that moment I have felt I have lost your confidence. Was I not right? The question is whether the King thinks my advice can be of use. If so, all the better. M. de Choiseul has qualities which I do not possess, and perhaps I have some which he lacks. Let us stick together, you, he and I, and all will be well. Otherwise I foresee the gravest evils at home and abroad. All I desire is the satisfaction of the King, the good of his state, and your friendship.

Bernis was fighting a losing battle and on December 13 the blow fell. At the time of the Damiens incident nearly two years earlier the stricken King remarked to him: 'Mme Infanta (Duchess of Parma) believes in you and she is right, for you are *bien honnête homme.*' Now, however, he was tired of the faint-heart who could only bleat Cassandra-like prophecies of doom.

Your reiterated requests to leave the Foreign Office are accepted [he wrote]. But I have also felt that you did not respond to the confidence I placed in you in such critical circumstances nor to the exceptional favours I have heaped on you in such a short time. I therefore order you to withdraw to one of your Abbeys within forty-eight hours without seeing anyone till I order you to return. Send back my letters.

Sire [replied Bernis], I obey your orders with the greatest respect and submission. I only asked to resign the conduct of foreign affairs because I could not carry the burden. My sole thought has been your service. God has seen into the depths of my heart, and Your Majesty will do so some day. My only regret is to have displeased you. My consolation will always be that I never failed in my duties to you unless by error. I have burned all the letters in which you displayed your confidence. There are only some in a portfolio at Versailles and I will have them found. I beg you to confirm the arrangement made for payment of my debts and to look with favour on my family and my nephews who serve you with zeal. I hope that my resignation and respect will lead you to do justice to my intentions and to pardon my involuntary mistakes.

The same day Bernis composed a farewell letter to Mme de Pompadour.

I owe it to our old friendship and my obligations to you to renew the assurances of my gratitude. I commend to your kindness and sense of justice my nephews and near relatives, not because they are mine, but because they are good servants of the King. You know better than anyone the motives for my resignation. My

intentions have always been honourable. I shall not forget my
obligations to you. I have lived too long and reflected too much to
expect to avoid attacks from my foes, though my only offence was
my too rapid ascent. I pardon them with all my heart. The King
never possessed a more faithful servant nor you a more grateful
friend.

Her reply is lost but it seems to have been friendly enough.
'Your letter has consoled me a little. You have not abandoned
me. The wound in my heart will never heal, for I thought
it impossible to displease the King. I shall always love him,
the State and you, Madame, for you are still one of my friends.'
Despite these affectionate words he felt that she had some part
in his fall, and the intimacy of twenty years was at an end. 'The
Marquise,' he wrote with cool detachment in his Memoirs, 'had
none of the faults of ambitious women but all the little failings
and levity of women obsessed by their figure and a superiority
complex. She made mischief without malignancy and did good
in a spirit of favouritism. Her friendship was as jealous as love,
superficial and unreliable.' He recalled his successful intervention
on her behalf some months earlier when the King was attracted
to the Marquise de Coislin, imploring him not to estrange Vienna
by dropping the champion of the alliance.

Mme de Pompadour neither contributed to his fall nor lifted
a finger to save him, for by losing his nerve he had dug his own
grave. Convinced that France was doomed if she continued the
costly struggle, he was not the pilot to weather the storm. His
instinct was sound enough, but his will was weak and his health
was poor. He had never really liked the Austrian entanglement,
and when his gloomy forecast was realised he patriotically proposed Choiseul as his successor. But he completely misjudged
his position in suggesting a condominium, in which he would
have less work and less responsibility, and the King was right
to reject the plan. If the Austrian partnership was to continue—
and the King never dreamed of dropping his ally—a firm hand
was needed at the helm. The fall of Bernis was welcomed by
Kaunitz, and a jewelled miniature arrived from the Empress for
the Favourite in gratitude for her unwavering support. After a
few years in the shadows the Cardinal was appointed Archbishop
of Albi and shortly afterwards to the Embassy at Rome, a post

far better suited to his timid nature. Though he kept in touch with his successor, he ceased to count in the life of the State. The long reign of Choiseul had begun. For the remainder of the Seven Years War France was governed by a triumvirate—the King, Choiseul and Mme de Pompadour. Ministers came and went, but the Favourite retained her influence till the day of her death.

9

CHOISEUL IN CONTROL

I

WHILE Fleury owed his position to the fact that he had been tutor to the King, Choiseul rose by his talents and piloted the ship of State for almost twelve years with courage and resource. Till then it had drifted along with the tide, for the initiative to the *renversement des alliances* had come from Vienna. Had it not been for the choice of Mme du Barry as the last and the lowest of the King's *maîtresses en titre*, he might have remained at the helm till the death of his master, who liked him as an entertaining companion and trusted him as a statesman. None of his servants since Maurepas transacted business with greater speed and efficiency or bored his master with fewer details. Though no one has ranked him with Chatham and Kaunitz, he stood out among the throng of mediocrities on the French public stage. The core of his programme was the maintenance of the Austrian alliance as an essential condition of victory in the unending colonial struggle with England. Never overawed by royalty, he expressed his views without arrogance but without reserve. That his private morals were as loose as those of his master was no disqualification in the France of Louis XV. Ambitious as he had every right to be, no one was less of an *arriviste*. For the first and last time the King chose the best available pilot to weather the storm.

The Duc de Choiseul, born in 1719, belonged to a branch of

the Stainville family, one of the oldest in Lorraine. Like most impecunious aristocrats he entered the army and served with distinction in Italy, Bohemia, and the Low Countries during the War of the Austrian Succession, rising to the rank of Lieutenant-General. 'I liked war,' he confesses in his Memoirs, 'and I dreaded the return of peace. I greatly enjoyed passing seven months of the year in the field and the remaining five in Paris.' On the return of peace he married the fifteen-year-old daughter of Crozat, who had made his fortune as a war contractor, and what began as a *mariage de convenance* grew into something like a love match. 'Her virtue, her charms, her feeling for me and mine for her, have brought happiness in our union much superior to the advantages of fortune.' She ranks with the Duchesse de Luynes among the few women of spotless reputation in the frivolous Court of Louis XV. Though, in the words of Horace Walpole, gallantry without delicacy was her husband's constant pursuit, she stood by him in sunshine and storm, winning and keeping a host of friends by her simplicity and charm. We come closest to her in the copious correspondence of Mme du Deffand, who, though generally more attracted by brains than by character, pronounced her an angel without a failing and took her to her heart. Among the factors of Choiseul's success, as he gratefully recognised, was his wife's money which enabled him to entertain on a lavish scale.

When the War of the Austrian Succession ended in 1748 his thoughts turned to a diplomatic career, for no fresh conflict was in sight and, deeply though he prized the glitter of the capital, he was not content to idle his life away. Since he had no influential friends at Court, the prospect seemed bleak enough till the incident at Fontainebleau in 1752 already described opened the way. Soon after the *rapprochement* with the Favourite she secured his appointment as Ambassador to the Vatican. Though he possessed no experience of diplomacy, he was exceptionally qualified for a profession where social accomplishments count scarcely less than ability. 'As delightful as ever,' reported Mme du Deffand after one of their many meetings. 'No one possesses more charm, grace, and gaiety. Compared with him everyone seems stupid or pedantic.' He was quickly at home in the Eternal City, entertained in lavish style, and won the confidence of

Benedict XIV. Undersized, ugly and snub-nosed but with piercing eyes, he held his own by quickness of mind and colourful talk.

The main task of Choiseul's four years in Rome was to liquidate the dispute about the Bull '*Unigenitus*' which had plagued France for forty years. Though the Bull had always been detested by the Jansenists against whom it was aimed, and was disliked by the *Parlements* who championed the Gallican tradition, the Jansenist tide was ebbing when the Ultramontanes under Jesuit leadership revived the struggle by a provocative act. In an effort to stamp out what was left of Jansenism the French hierarchy, with Christophe de Beaumont, Archbishop of Paris, at their head, demanded certificates of confession from all who wished for the last sacraments and refused them to those who had received absolution from Jansenist priests. In 1752 the *Parlement* denounced this practice and ordered the arrest of priests who refused to comfort the dying except on terms. The King, weary of the strife, exiled both the Magistrates who opposed the certificates and the Archbishop who supported them, and enjoined silence on both parties. The Magistrates were recalled in 1754, and in 1755 the quinquennial Assembly of the French clergy was summoned to decide whether acceptance of the Bull was essential to membership of the Church. Worried by the bitter conflict and by the threat of some of the Bishops at the instigation of the Jesuits to form a schism in the event of any tampering with the Bull of 1713, Choiseul consulted the Pope. 'I told the Pope that if there were no more objectors to the Bull they would invent some other bone of contention in order to form two parties in the State, and thus to have enemies to fight and blind proselytes to govern. For they do not wish to be a simple religious order like the Capucins. In France they have to intrigue, make a stir, govern the King, the Royal Family and the Bishops, and give rein to their vanity.' The Pope, he adds, did not contest this indictment, and was easily persuaded to ignore the intriguing fanaticism of most of the French Archbishops whose only merit was that they lived good lives. He was well aware of the ignorant obstinacy of Christophe de Beaumont who, limited though he was, desired to dominate the French clergy while his vanity was nourished by the admiration of the Royal Family. A new Bull, which the Ambassador helped to draft, modifying the provisions of '*Unigenitus*', was declared contrary to the liberties of the Gallican Church, but a *lit de justice* ordered the *Parlement* to register it. Neither Jansenists nor Jesuits were satisfied by the compromise, but tempers cooled and nothing more was heard of the certificates which had caused the storm. The French Ambassador, himself an *esprit fort*, had the good fortune to deal with Benedict XIV, the most tolerant Pope of modern times. When the issue was decided he returned to Paris where he received the congratulations of the King and the courtiers on the success of his mission.

Having experienced the fascinations of diplomacy, Choiseul was delighted to accept the Embassy at Vienna, where he was warmly welcomed by the Empress, Kaunitz, and the Emperor. Though he had not initiated the *renversement des alliances*, he approved it and strove to keep it in repair. 'The Empress,' ran his first dispatch to the King, 'talked of Your Majesty with lively interest, inquired about the people in your confidence, and displayed much friendship and esteem for Mme de Pompadour.' Maria Theresa's references to the Favourite may not have been quite so cordial as he reported, but zeal for the success of his mission seemed to justify a little exaggeration. In addition to his political sympathies his birth made him *persona grata*, for his father had been in the service of Duke Francis of Lorraine, now the Emperor Francis. His task of cementing the alliance of the Courts and the co-operation of the armies in the Seven Years War was complicated by the military disasters of France which incurred a good deal of criticism. His friend Bernis, who was in control of foreign policy, wrote that the King and the Council rendered full justice to his talents and zeal, and the seal was set on his favours by his promotion to the dignity of Duke in August, 1758. As the sky darkened Bernis lost his nerve and begged the ablest of French diplomatists to share his burden. The idea of a *consortium* was a dream, and by the end of 1758 Bernis was banished from the Court and Choiseul ruled in his place.

In his fortieth year the new Foreign Minister was at the height of his powers. No one could speak with so much authority on policies and personalities in Vienna, and no Minister of the reign brought such a fund of energy to his task. The military weakness of France had been exposed when the rout at Rossbach echoed round the world. The first duty was to restore the morale of the army, the second to enlarge the navy, for the British foe could never be crushed on the Continent. The capacity of the new pilot was quickly recognised at home and abroad, and Catherine the Great saluted him as *le cocher de l'Europe*. For the next decade he stood forth without a rival as the effective ruler of France, trusted and liked by the King and the Favourite. The political *rôle* of the latter ended with the promotion of her *protégé*, who was determined to be master in his own house but was quite willing to leave control of the arts and a share in the distribution of Court favours in her hands. Their association was strengthened by the fact that his brother-in-law the Duc de Gontaut was among her most intimate friends. With his easy morals and his friendship with the *Philosophes* he could not expect to earn the favour of the Queen or the Dauphin, but neither of them ventured to challenge the authority of the King. Taking over the Ministry of Marine in 1761 he transferred the Foreign Office to his cousin the Duc de Choiseul-Praslin for the remainder of the war, while retaining the supreme direction of affairs.

With Choiseul at the helm the Favourite reached the summit of her career, and the two friends worked together in unbroken harmony till her death. The Minister, as she was well aware, was the predominant partner. 'I am credited with a great deal of influence,' she remarked to Gontaut, 'but without the friendship of M. de Choiseul I could not obtain even a Croix de Saint-Louis.' It was owing to her patronage that Soubise, the commander on the fatal field of Rossbach, retained his post in the army and was given another chance. Wagging tongues spoke of a *liaison* with Choiseul, but she was one of the least sensual of women and Choiseul had plenty of choice elsewhere. That his gentle wife made friends with her was no surprise, for she made friends with almost everybody. The innermost circle was completed by his formidable sister the Duchesse de Gramont, who made up by her wits what she lacked in feminine qualities. At the wish of her brother she had married a wealthy profligate, from whom she was separated after six months. She retained the title and her husband's money, and henceforth made her home with the brother she adored. Every evening the King appeared in the apartment of the Favourite, happy and carefree now that Choiseul was in command. Duke and Peer, Governor of Touraine, possessor of the Golden Fleece, he enjoyed a fantastic income of 800,000 livres in addition to the ample dowry of his wife. For a man of his generous nature and extravagant tastes, however, no sum sufficed. He loved to assist his relatives and hated to refuse applications for help. 'In his home he was the most amiable of men,' testifies Dufort de Cheverny. 'He received innumerable requests and only refused them when they were impossible of fulfilment.' Vast sums were spent in building and landscape-gardening at Chanteloup on the Loire which he purchased in 1761. Unlike his master and the Favourite, who were often in low spirits, he was always cheerful and serene. His heart, declared Bernis who knew him well, was kind and tender. With his buoyant temperament, enjoying the material pleasures of life to the full, he was one of the happiest of men.

Since not even the optimism of Choiseul could envisage a happy ending of the Seven Years War, his thoughts turned to the reconstruction of the power of France after the restoration of peace. Never for a moment did he waver in support of the Austrian alliance, but that was not enough. England had proved stronger than he expected, France needed other allies, and where could they be found except in the south? Since Bourbon princes sat on the thrones of Spain, Naples and Parma, why should they not supplement the Hapsburg alliance and thus balance the Anglo-Prussian partnership in the north? Though Spanish military power was waning, her navy might be useful in restoring the equilibrium at sea. With these considerations in mind Choiseul planned the *Pacte de Famille* secretly signed in August, 1761, the principal diplomatic achievement of his tenure of office. In addition to the permanent association of France and Spain, the latter undertook to declare war against England in the following spring if the conflict was still in progress, and France would hand over Minorca in return. Of equal importance for the future was the rebuilding of the navy which had shrunk to a shadow during the war.

Next in significance to the Favourite among the friends of Choiseul was Voltaire, who cherished the hope of being recalled to the Court through their influence. The Minister shared the general outlook of the *Philosophes* and removed the ban on the publication of the *Encyclopédie*. A further point of contact was their common dislike of Frederick the Great—Choiseul for reasons of *haute politique*, Voltaire on account of personal affronts. Despite his temporary arrest in Frankfurt on leaving Germany for ever in 1753, he resumed correspondence with the ruler and remained in contact till the end of his life, since the admiration of the two most famous men in Europe for each other's genius survived their contempt for each other's character. Even the Seven Years War failed to break the association, and in 1759 a selection of prose and verse was dispatched by Frederick from the front. Among them was an ode on the French troops whom, with memories of Rossbach fresh in his memory, he saluted with bitter irony: 'as valiant in pillage as cowardly in battle'. Further barbed arrows were launched at the King and the Favourite. 'Quoi! votre faible monarque, jouet de la Pompadour.' Voltaire forwarded the latest stinging nettle—as he forwarded all his political correspondence with Berlin—to Choiseul, who decided not to show it to the King. Voltaire congratulated the royal author on his verses, but advised him not to give them to the world.

Though his sympathies in the Seven Years War were wholeheartedly with France and Austria, Voltaire had no more desire for the total defeat of his old patron than the Minister who, like all statesmen worthy of the name, had the Balance of Power in mind.

If Luc were a different person [wrote Choiseul in July, 1759], and possessed some of the ordinary virtues in addition to his talents, I think it would be best that he should not be annihilated, in view of the equilibrium not only of Germany but of the North. The Prussian power, wisely directed, was excellently designed for a wise, pacific and just system. The alliance of France and Prussia was a very wise arrangement. I confess I was a supporter of the system which we followed before the present war, whereas now we cannot say we have a solid foundation; on the return of peace we shall have to fashion a new system, always a delicate problem for large states. It matters little to a kingdom whether Pierre or Paul is Minister, Jeanne or Marguerite the mistress. But if one is not crazy, one ought to tremble at the thought of helping to upset the edifice constructed by Richelieu and Mazarin, which was maintained for sixty years by Louis XIV, and contributed to the success of his reign and the lustre of his nation. One must be very presumptuous to imagine that one can find an equivalent for the system of these great men. Fifty leagues of Canada, Silesia and Prussia, more or less, do not trouble me, but the creation of a new system alarms me and fills my thoughts day and night. I have reason to reflect deeply on the situation of Europe after the peace, for on that depends the weal or woe of the universe for a century. As for Luc, he is a mad dog and we must let him bark; that is his only consolation. I pity him: lies and insults are the only weapons he will soon have left. Tell me any views you have on politics: I am only too happy to learn from the ideas of someone like you whose abilities I respect.

While they agreed about Prussia, they disagreed about England, for which Voltaire always kept a warm place in his heart. 'The more zealously they support Luc and the more they ruin themselves for him,' wrote Choiseul, 'the more I shall laugh. If he no longer existed, we should be too happy to have a war with the English alone. They would soon be brought to heel, despite their four hundred vessels. It is incredible how their commerce has suffered this winter from our ships. England ought to choose between commercial and military power, as one cannot have both.' Writing in 1759 he could not foresee that the Peace of Paris, still four years ahead, would leave the island kingdom in possession of France's fairest colonies.

Like all friends and admirers of Voltaire, Choiseul was well aware of his failings. Possessing not only the sharpest tongue but the thinnest skin in Europe, the Sage of Ferney suffered as much pain as he inflicted, and he made no attempt to conceal the smart. In 1768, at the age of seventy-four, he received some excellent advice from a man of imperturbable temper who was young enough to be his son. 'I am always surprised,' wrote Choiseul, 'at the heat you display in the smallest matters which concern you, and that you do not feel that this heat, which is an annoyance for you, is precisely the object of your enemies. They cannot have your tongue cut out, but they make you unhappy.' But Voltaire was too old and too self-centred to mend his ways.

II

The health of the Favourite, never good, worsened during the disasters of the long war, and when peace returned in 1763 she had only one year to live. She had occasionally vomited blood since her childhood, and suffered from feverish colds, cough, and palpitations. It was a case of premature physical decay, for she was only just over forty. She lost colour and flesh and sometimes spent the whole day in bed. She had been so ill in 1757 that she made her will, and she was poorly again at the close of 1763. 'Rejoice with me,' wrote the Duchesse de Choiseul to Mme du Deffand, 'she is out of danger.' Anchored in the confidence of the King, who hated changes in his entourage, and trusted by Choiseul, her position appeared secure enough, but the strain was becoming almost too heavy to be borne. Once again she consulted a fortune-teller, who assured her that her death would not come without warning. She worried not only about herself but about the state of France, and Choiseul, who felt a genuine affection for her, told Mme du Hausset that he feared that she would die of grief. When Mme de la Ferté, daughter of Mme Geoffrin, who had known her in her Paris days, visited her early in 1764, she complained of sleeplessness, indigestion and breathlessness on mounting the stairs. Referring to her latest achievement in securing the return to favour of Cardinal de Bernis—an old friend of them both—she remarked that he had always been a good sort, but the misfortunes of France had saddened him and he had got on the nerves of the King and herself.

> Then she told me how grieved she was by the deplorable state of the kingdom. Only her affection for the King kept her at his side. She would be a thousand times happier alone and serene at Menars, but the King could not spare her. Then, speaking with an energy I had never seen in her, she poured out her heart on her torments. I never heard a finer sermon on the nemesis of ambition. She was by turns so miserable, so insolent, so violently agitated, so embarrassed by her supreme power, that when I left after an hour I felt that death was her only refuge.

She was also oppressed by money troubles, eking out her uncertain allowance by the sale of jewels and occasional windfalls at the card table. At her death only thirty-seven louis (pounds) were found in her dressing-table.

Mme de Pompadour faced the approach of death calmly, for she had drunk the cup of ambition to the dregs and was ready to depart. 'I am told there is no danger,' reported the Duchesse de Choiseul, in March, 1764, 'but I am anxious because I love her. How should I not? I add esteem to gratitude, and she has no better friend at Court.' The King and the Favourite were at Choisy when her hour struck. She was taken back to Versailles, where the King visited her several times a day. At the suggestion of the doctors he broke it to her that the moment for Supreme Unction had come. In obedience to orders she sent for her husband, who replied that he was ill. The faithful Quesnay did his best, but her frail body was beyond repair. 'Shall I see a confessor?' she asked the King, who expressed a wish that she should be reconciled with God. On the morning of her death her wills of 1757 and 1761 were read to her with a long list of legacies to her staff, and she dictated a codicil to her secretary Collin, leaving jewels and *objets d'art* to Choiseul, Gontaut, Soubise, and other close friends. Choiseul paid several visits to the sick-room and removed a large portfolio containing state papers. Feeling that every agonising breath might be the last she exclaimed: 'The end is near, leave me alone with my ladies.' A *curé* was summoned, and a few minutes later she was gone. As the King watched the funeral *cortège* leave for Paris he murmured 'une amie de vingt ans', and two big tears rolled down his cheeks. Though his passion had long since cooled he missed her company and felt strangely alone. Every woman in society was willing to respond to his advances, declares Dufort de Cheverny. None of them appealed to him, for no one combined the qualities which had made her a friend and counsellor no less than the brightest ornament of the Court.

Broadly speaking [testifies the Duc de Croÿ], she was regretted, for she was kindly and helpful to almost everyone who approached her. Rarely was a post filled or a favour granted without her intervention. She only secured the dismissal of three or four Ministers who had tried to overthrow her. Yet France suffered many misfortunes in her time and many useless expenses were incurred. Her death was almost the greatest event one could imagine. It remained to be seen to whom the King would give entire confidence, for he needs someone to help him make up his mind. That might alter the whole system of the Court and even destroy the Austrian alliance.

In the Royal Family no tears were shed except those of the King. There was no more talk of her, wrote the Queen to President Hénault, than if she had never lived. The Dauphine spoke in gentler tones. 'We have lost the poor Marquise. She received Supreme Unction, and it only remains for us to pray for her. The King is very distressed and controls himself with difficulty in public. Our greatest hope is that he will now concentrate his affection on his children and find happiness with us, and that *le bon Dieu* will touch his heart.' Even her old enemy the Dauphin admitted that she died with a courage rare in either sex. In Paris her passing merely produced a few ribald *Poissonades*. Her books and *objets d'art* were sold under the direction of her brother, her sole trustee. Though she had been reviled in the streets of Paris and in certain quarters of the vast palace, she was liked and regretted by most of those who knew her best.

The passing of the Pompadour left a blank in the King's life but had no effect on the structure of French policy as determined by the *renversement des alliances*. As Maria Theresa had regarded the Treaty of Aix-la-Chapelle in 1748 as merely a breathing space in her struggle with Prussia, so Choiseul envisaged the humiliating Treaty of Paris in 1763 as nothing more than a pause in the world-wide colonial conflict with England. 'England is and always will be the enemy of your power and your State,' he declared in a memorandum to the King. 'Her commercial greed, her arrogance and her envy of your power should warn you that many years must pass before we can make a lasting peace.' He had laid the foundation of France's recovery in the *Pacte de Famille* with Spain in 1761. The next task was to revitalise the army, rebuild the navy, and reform the finances in preparation for the next round which could not be far away. Of these three objects the first and second were achieved. 'I think it was a very good job,' he told the King, 'and it needed courage to undertake it; for all the officers and even the civil servants in the department did their utmost to wreck it. Nothing intimidates me when I feel I am on the right course, and I have surmounted every obstacle.' His reforms in the navy challenged fewer vested interests. At his fall in 1770 a powerful fleet was once more in being and the storehouses were full of supplies. He lived just long enough to witness the triumph of the American colonies with the aid of France and Spain, and to reflect that at any rate in the sphere of national defence his labours had not been in vain.

The closing decade of the reign was cheered by two additions to the dominions of France, all the more welcome after the loss of Canada and India. The first was the incorporation of Lorraine on the death of Stanislas in 1766, in accordance with the arrangement when he succeeded Duke Francis in 1737. That the little Duchy contained the richest iron mines in Western Europe was unknown, but its strategic position on the eastern frontier made it a valuable asset for the purposes of offence or defence out of all proportion to its population and its size.

Of scarcely less significance was the conquest of Corsica. The waning power of the Republic of Genoa, to which it had belonged since the fourteenth century, encouraged the appetite of the House of Savoy and other Powers, and the inhabitants frequently rebelled against foreign rule. But the island was too small to shape its own destinies and it was weakened by the hereditary vendettas which had earned it a bad name. The attack on the Genoese garrisons was begun by Paoli during the Seven Years War, and the island, with the exception of some coast towns, was soon in his hands. Feudalism was suppressed, the vendetta was curbed, and a popular constitution was granted. The name of Paoli echoed through Europe as the symbol of liberty, and Boswell, who had a passion for celebrities, journeyed to Corsica to pay his respects. Too weak to reassert her sway, Genoa turned to France for support. In 1764 French troops were authorised to garrison three fortresses for four years under Genoese sovereignty, after which Genoa, realising that her day was over, sold the island to France. The gallant Paoli, supported by his secretary Carlo Buonaparte, father of Napoleon, had no wish to substitute one foreign master for another; but though he turned his arms against the French, the unequal struggle could have only one end. In 1769 he and his chief comrades sailed in a British ship to Italy, and in September 1770 a general assembly met and swore allegiance to Louis XV. Though neither Corsica nor Lorraine was to be despised, France owned less territory and possessed less influence in the world at the end than at the beginning of the reign.

Next to rebuilding the power and prestige of his country after the disasters and humiliations of the Seven Years War, the principal achievement of Choiseul's later years of office was the suppression of the Jesuits. That he was an *esprit fort* was not the cause of his hostility, for no one was less of a fanatic than this easy-going Epicurean. The Jesuits had powerful friends in France as well as powerful foes, and the two sides—Ultramontanes and Gallicans—seemed not unequally matched. In one camp stood the Queen, the Dauphin and the majority of the higher clergy with the Archbishop of Paris at their head; in the other the *Parlements*, the lower clergy, members of rival Orders, the Jansenists and Choiseul. Though the King had always been regarded as a friend of the Order, he took little part in a struggle which he regretted and which would have been unthinkable in the days of Louis XIV. The conviction that it had grown too powerful and constituted a standing challenge to the authority of the State, an *imperium in imperio*, was widely held in Western Europe, and the severity of Catholic rulers proved that dislike of the Jesuits could not be dismissed as hostility to the Church. That the Order had engaged in large-scale commercial transactions showed how far it had strayed from the ideas of its founder. Mme de Pompadour took no part in the campaign, being content to follow the lead of the King. 'I believe the Jesuits are good people,' she remarked, 'but the King cannot sacrifice his *Parlement* to them just when he needs it so much.'

The campaign, which swelled into a crescendo of condemnation and culminated in the suppression of the Order by Clement XIV, opened in Portugal in 1759 when Pombal, the omnipotent Minister, charged its members with complicity in a plot to murder the King and evicted six thousand Jesuits from Portugal and her colonies. When the Pope retaliated by expelling all Portuguese residents in his dominions, Pombal confiscated the property of the Order and urged other Courts to join in demanding its suppression.

The second act of the drama was staged in France where the lead was taken by the *Parlements*. When the commercial enterprises of Père de La Valette, the Jesuit administrator of the

o

island of Martinique, failed for two million francs owing to the capture of five richly laden merchant ships by the English, some French commercial houses suffered from the bankruptcy. Ricci, the General of the Order, who repudiated the debt on the ground that La Valette had acted without authorisation, was sued by the creditors, lost his case, and appealed to the *Parlement*, which, with its Jansenist colouring, confirmed the judgment of the lower tribunal. At this stage Choiseul ordered an inquiry into the constitutions of the Order by the Archbishops and Bishops, who reported by a large majority that the autocracy of the General infringed the rights of France and urged the appointment of a resident Vicar-General subject to the laws of the kingdom. Ricci's defiant rejoinder: *sint ut sunt aut non sint* provoked a decree of suppression in 1764. Members of the Order were allowed to remain as secular priests till 1767, when they were expelled from France. A flood of pamphlets testified to the depth of feeling aroused by the activities of the most militant Order in the Church. Choiseul, who detested persecution, had rescued a few Protestants from the galleys, but he differentiated between a small persecuted minority and a powerful Order. In view of the strong feelings of the *Parlements* and his principal adviser, the King gave way, merely pleading for lenient treatment. 'I am not in love with the Jesuits,' he noted on a memorandum of Choiseul, 'but all the heretics have always detested them, and that is to their credit. If for the peace of my kingdom I unwillingly send them away, I do not wish people to think that I approve everything the *Parlements* have done or said against them.' The Edict drafted by Choiseul confined itself to a declaration that the Society no longer existed in France, and that its members would henceforth live as simple individuals subject to the spiritual authority of the ordinary clergy.

None of the *Philosophes* had applauded the campaign so rapturously as d'Alembert. 'Perhaps the hour is approaching when Philosophy will have its revenge on the Jesuits,' he wrote in 1761. 'At the present moment I see everything in the rosiest colours,' he added in 1762. 'I see the Jansenists dying peacefully next year after preparing the way for the violent death of the Jesuits this year. I see toleration introduced, the Protestants recalled, marriage of the clergy, confession abandoned, and fanaticism quietly uprooted.' Voltaire, who detested every form of persecution, clerical or anti-clerical, was rebuked by d'Alembert for his luke-warm support of the campaign against the teachers of his youth. 'Away with human weakness. Let the Jansenist *canaille* rid us of the Jesuit *canaille* and let these spiders gobble each other up.'

The third act opened in Madrid in the same year 1767 when Charles III suppressed the Society throughout his vast dominions on the ground that it challenged the authority of the Crown by opposition to a tax. Following the Portuguese precedent, Spain deported thousands of priests to the Papal states, where they were forbidden to land and were finally dumped into Corsica. The example of the rulers of France and Spain was followed by the Bourbon Courts of Naples and Parma. Selecting the weakest of the Order's foes for his counter-attack, Clement XIII declared the Duke of Parma to have forfeited his rank and title, whereupon France occupied Avignon, still a Papal possession, and a demand for the suppression of the Order was presented by Cardinal Bernis, French Ambassador in Rome, in December, 1768, in the name of France, Spain, and the Kingdom of Naples. 'The extinc-tion of the Jesuits is necessary,' wrote Choiseul to Bernis in 1769, 'for the King of Spain has just sent a courier to say that the tranquillity of his kingdom and his person demands it.' If the Minister had ever entertained any doubts about such a drastic solution, they would have been removed by the attitude of Madrid, since the *Pacte de Famille*, of which he was the architect, was in his opinion as vital as the Austrian alliance to the position of France as a Great Power. 'For ten years the Jesuits have persecuted me. In France they said I expelled them, in Spain that I am their friend. Both are untrue. Nothing has mattered less to me in life, but we have had enough of them. They have got on the nerves of the Courts to such an extent that at Madrid they forget England and Pitt in their obsession with the Jesuits and are worrying me about them. Let them all go to the devil, and the Pope too if he does not rid me of them.' Even Cardinal Bernis, the mildest of men, told Choiseul that he detested their intrigues, their despotism, and their fanaticism.

The crisis proved fatal to the aged Pope, a staunch supporter of the Order, and the reply to the demand fell to his successor, Clement XIV, a man of softer metal, who had no love for the

Jesuits and even feared they might poison him. No one save a Hildebrand or an Innocent III could be expected to resist the most powerful Catholic rulers in Europe who were now joined by Portugal. When Maria Theresa yielded unwillingly to her son Joseph and Kaunitz, the House of Savoy remained the only friend of the Order. The final blow fell in 1773 when it was suppressed by a Papal Bull on the ground that it had infringed its constitution by its political activities, that its abolition was demanded by Catholic sovereigns and high ecclesiastical dignitaries, and that it was necessary for the peace of the Church. Ricci was imprisoned in the Castle of St. Angelo where he died two years later. One of the paradoxes of history was witnessed when members of the most ultramontane Order in the Church found refuge in the dominions of the free-thinking rulers of Prussia and Russia. Though Choiseul had fallen from power before the dissolution, he witnessed with satisfaction the triumph of his policy from his peaceful country home.

The suppression of the Jesuits was received with mixed feelings in France. There was a widespread sentiment that they had been treated more harshly than they deserved. The closing of their colleges created a vacuum in the educational life of France which proved difficult to fill. Voltaire provided hospitality for a Jesuit Father at Ferney which was gratefully accepted. The sympathy was shared by Louis XV who, like the Queen and the Dauphin, had retained his Jesuit Confessor, and when the plight of the Order was described to him by his daughter Louise, one of the most ardent of their champions, he determined to act. Choiseul's successor at the Foreign Office, Aiguillon, drafted a royal declaration recalling the Jesuits expelled by the *Parlements* and allowing them to be employed by the Bishops or under their authority. Since this would contradict his previous action and threaten a breach with Spain, Aiguillon argued that the Jesuits had submitted to the Bull of suppression and would not carry on the Society. When, however, the King learned from Rome that a circular by the Jesuit General desiring the Jesuits to live according to their rule and to receive novices, he withheld his signature at the wish of the Pope. Since the Order and their champions, faithful to Ricci's formula, rejected limited concessions and demanded integral restoration, the project was abandoned. Not till the storms of the Revolution and the Napoleonic era were over did the Order re-emerge with its constitution unaltered and its militancy unimpaired.

Choiseul's position was strengthened by the knowledge that no serious rival was in sight, but an attempt to overthrow him was made under the auspices of his most influential enemy at Court, Comtesse d'Esparbès, who hoped to succeed Mme de Pompadour as the ruling Favourite. Without waiting for a frontal attack he drafted a long memorandum defending his record since his appointment in 1758 and offering his resignation. The King begged him to stay, and the ambitious Duchess was exiled to her country home. 'I remain,' commented Choiseul when the storm blew over, 'but one day Your Majesty will exile me too.' Another potential danger disappeared when the Dauphin died in 1765, for everyone knew that his accession would have involved instant dismissal. Danger could only threaten if some pretty face were to catch the fancy of an ageing sensualist and drive every competitor for influence, whether male or female, out of the field.

10

SECRET DIPLOMACY

THE traditional notion of Louis XV as little better than an indolent rake was modified nearly a century after his death by the publication of four substantial works which revealed him as keenly interested in his armies and eagerly engaging in secret diplomacy behind the back of his Ministers. The veil was lifted in 1865 in Boutaric's *Correspondance secrète de Louis XV*—discovered in the Foreign Office secret files. The outlines were filled in by the Duc de Broglie in *Le Secret du Roi*, based on the archives of his family, and by Vandal's *Louis XV et Élisabeth de Russie*. Of equal significance to students of his character was the publication in 1865 of the *Correspondance de Louis XV et du Maréchal de Noailles*, preserved in the War Office, with a lengthy Introduction by Camille Rousset, the biographer of Louvois. Of the relatively few surviving letters of the King in his own hand the larger number were written to the old Marshal. No fair assessment of his complex personality is possible if we forget the long hours alone in his study reading and commenting on diplomatic reports from various European capitals from his secret agents—described by the Prince de Conti as his pocket viziers—and the bulletins and memoranda of Marshal Noailles from the eastern front. How he toiled at his papers was unknown to the diarists of his reign and was never fully grasped by Mme de Pompadour herself. In domestic affairs he may justly be dismissed as a *roi fainéant*, a passenger in the royal coach, not the charioteer. In the wider sphere of European relations, on the other hand, he had ideas of his own and laboured, though without success, to carry them out. Distrusting all his Foreign Ministers before Choiseul, and hiding a good deal from Choiseul himself, he pursued an independent course, not from love of double-dealing but for purposes close to his heart, above all the election of a French prince to the Polish throne. He corresponded with his secret agents in Warsaw, Stockholm, London, St. Petersburg and Constantinople through the Prince de Conti, the Comte de Broglie, and Tercier, Permanent Under-Secretary of the Foreign Office, leaving his Ministers to guess what was going on.

I

The publication of the voluminous correspondence with Marshal Noailles revealed that the chief counsellor for the first year or two after Fleury's death was the veteran survivor from the age of Louis XIV who held no departmental post. The son of a Marshal, nephew by marriage of Mme de Maintenon, campaigner in the War of the Spanish Succession, President of the Council of Finance under the Regency, brother-in-law of the royal bastard the Comte de Toulouse, Noailles became First Minister in all but name. The confidence he had inspired in Louis XIV was shown by entrusting to his care political memoranda for delivery to his successor on reaching maturity. Though a *bête noire* of Saint-Simon and d'Argenson, the old Marshal was a man of integrity and ability, and the correspondence with Louis XV does honour to both. For practical purposes the reign opens with the death of the Cardinal at the beginning of 1743, but as his old tutor began to lose grip he turned to Marshal Noailles, then serving at the front. The correspondence, which is particularly full in the first two years, opens with a memorandum in October 1742 on the defence of the frontiers, and a covering letter. 'Please believe I have no other aim than your service, your personal glory and the happiness of your State. You know my tender and respectful attachment which I should like to prove with my blood.' 'I have read your memorandum and will read it again before M. de Breteuil (Minister of War) replies to it,' answered the King. 'I shall be very glad to have your ideas and to carry them out if they appeal to me. I do not doubt your attachment to my person and to the well-being of my State.' A month later the Marshal wrote in a strain of increasing anxiety about the military situation and implored his master to assert himself.

Firmness and courage alone can help. I realise the exhaustion of your peoples, the depopulation of the countryside, the need for relief from the burden of taxation. Yet the welfare of the state and your glory and honour demand the preservation of its rank and reputation in Europe. There is not a moment to lose in placing this frontier in a state of defence for the next campaign. Troops must be recalled from Germany. But your most faithful servants will waste their time on memoranda and projects unless you support them and, if you approve them, order them to be carried out. Only the will of the master can generate the energy needed to avert the evils which threaten us. The situation must be surveyed as a whole before any particular plan can be formed. I shall, however, confine myself to the frontier you have given me to command, though if desired I am always ready to explain my views based as they are on the experience of nearly fifty years. If you wish me to break silence it is for you to command.

'The late King, whom I wish to imitate so far as I can,' replied the monarch, 'advised me in his last days to seek counsel in everything and to follow the best advice, so I shall be delighted to have yours.' He was anxious, he added, to understand the art of war which his ancestors had practised with so much success. Making full use of this authorisation, the Marshal continued to press the King to play his part. 'After the death of Mazarin, Louis XIV had no First Minister and governed alone with his Council, to which he never admitted ecclesiastics. Every member was free to speak but the King made the decisions. You need competent and disinterested councillors. Fill the hearts of your people with joy.'

The King's letters to Noailles reveal more feeling than he usually displayed. 'I know you have been poorly,' he wrote in May 1743, 'but your heart has given orders to your body. Take care of both. I know you serve me well. Always count on my friendship.' The defeat at Dettingen a month later failed to shake his master's confidence. 'I know it is not your fault that the battle was not more successful. It was a draw, not a defeat. Keep your eye on the young officers so that they grow into good generals which everyone agrees we do not possess.' That someone was to blame seemed clear enough, and Noailles fired a broadside at the soldiers and civilians alike.

I grieve to see you, who deserves love and good service, so badly served. In all branches of the administration there is torpor, indolence and insensibility which require prompt remedies if your kingdom is to escape great misfortunes. The Foreign Office, for instance, is very badly run. Most of the Ambassadors are unsuitable as they usually owe their posts to favour, not to merit. There is no chance of securing a reasonable peace unless the troops are increased. We must sustain the Emperor and pay him, preserving this phantom in order to prevent Germany from forming a league against us and supplying soldiers to England. He is amiable, honourable and resolute, but he has no military or political experience, no judgment, and only cares about recovering Bavaria. France is in danger. We must try to hold out till winter and then increase our troops and try to end a war in which we have had nothing but misfortunes.

Marshal Broglie was relieved of his command, but that was all.

You know [replied the King], I do not like heavy punishments. With mild punishments and small rewards we achieve more than by greater harshness and richer rewards. I know our Ambassadors are a poor lot, but how am I to replace them? It is true we have had thirty years of peace; but consider events, of which speculation is not the least since it has made people lose their heads and has destroyed credit. To restore it would take a long time. And are we not paying the debts of the late King, and for costly maladies and famine? And if we have to defer payments and make some bad bargains, as we must, good-bye to all credit, and money, already in so short supply, will be even scarcer. I write all this, not to avoid doing what is needed, but to do it properly, not wastefully and subject to robbery as hitherto. An increase of cavalry has been ordered. As for the Emperor I am convinced we must support him as much as possible by a subsidy for himself but not for his troops. I will lose no chance of peace.

The most important result of the Marshal's admonitions was the decision to employ the best soldier in Europe, Marshal Saxe.

That a German Protestant should command the troops of the *Roi très Chrétien* made the King hesitate, but he withdrew his objections on condition that he should serve under the orders of Noailles. It was a wise decision, for what little glory was won in the War of the Austrian Succession was due to the gifted bastard of Augustus the Strong, Elector of Saxony and King of Poland. A second resolve gave Noailles no less pleasure.

> I cannot express my infinite satisfaction [he wrote on August 6, 1743]. I recognise the blood and the sentiments of Louis XIV and Henri IV, and I congratulate Your Majesty, his state, and all who, like myself, desire his glory. Your decision to go to the front is indispensable: it is the only way to save the state. Your personal honour is engaged. A King is never so great as at the head of his troops. That is where his subjects desire to see him. There he is the most worthy of respect, especially when it is for the defence of the state and its frontiers. The rehabilitation of your troops demands it. Your authority and presence are the sole means of restoring order, the spirit of obedience, and the morale which are absolutely destroyed. You realise that to make war by proxy has not been a success, and I venture to say that it is and will be the same in all branches of the administration. The success of all your enterprises will always depend on you taking the lead and not leaving everything to others. Your subjects will rejoice and foreigners will feel more confidence. Every sovereign in Europe has been at the front. You, Sire, are the first and only member of your house who has not taken command. Not to do so would be the less excusable because more reasons demand it. Moreover, everyone recognised in Your Majesty the talents and qualities needed for war. Your kingdom is purely military. Glory and the love of arms have always distinguished the French nation above all others. When you are resolved to learn and practise this profession, the glory and aggrandisement of your state will be your reward. You cannot see your troops too much or too often, both in peace and war.

The project of a visit to the front had to wait till the year 1744.

The King and the Marshal could do little more than deplore the plight of France. 'If everyone were like you and me, above all *le bon Dieu*,' wrote the King in September, 1743, 'all would go well. There is plenty of good will but the moment is very critical. I am sorry your health has suffered. Mine is very good.'

> My health is very bad [replied Noailles] because I sacrificed it to you

long ago. I am old, the fatigues are constant, and grave anxiety weighs me down. If I were not so tenderly attached to you I should not worry so much. I cannot discern any remedies for the misfortunes of your kingdom. We have no Eugenes or Marlboroughs among us. France is not fruitful in great men, and it would be the worse for us if we alone suffered from this sterility. I think we have the raw material. We must aid nature, inflame zeal, provide opportunity. This is an essential part of the duties of royalty and not the least difficult, though not for you, with your talents to make yourself beloved. Promotions without merit diminish zeal, so please consult me first.

At the close of 1743 the Marshal compiled a long letter and a still longer memorandum.

Our troubles in recent years are not due to necessity or chance. There were two chief causes. Firstly the Government has never formed a general plan of conduct. It has acted from hand to mouth, without considering the goal, our engagements, and our resources. Thus we have had deliberation in place of action, pernicious vacillation—almost always only half measures. Secondly, discredit abroad. I hardly dare tell you how other states shrink from making engagements with France. I beg you to use your authority, to speak, to decide, to tell your Ministers what to do. The first task is to form a general plan to which all details must conform. That would be the duty of a First Minister if you were weak enough to have one. A great King should know the capacity of his Ministers and try them out.

An accompanying Memorandum developed the argument and renewed the appeal. The root of the trouble was the lack of a general plan. Several people had urged him to draft one, in which military and political considerations would be combined. The King should invite each of his Ministers to prepare a draft. At the moment, since peace was impossible, the military effort should be redoubled. That the reign was a failure was not due to lack of sound advice.

The summer of 1744 witnessed the long-heralded royal visit to the front, immediately followed by the critical illness at Metz. 'I was at the gates of death,' wrote the King to Noailles after his recovery. 'God is master in all things, but a good master.' From this point the correspondence which had flowed in a spate since the close of 1742 becomes a trickle. Whether Noailles lost the

King's confidence, and if so for what reasons, we cannot tell. Perhaps it was merely owing to age and failing health, for he retained his place in the Council. An occasional memorandum was dispatched, for he loved to use his pen. In 1749, after the return of peace, he wrote: 'My strength is waning, but not my zeal for your glory. Peace has come, but the envy and animosity of certain neighbours remain.' In 1756 he reported that the hour of retirement had struck. 'My sight and hearing are failing; it is difficult to read, write, and walk; I am losing grip and my memory is going. I should hate to vegetate at your Court. To outlive oneself is humiliating. I beg leave to retire. I also beg leave to retain my apartment so that the oldest of your servants can pay homage several times a year.' The King replied that he might keep his apartment, adding 'my sentiments for you will never change.' The tough old soldier lingered on for another decade, passing away in 1766 at the age of eighty-seven. Never again was the King to find a counsellor whom he could unreservedly respect and trust.

II

The *Secret du Roi*, as revealed a century after his death, confirms the impression derived from the correspondence with Noailles that Louis XV was a man of average intelligence, genuinely interested in foreign affairs but lacking the energy and self-confidence to argue with his Ministers or to implement his plans. Though in no way ashamed of his backstairs activities, he paid his agents from his privy purse and trembled at the thought of his double-dealing being discovered. His secret diplomacy was doomed to failure not merely by his own infirmity of purpose but by the fact that it was never underwritten by the Government and the nation.

When he began to assert himself in the sphere of foreign affairs after the return of peace in 1748 he was faced by a difficult decision. The traditional policy of France was to support Poland, Sweden, and Turkey with the object of keeping the growing might of Russia in check, and to this policy he was inclined to adhere, though the danger of antagonising the Colossus of the North could not be overlooked. Moreover, Peter the Great had been strongly attracted to France on his visit in 1717, and his daughter Elizabeth inherited his sympathies. Her name was on the list of candidates for the coveted prize of Queen of France, and she entertained a romantic affection for Louis XV till the day of her death. As allies of Austria in the Seven Years War the paths of France and Russia ran parallel for several years, and the growing power of Russia as revealed in the campaigns suggested reconsideration of the patronage of her weaker neighbours. The rivalry of pro-Polish and pro-Russian policies in France came to a head when Choiseul was called to the helm, for to the greatest Minister of the reign, obsessed by the rivalry of England, the fate of Poland was of little account. This division of opinion, added to the lack of muscle in the King, prevented either party from taking a firm and consistent line in foreign affairs.

The curtain rises on the visit to Paris of a party of anti-Russian and anti-Saxon Polish noblemen in 1745, in view of the uncertain health of Augustus III, to invite the Prince de Conti to stand as a candidate at the next vacancy. Conti informed the King, who authorised him to go ahead behind the back of his Ministers and promised financial support. It was not merely family ties which aroused his interest, for French contact with Poland dated back to the Valois kings. Conti advised the appointment of Ambassadors in Eastern Europe instructed to report direct to himself independently of their routine dispatches to the Foreign Office. Thus the foundations of the *Secret du Roi* were laid. On one occasion a Polish agent handed confidential reports direct to d'Argenson, the Foreign Minister, who dared not raise the matter directly with the King but drafted a dispatch favouring Saxon claims and showed it to the King who made no comment. No further step was taken till 1752, when a new Ambassador to Poland was required.

At this point a fresh performer appears who was soon to take Conti's place as conductor of the King's private orchestra and to hold it for the rest of the reign. The Comte de Broglie, second son of the Marshal, an officer aged thirty-two, received two sets of instructions for Warsaw, one from the Foreign Minister, Saint-Contest, the other from Conti on behalf of the King, and was charged to send separate reports to each. 'The Comte de

Broglie,' wrote the King, 'will believe what the Prince de Conti tells him and will not speak to a living soul.' Money was provided for special purposes independently of the normal expenditure of the Embassy, and he alone of the Ambassadors was aware of his master's plans for a French prince on the Polish throne. It was a delicate situation, for the Dauphine, a Saxon princess, received complaints from her parents of the Ambassador's activities in building up French—in other words anti-Saxon—influence in Warsaw. The public and private Instructions agreed on the importance of reviving French prestige, but the Foreign Minister was unaware of the Conti candidature. He would not have approved it, since he desired the continuance of the Saxon-Polish union on the ground that the Elector's well-known Francophil sentiments were cemented by the marriage of his daughter to the Dauphin. That the rival schemes for dealing with the next vacancy were mere wishful thinking since they ignored the intentions of Russia and Austria in no way diminished the zeal of the King.

The invasion of Saxony in 1756 by Frederick the Great unleashed the Seven Years War and threw the fortunes of Poland into the melting-pot. France, Russia, and Austria were now allies, and a working partnership with Russia, who regarded Poland as within her sphere of influence, involved the soft-pedalling of anti-Russian propaganda in Warsaw. Though Louis XV accepted the temporary necessity of co-operation with Russia, he never abandoned the dream of playing the part of protector of Poland, though the prospects of success waned from year to year. Broglie was recalled from Warsaw and Conti's influence faded away. On his return Broglie expected to play a leading part in the shaping of French policy, but he found Mme de Pompadour, Bernis and Belle-Isle in general control. While the Favourite was an ardent champion of the Austrian alliance, Broglie desired France to consult her own interests at Warsaw. Despite these cross-currents he was sent back to Warsaw in 1757 in the hope of persuading Saxony to abandon her ambition to place a third member of the family on the Polish throne in return for a share in the prospective spoliation of Prussia. Once again he carried two sets of instructions. 'If it proves impossible,' declared Louis XV through Tercier, 'to reconcile consideration for Russia with the sentiments

the King has always entertained for Poland, give preference to
the interests of the latter.' Russia resented the envoys' pro-
Polish attitude, Brühl, the omnipotent Minister of Augustus III,
complained to the French Government, and Broglie was scolded
by Bernis, the new Foreign Minister, who knew nothing of the
Secret du Roi. Realising the improbability of securing a French
or Francophil ruler at the next vacancy, Broglie asked the King
if he wished him to resign. No, was the reply: he could not be
sent back to Warsaw owing to the hostility of Brühl, but he
would receive the secret reports from Warsaw, St. Petersburg,
and Turkey, while Durand, his successor in Poland, would strive
to maintain contact with the friends of France. Broglie's wish
to rejoin his brother in the army was vetoed by the Favourite
and her military *protégé* Soubise. That he retained his master's
confidence was proved in February, 1760, when the King wrote
to Breteuil, the new Minister at St. Petersburg: 'You will report
everything to the Comte de Broglie. Tercier will send you his
instructions. I enjoin the strictest silence except in regard to
Broglie and Tercier.' Two years later the Marshal and the Count
were exiled to their country estates—the latter doubtless a victim
of Choiseul's resentment of the secret activities at which he could
only guess. The transfer of Tercier from his high post in the
Foreign Office to the minor position of Keeper of the Archives
registered the Minister's displeasure but failed to sever his sub-
terranean contacts with the King. When Tercier asked if the
secret reports were still to be forwarded to Broglie the reply was
in the affirmative.

The King's interest in Poland never flagged, though he now
preferred Prince Xavier, the Francophil brother of the Dauphine,
to Conti as a candidate for the throne. But he was too weak-
willed and too far away to compete with Russia's candidate,
Stanislas Poniatowski, a former lover of Catherine the Great,
an admirer of French culture, and a friend of Mme Geoffrin. In
the absence of vigorous support for a rival candidature Russian
pressure, strengthened by the presence of Russian troops, carried
off the prize. In any case the humiliation of Rossbach would
have sufficed to paralyse French influence in Eastern Europe.
Refusing recognition of Stanislas, France withdrew her representative. Poland had always been the core of the King's secret

diplomacy, and little remained to be done. Choiseul's position appeared impregnable, and the King dreaded a collision with his masterful Minister. When Tercier died in 1768 the timid ruler was alarmed lest his papers should fall into his hands and begged Broglie to rescue them. 'The Duc de Choiseul is very clever and he may know a good deal. I think we must go on as we are and not give away anything more. Tell him that his suspicions are groundless and that you have no thought of opposition. Perhaps that was not always the case, but you must keep on good terms with him.' The letter was in answer to Broglie's suggestion to tell the Minister everything and end the mystery which no longer deceived anyone and which weakened the policy of the State. Now that Tercier was gone Broglie became the sole director of what little was left of the secret system.

Though the King's attachment to Poland excluded intimacy with Russia, he was never a Russophobe. After many years in which diplomatic contacts were broken off, and after feelers on both sides, a Jacobite exile in Conti's entourage who called himself the Chevalier Douglas was chosen in 1755 to reconnoitre the ground, carrying with him a snuff-box with a double bottom in which his instructions and itinerary were concealed. The mission was a failure since the envoy posed as a simple tourist, and his request to the British Ambassador, Sir Charles Hanbury Williams, to present him to the Empress was declined. He returned to Russia in the following spring, no longer as a secret agent but as an accredited representative, accompanied by a secretary whose name was soon to become familiar throughout Europe.

Though the elaborate mystery of his sex* has kept his memory alive, the Chevalier d'Éon de Beaumont claims a place in history as a secret agent of Louis XV. Starting his career as a lawyer, author and *protégé* of Conti, he received his first diplomatic assignment in 1756 at the age of twenty-eight. Despite the hostility of the Chancellor Bestucheff the envoys were welcomed by the Vice-Chancellor Woronzow, whose influence was increasing, by Shuvaloff the Favourite, and by the Empress Elizabeth herself. While the official instructions were to convert Russia from a pro-English to a Franco-Austrian orientation, the secret

---

* That he had accompanied Douglas on his fruitless errand in 1755 disguised as a woman is a legend.

purpose was to win support for a French candidate or for a marriage of the Empress to Conti. Two sets of reports were dispatched, one to the Foreign Office, the others through Tercier to Conti and the King. D'Éon had been supplied with a copy of the *Esprit des Lois* with a double binding in which were concealed letters to the Empress and ciphers for the correspondence of the two rulers behind the back of their Ministers and Ambassadors. The Empress responded with an offer to make Conti Duke of Courland and commander of the Russian troops if the King approved. At this moment, however, Conti lost favour at Versailles and the project was dropped. Though the Douglas mission was a failure so far as Conti was concerned, it helped to win Russia for the Franco-Austrian coalition. D'Éon's share in the *rapprochement* was recognised by his official superiors, by the King, and by the new Ambassador the Marquis de l'Hospital. He declined a flattering offer to enter the Russian service, convinced that the brightest prospects were to be found in the land of his birth. Requesting his recall on the plea of ill-health, he left St. Petersburg loaded with compliments and presents. He was rewarded by a pension of 2,000 francs, appointed aide-de-camp to Marshal Broglie, and distinguished himself in the Rhineland campaign of 1761. He could look back on his years in Russia with pride, for he had established his reputation as a diplomat at an unusually early age.

When Breteuil succeeded L'Hospital as Ambassador in 1760, the King instructed him to correspond direct with himself and requested D'Éon to supply a description of the Russian Court. On the accession of Peter III in 1762 Russia withdrew from the Seven Years War and transferred her support to his hero Frederick the Great, and on his deposition Catherine continued the policy of co-operation with Berlin as the best method of dominating and partitioning Poland. French policy, official and unofficial, failed in Russia as it had failed in Poland. Choiseul was much more interested in the West, the Mediterranean, and the New World, and the King lacked the strength of will to challenge his control.

Next to Poland and Russia the chief arena of the *Secret du Roi* was England. Though he had no love for the island kingdom, Louis XV never shared Choiseul's conviction that she was the

P

eternal enemy, and in his relations with her he used the same underhand methods which he had adopted in Eastern Europe. The record of these relations in the middle years of his reign is largely the story of the two most mysterious personages of eighteenth-century Europe, the Comte de St. Germain and the Chevalier D'Éon. Despite the celebrity of the former during his lifetime not a scrap of evidence has come to light on the place or time of his birth, his parentage, his relatives or his early career, and he firmly declined to reveal his name. He may well have been a Spanish Jew with a dash of royal blood in his veins. Nothing but unusual abilities—chemist, musician, painter, linguist, brilliant talker—combined with the adventurer's belief in his star, could have sustained the imposture of his title, won him entry into the Courts of Europe, and enabled him to become the trusted agent of Louis XV. Crystal-gazing, astrology and necromancy, which had been rampant during the Regency, survived the jeers of the *Philosophes*, smoothed the way for Freemasons, Rosicrucians and Illuminati, for clever impostors of the type of St. Germain and Cagliostro, and for more serious pioneers such as Mesmer. The eighteenth century was an age of superstition no less than an age of enlightenment.

The Comte de Saint-Germain enters the orbit of history in 1740 as a *protégé* of Belle-Isle, who was addicted to various forms of occultism. Having dabbled in chemistry and medicine he purveyed drugs and face creams to minor German Courts, and volunteered advice on his patrons' health, such as not drinking at meals. Taking him to Paris the Marshal presented him as the son of his old age, adding: 'He is a great doctor and I hope he will never leave me.' While living with Belle-Isle at Versailles he was provided with a laboratory in Paris for chemical research. With such influential backing his pretensions waxed as rapidly as his fame. The infancy of medical science left the field to quacks, and when the Duchesse de Châteauroux was stricken by mortal sickness he was summoned to her aid. Recognising that nothing could be done, he replied that he was called in too late. He found himself on the horns of a dilemma. To undertake a hopeless case was to saddle himself with the odium of failure, while to refuse his services was to admit that there were limits to his skill. His choice of the latter alternative damaged his prestige, and he decided to leave France, confident that wherever he found himself he could live by his nimble wits.

Though the forces of the Young Pretender had not marched nearer London than Derby, the nerves of the capital needed time to recover.

> We begin to take up people [reported Horace Walpole to Sir Horace Mann on December 9, 1745], the other day they seized an odd man who goes by the name of Count St. Germain. He has been here these two years and will not tell who he is or whence, but professes that he does not go by his right name. He sings, plays on the violin wonderfully, composes, is mad, and not very sensible. He is called an Italian, a Spaniard, a Pole; a somebody that married a great fortune in Mexico and ran away with her jewels to Constantinople; a priest, a fiddler, a vast nobleman, the Prince of Wales has had unsatisfied curiosity about him, but in vain. However, nothing has been made out against him; he is released, and what convinces me that he is not a gentleman, stays here and talks of being taken up as a spy.

The description of this rather shadowy being as mad may have been due to his entertaining habit of romancing about distant times as if he had been an eyewitness.

The next appearance of St. Germain was as a *protégé* of Clive in India, where he increased his store of precious jewels. Returning to France after a decade of absence he soon recovered his footing at Versailles. Casanova met him at dinner in 1757 and describes him as enjoying the favour of the King and the Pompadour. Louis XV, tepidly interested in science and magic, was intrigued by his claims to transmute metals and prolong life. After the death of Marshal Saxe he was provided with an apartment at Chambord and allotted funds to design colours for textiles. Both the pious Dauphin, who hated sorcery, and Choiseul, a notorious sceptic, frowned on the adventurer, but the Favourite delighted in his colourful talk. 'A man as amazing as a wizard,' records Mme du Hausset, 'often came to see Mme de Pompadour, the Comte de St. Germain, who wished people to believe that he had lived for centuries.

> MME DE POMPADOUR: What sort of man was François I, a King whom I could have loved?
>
> ST. GERMAIN: A good sort, but too fiery.

He then described Mary Queen of Scots and Queen Margot.

MME DE POMPADOUR: You seem to have seen them all.

ST. GERMAIN: Sometimes I amuse myself by letting people believe that I have lived for ages.

MME DE POMPADOUR: But you don't tell us your age.

The Count, testifies Mme du Hausset, looked about fifty, was neither thin nor stout, and dressed simply in good taste. Since he claimed to remove flaws from diamonds the King handed him one valued at six thousand francs which if flawless would have been worth ten thousand. The wizard undertook to remove the flaw in a month and brought it back flawless. The probable explanation was that it was another gem, and his claim to increase the size of pearls was doubtless sustained by the same cunning method. The adventurer who had refused his services at the deathbed of Mme de Châteauroux displayed no less prudence in declining Mme de Pompadour's suggestion to supply the King with an elixir of life. 'He is a quack,' exclaimed Dr. Quesnay, 'for he says he has an elixir.'

Louis XV was so impressed by his ability that he decided to employ him as an agent of his secret diplomacy. The disappointments of the Seven Years War, above all the catastrophe of Rossbach, turned his thoughts to peace—if possible a general peace—for he had no wish to betray his Austrian ally. Since Choiseul favoured a resolute prosecution of the struggle, the timid monarch was driven to act behind his back. The first assignment was a mission to Holland in February 1760, nominally to negotiate a loan, but in reality to establish contact with England, the principal enemy, in a neutral state. Choiseul tried in vain to extract information from Belle-Isle, the chief patron of St. Germain, now Minister of War. The French Minister at the Hague reported what he could learn of the movements of the secret agent, but he failed to discover that his main object was to make peace. The Austrian Minister at the Hague reported to Vienna alarming rumours that France was feeling her way towards a settlement. Choiseul detested the idea of negotiations with England, official or unofficial, spoke scornfully of St. Germain as *ce fils de juif*, and instructed the French Minister to disavow him. Though aware of Choiseul's hostility, the mysterious agent counted on the steady support of the King. Incensed by the double-dealing of his master, the Foreign Minister resolved to bring the issue to a head at a meeting of the Council. 'I have ordered our representative at the Hague,' he announced, 'to stop the activities of the Comte de St. Germain. I have not sought the King's orders because I feel sure that no one here would have dared to negotiate for peace without my knowledge.' When he requested the approval of the Council all eyes turned to the King and Belle-Isle, who sat silent under the rebuke. Choiseul described his victory in a letter to the Minister at the Hague, and suggested that the Government of the United Provinces should be requested to arrest 'ce fripon' and hand him over to France for punishment. A Dutch friend warned him of the danger and urged him to escape to London. After a brief stay—for a French secret agent was naturally an object of suspicion in England while a war was in progress—he found refuge in Russia, where he consorted with the conspirators who deposed and murdered Peter III. But the days of his diplomatic service were over, and for the remaining twenty years of his life he played no further part in the history of France. Once again the King's secret diplomacy had failed.

A fresh chapter in Anglo-French relations opened when D'Éon accompanied the Duc de Nivernais to London as Secretary of Legation in 1762 to discuss terms of peace at the close of the Seven Years War. After completing the negotiations the Ambassador returned to France leaving D'Éon as interim Minister, and he was commissioned by the British Government to convey to Paris the British ratification of the treaty. He was rewarded by the King with the Order of St. Louis, and was appointed Minister Plenipotentiary till the arrival of a new chief.

Since the Treaty of Paris was widely regarded as little more than a truce, Broglie drafted a plan for the invasion of England if the war was renewed, despatched officers to survey possible landing places on the south coast, and instructed D'Éon to collect information. 'The Chevalier D'Éon,' wrote the King, 'will receive my orders through the Comte de Broglie and Tercier on the reconnaissance in England, and will carry out his orders in this connection as if they came direct from myself. He must observe the strictest secrecy in this affair and not inform anyone alive, not even my Ministers.' The need for secrecy was reiterated by Broglie, above all for the safe keeping of papers, and he expressed his pleasure in having D'Éon as his lieutenant 'in such an important task which may result in the safety and even the glory of the nation'. The possession of the document concerning the plan of invasion furnished D'Éon with his most effective weapon in his attempts to extract funds from his royal employer in order to pay his debts and keep up his opulent standard of living.

> The King sent for me this morning [reported Tercier to D'Éon on June 10, 1763], and I found him very pale and agitated. He told me in a strained voice that he feared the secret of our correspondence has been betrayed. Having supped alone with Mme de Pompadour a few days ago he dozed off after a slight excess for which he believes her responsible. She took the key of a desk and discovered your relations with the Comte de Broglie. This he infers from indications of disorder among his papers. So he bids me enjoin on you the utmost discretion towards the new Ambassador whom he regards as devoted to Mme de Pompadour. He counts entirely on you.

The duplicity of the ruler was equalled by his terror of exposure. It was the most brilliant chapter in the life of *le petit D'Éon*. As Minister Plenipotentiary he lived in style and entertained as lavishly as if he had been the new Ambassador. His head was turned by his promotion, and to meet expenses he applied to his official chief, Choiseul, to pay his debts and save him from bankruptcy. The Foreign Minister, never his friend, rebuked his extravagance and declined his request.

When the arrival of the new Ambassador, Comte de Guerchy, reduced him to his former rank D'Éon fought hard to avoid stepping down. Despite his youth and modest birth he appears to have expected the appointment himself, and his attitude to the new Ambassador was hostile from the start. At their first interview a struggle began which ended with his political eclipse, for Guerchy handed him a letter of recall. 'The arrival of the Ambassador,' wrote the Foreign Minister, 'terminates your commission as Minister Plenipotentiary. Inform His Britannic Majesty and return to Paris without delay, but without appearing at Court.' Since the letter of recall was not signed by the ruler, D'Éon announced that he would ignore the summons. He sent

letters to Tercier to be shown to Broglie and the King, describing
plots he had discovered to poison or kidnap him. He claimed to
have humiliated and mystified the Ambassador and to have
'fought like a dragon' for the King and his secret and Comte de
Broglie. Alarmed by the vehemence of these letters and fearing
that the angry Ambassador might seize D'Éon's papers, the King
ordered Guerchy to keep secret any documents which might
come into his hands and to transmit them under seal to himself.
When Tercier and Broglie remonstrated on the ground that the
Ambassador might discover and reveal their secrets, the King
replied: 'If Guerchy betrays the secret he would be ruined. If he
is honest he won't do so. If he is a rascal he must be hung. I
see you and the Comte de Broglie are alarmed. Be reassured.
I have a cooler head.' Choiseul vainly invited D'Éon to re-enter
the army, and when Guerchy requested his extradition it was
refused by the British Government. 'Let him keep quiet,'
declared Lord Halifax; 'tell him that his conduct is execrable
but his person is inviolable.' 'M. D'Éon is not mad,' wrote the
King to Tercier, 'but proud and very eccentric. We must let
time pass, give him some money, and keep him where he is, and
no more affairs.'

D'Éon, a born fighter, had no intention of abandoning his
vendetta, and in March 1764 he published a quarto volume against
the Ambassador containing their correspondence. 'Mad with
pride, insolent, insulting, dishonourable, a real mixture of
abominations, at first too well treated by his Court and then too
ill,' commented Horace Walpole, 'he is full of malice and knows
how to turn it to account. Many people think nothing can be
done. I should welcome severity.' Though the book was not
libellous in a strict sense a charge of libel was brought by the
Crown. At this stage the King feared that the man who had
published the correspondence of the Ambassador might commit
even graver indiscretions for the purpose of self-vindication,
though he could scarcely believe that he would turn traitor.
Condemned for libelling Guerchy, D'Éon hit back by charging
his enemy with attempts on his life. When the case was heard at
the Old Bailey in March, 1765, the jury returned a verdict of
attempted assassination. 'In France he would be broken on the
wheel,' wrote the exultant plaintiff to Broglie; 'here he will only

be hung.' The Ambassador was saved by his diplomatic immunity, but the trial cost him his post and he died soon afterwards.
The long battle was over. D'Éon was granted a pension of
12,000 francs after his official recall in return for surrendering the
most compromising of his papers, including the instructions to
report on the possibility of invasion. The verdict at the Old
Bailey restored his popularity in England, and Broglie resumed
friendly correspondence. Though holding no official post he
decided to remain in the land where he had made many friends,
and the King welcomed his secret reports on the English scene
through Broglie as before, though even now he felt a little
anxious about his activities. 'You know D'Éon is mad and perhaps dangerous,' he confided to Broglie in 1767, 'but with mad
people the only thing is to shut them up. Surely in England he
is recognised as such, and the English can only make use of him
as a diversion and to mock M. de Guerchy.'

In the course of his wordy warfare with Guerchy an agent of
the Ambassador hinted that the uniform of a dragoon who was
also a noted duellist concealed a female or a hermaphrodite, and
the rumour gained credibility from his feminine voice and the
absence of amorous escapades. The new Ambassador believed
it and reported it to Versailles as the talk of the town. In his
diary in 1771 Barbier notes the belief that 'this fiery person, so
celebrated for his adventures, is a woman in man's clothes',
and that large sums were staked on the issue. To D'Éon, who
thirsted for publicity as a consolation for the loss of his official
post, the revival of interest was not unwelcome, but his mood
changed when he was charged with profiting from the specula-
tions. He demanded an apology from a banker who had started
the rumour and vainly challenged him to a duel. Once again,
as at the height of his feud with Guerchy, he feared kidnapping
and buried himself in the country under a false name. After thus
angrily repudiating the charge his mood veered once again, and
he resolved to accept the imputation and turn it to account.
When Drouet, the secretary of Broglie, was on a visit to London
he referred to the gossip and was amazed at D'Éon's admission
that it was true. Drouet was convinced, he told Broglie, who in
turn informed the King. 'The suspicions about the sex of this
extraordinary personage are well founded. Drouet, whom I

begged to find out, assures me that he is indeed a woman. He begged Drouet to keep the secret, observing that otherwise his *rôle* would be finished.' Beaumarchais, who visited him in 1775, was of the same opinion, but the King knew his agent too well to be deceived. After this curious transaction he was allowed to return to France and wear the Order of St. Louis. Though he was hailed as a new Maid of Orleans he saw no prospects in his native land and returned to England where he spent his last twenty years in female attire. The origin and purpose of this strange mystification has never been satisfactorily explained.

Louis XV continued to dabble in secret diplomacy long after he had any definite object in view. One day in 1769 Mme du Barry, who took more liberties than any of her predecessors, noticed a big packet on his table and asked what it contained. 'I refused to show it to her,' he reported to Broglie. 'Next day she returned to the charge. I told her it was about Poland, and, as you had been Ambassador, you still had contacts on which you reported to me. That is all I have said and done. I don't think she will tell Choiseul.' His main concern in his closing years was with England which he agreed with Choiseul in regarding as enemy number one. 'M. Pitt is a madman, a dangerous mad-man,' he wrote to Broglie in March, 1770. 'What he has said about us would deserve death in any other country. What cruel neighbours they are!' Yet he dreaded nothing so much as another conflict, and among the causes of Choiseul's dismissal was a feeling that he might be playing with fire. Broglie continued to provide lengthy memoranda on the state of Europe, but his influence was at an end for there was nothing more for him to do.

The King's interest in Poland was unabated long after he had realised his impotence in Eastern Europe. The revolt of a section of the Polish nobility in 1768 against Russia's domination of their country through her puppet Stanislas Poniatowski prompted the dispatch of Dumouriez in 1770 to Warsaw in order to assist the Russophobe party. The envoy, operating independently of the French Ambassador, quickly discovered that an even more deadly enemy of the Polish nation than Russia was the character of the nobility. They were proud and extravagant, reported the young French officer, great talkers, great liars, ignorant, super-stitious, possessing little intelligence and even less courage, passing their life in amours, drinking, fêtes, gambling for high stakes and plotting against each other. His dislike of the nobles was fully reciprocated, and he was glad to be recalled in 1771. Two years later Louis XV witnessed the First Partition with a regret sharpened by the spectacle of his Austrian ally joining in the spoliation. For thirty years his Polish policy had proved as unfruitful as chasing a will o' the wisp.

The King's underground methods brought him more anxiety than satisfaction. When a new war with England seemed to threaten in 1772 the soldier-diplomatist Dumouriez proposed to raise volunteers in Hamburg for a landing in Sweden. The King approved the suggestion on condition that his Foreign Minister d'Aiguillon was not informed. 'The King will abandon us,' exclaimed Dumouriez to the War Minister, an enemy of the Foreign Minister, 'and I shall be hung. At any rate he must tell me his orders himself.' Accordingly verbal instructions were given, including an arrangement that the secret correspondence should be addressed to a third party, and that Broglie, the head of the Shadow Cabinet, should not be told. At this moment French diplomacy for the first and last time was conducted at three levels—officially through d'Aiguillon, semi-officially through Broglie, and secretly through an officer without the knowledge of either. In his attempt to emulate the skill of a conjurer tossing several balls into the air and catching them as they fell, the ruler undertook a task beyond his strength. The success of secret missions depends on the tact and resource of the agent no less than on the statesmanship and resolution of the employer, and the secret mission of Dumouriez was compromised from the start. Breaking the journey to Hamburg at Brussels he gave parties to some of the French magistrates who had been disgraced for their resistance to Maupeou, the Chancellor, who was backed by the King. The news was reported to d'Aiguillon, who wondered what Dumouriez was doing and gave orders to have him watched. On arriving at Hamburg he paid his respects to the French Minister who had been instructed to tap his correspondence. It was soon discovered that friends in Paris were sending him the gossip of the Court under cover of code names. D'Aiguillon figured as *le charlatan*, the King as *le chef de la librairie*, who was described as knowing the writers by name and affording them his tacit permission. The letters of Dumouriez were equally indiscreet, for he found little pleasure in serving a spineless master who seemed afraid of the sound of his own voice. 'I am expecting the great revolution in 1780,' he wrote; 'it is time to shake off this lethargy, otherwise the awakening will be fatal, abroad as well as at home.' An intercepted letter requesting an audience of the King of Prussia, whom he had admired ever since the campaigns of the Seven Years War, exposed him to the charge of treason and secret negotiations with a foreign state. Delighted at the chance of asserting his authority, d'Aiguillon instructed his Minister at Hamburg to arrange for his arrest, and requested the Senate of the Free City to issue the necessary orders. Dumouriez was arrested and a fortnight later found himself in the Bastille. Confident that his master would avert serious penalties he took his imprisonment calmly, was treated with every consideration, and regained his liberty when d'Aiguillon lost his post on the accession of Louis XVI. The whole episode illustrates the weakness of a monarch who lacked the courage to avow and defend his agents.

D'Aiguillon had used his discovery of the secret activities of Dumouriez to strike at Broglie, who was exiled to his estates. The faithful servant wrote to remonstrate, and his wife journeyed to Versailles where she vainly implored the King to investigate the charges. On the death of his old master he protested against his exclusion from the Court and forwarded evidence that he had merely obeyed the royal commands. Louis XVI ordered the new Foreign Minister Vergennes to examine the documents and to interview the plaintiff. A published letter from the new ruler recognised his innocence and ordered him to destroy the secret correspondence, but, yielding to his protest, he ordered it to be transferred for safe keeping to the Foreign Office.

On the death of Louis XV D'Éon confided to Broglie his opinion of their old master.

He was endowed with great penetration, great judgment and a profound knowledge of men and things. All he lacked was strength of character to control his Ministers and Ambassadors as befitted a King. In the midst of his own Court he possessed less power than a prison official. With incredible weakness he permitted his disloyal servants to triumph over the faithful, and he always did more for

his open enemies than for his true friends. You should inform the
young King that you were the secret Minister of Louis XV and I
the Assistant Minister under his orders and yours.

Though his pension was continued, D'Éon was never satisfied
with the rewards of his services. The curious story of double-
dealing confirms the verdict of the Duc de Broglie that his ancestor
deserved a better master.

II

MME DU BARRY

Since the death of Mme de Pompadour in 1764 Louis XV lacked a friend in whose company he could find happiness and peace. He felt no affection for his Ministers or the members of his Household. For a brief space Mme d'Esparbès seemed a possibility, but her candidature was frowned on by Choiseul, still at the height of his power, and her charms were unequal to her claims. Other women were available in plenty, but he had always craved for something more than physical delights. Would he ever again find someone who could combine the *rôles* of mistress and familiar friend? Looking round the Court he discerned no one with the requisite qualifications. Why then should he not once again explore beyond the walls of his gilded cage? The news of Mme de Pompadour's charms and accomplishments had reached him from the bourgeois world of Paris, and sharp eyes —particularly those of Richelieu, First Gentleman of the Bedchamber—were on the lookout for a successor. A second Pompadour could scarcely be expected, for her gifts were unique; but a combination of youth, beauty, and vivacity might outweigh disabilities of education and lowly birth. That at last, at the age of fifty-nine, the *blasé* ruler found what he needed—comradeship and *joie de vivre*—was a landmark in the history of France. If the two middle decades of his life may be labelled the reign of the Pompadour, the last quinquennium carried the bright standard of his Nell Gwynn, Mme du Barry.

The parish register of Vaucouleurs, a little town in Champagne, records that *Jeanne, fille naturelle d'Anne Bécu*, was born on August 19, 1743, and baptised on the same day. At her father's identity we cannot even guess. Her mother, daughter of a cook and herself a dressmaker, soon gave birth to a second child, also of unknown paternity, and migrated to Paris in the hope of earning a higher wage. In the capital she found not only a situation but a husband, and her daughter was educated at a convent at the expense of a rich friend. Returning home at the age of fifteen the beautiful girl was apprenticed to a fashionable hairdresser who fell violently in love with her. Forced to leave owing to a quarrel between the respective mothers, she became *lectrice* to a wealthy widow living near Paris, whose two inflammable sons competed for her favours; and once again the peace of a household necessitated the dismissal of the charmer. Her third situation was in a fashionable showroom where at the age of eighteen temptations surged over her like a flood. Among the dissolute throng which frequented the establishment was Comte Jean du Barry, a successful army contractor whose flagrant debaucheries earned him the nickname of *le Roué*, a title reminiscent of the orgies of the Regency. Jeanne Bécu was added to his conquests, and the dressmaker's daughter sailed into society as the Comtesse du Barry, a title to which she possessed no claim since the neglected wife of the *Roué* was alive. In his spacious mansion she met a crowd of aristocrats, for lavish entertainment could always fill a salon. Despite her plebeian origin and scanty education she took polish and looked the great world full in the face, unembarrassed and good-humoured, vivacious and radiant. Though she had always aspired to better herself there was little of the calculating schemer about her, and indeed there was no need to scheme. Nature's gifts, her face and personality, spoke for themselves. Her charm lay in her lack of pose, her childlike gaiety, her frank enjoyment of Vanity Fair. Amoral rather than immoral, she accepted the advances of her admirers and savoured every intoxicating hour as it flashed past. Who could set bounds to the fortunes of this woman so obviously destined to please?

When and where the King saw her for the first time we do not know, but it seems likely that contact was established soon after the death of the Queen in 1768 by the *Roué* himself with the aid of the valet Lebel and perhaps of Richelieu as well. The latter, who knew her, expected merely a nine days' wonder, convinced that when the King learned that the enchantress was an obscure illegitimate and that the so-called Comtesse du Barry was a mistress, not a wife, the scales would fall from his eyes. But he had never cared about trifles when they interfered with his pleasure, and now he had ceased to care at all. When Richelieu inquired what he found so alluring in his latest flame, he replied that she made him forget his sixty years. To the jaded ruler the dazzling creature seemed like a breath of spring after a long winter of loneliness and depression. Seeing her in chapel Horace Walpole described her as pretty but not striking, adding that he would never have inquired who she was. Unlike the Pompadour, who looked attractive in repose, the face of her successor needed lighting up.

No one was happier at the turn of events than the Comte du Barry, whose earlier attempts to secure a diplomatic post had been repelled by Choiseul and who now felt his feet on the ladder. That his pretty mistress must leave him was a trifle, for her place was easy to fill. The usual condition that a potential Favourite must be a married woman was met by a nominal marriage to his brother, the Chevalier Guillaume du Barry, a retired naval officer living in the depths of the country. A further service was rendered when the *Roué* furnished his ex-mistress with suitable clothes and jewels, carriages and lackeys, to build her up into a *grande dame*. Ambitious courtiers of both sexes climbed on to the band-wagon, including the cynical Richelieu who soon grasped that she had come to stay. Her *clientèle* was widened by the adherence of Choiseul's enemies who, after a decade of unavailing opposition, saw their chance at last. Her triumph was the talk of the town, and the *Chansonniers* were soon hard at work.

> *Quelle merveille!*
> *Une fille de rien.*
> *Une fille de rien,*
> *Quelle merveille!*
> *Donne du Roi de l'amour,*
> *Est à la Cour!*

Elle est gentille,
Elle a les yeux fripons.
Elle a les yeux fripons,
Elle est gentille.
Elle excite avec art

Un vieux faillard.
Le Roi s'écrie:
L'Ange, le beau talent!
L'Ange, le beau talent!
Viens sur mon trône,
Je veux te couronner,
Je veux te couronner.

The King cared little what his people said about him, and Mme du Barry, unlike the Pompadour, was too much a child of nature to trouble about satire, envy, and abuse. She lived for the moment and every day she felt the ground firmer under her feet. 'The lady lives in a residence near that of the late Comtesse de Pompadour,' reported the Austrian Ambassador to Maria Theresa. 'Her liveries are magnificent, and on Sundays and fêtes she is seen at the Royal Mass in a chapel reserved for her.' The King had once again found the intimacy, the relaxation, the stimulus which the de Nesle sisters and the Pompadour had once supplied and which his furtive visits to the *Parc aux Cerfs* could not provide. The older he became the more he longed to be rejuvenated by the magic of beauty and youth. Such was the fascination that the project of reviving the institution of *maîtresse en titre* floated into his mind. That she coveted the post was natural enough, but even the autocrat could not elevate his lady-love by a stroke of the pen, for tradition required a vital condition to be fulfilled. Some great lady had to be induced to present her at Court by the promise of substantial rewards. After the terms demanded by a Marquise and a Baronne had been rejected as too high, the Comtesse de Béarn volunteered for the ceremony if her debts were paid. When the date had been fixed for January 25, 1769, she lost her nerve, for the frowns of Mesdames were unconcealed. Alleging that she had sprained her ankle, she absented herself from Court and the ritual had to be postponed. A few days later the King was injured in the hunting field and was nursed by his

MADAME DU BARRY
from a painting by F. H. Drouais
(*Musée d'Agen*)

daughters who kept the enchantress at bay. Trusting in the favour of the King the Favourite met the weeks of waiting with a light heart, and her confidence was rewarded when the ceremony was fixed for April 22nd.

The presentation of Mme du Barry ranks among the most colourful episodes in the history of the French Court. While the Pompadour, with her more sensitive feelings, had found her début an ordeal, the du Barry took it in her stride. That the injured Queen had gone to her rest diminished the strain, and at fifteen the new Dauphin was too young to count. At the last moment it seemed as if the cup might again be dashed from her lips, for the elaborate *coiffure* took longer than expected and the King, annoyed by her unpunctuality, spoke of calling off the ceremony. A moment later her arrival was announced to the crowd in the Galerie des Glaces by Richelieu in his capacity as First Gentleman of the Bedchamber. At the sight of his mistress, radiant in a white gown and blazing with diamonds, the King's resentment melted away. She went through her paces without a trace of embarrassment, saluted Mesdames and the Dauphin, and retired in a blaze of glory. Whatever might be the stain of her birth, friends and foes agreed that such a lovely mistress had never been seen at Versailles. Once again France possessed the expensive luxury of an uncrowned Queen and her ruler a cheerful comrade for his old age. Apartments were allotted to her in all the royal palaces, the Château de Louveciennes near Marly became her property, and she found herself a European celebrity. Except for Choiseul, Mme de Gramont, and the Royal Family, the Court was at her feet, and Voltaire saluted her in sparkling verse. Two portraits of her were painted by Drouais, one as Flora, the other as a huntress in the man's attire she wore when she joined the royal hunt. Horace Walpole saw her again on September 17th and was struck by the absence of powder and rouge. Though she shared the prevailing passion for jewels and gambling, she learned to enjoy the *objets d'art* by which she was surrounded and to appreciate Shakespeare. In view of her origin it is astonishing how quickly she adapted herself to the minimum social requirements of the Court.

The first major result of her installation was the fall of the Minister who had held the reins of government firmly in his

Q

hands for nearly twelve years. Unlike Richelieu, who trimmed his
sails to every passing breeze, Choiseul realised too late that *la fille*,
la coquine, as he called her, was more than a butterfly and had
come to stay. His peril was increased by the tactless hostility of
his masculine sister, the Duchesse de Gramont, who was believed
to have aspired to the position. Even the Minister's gentle wife
found it difficult to conceal her feelings. 'The disdainful demean-
our and unguarded language of the Duchesse de Gramont and
and her intimate friend the Princesse de Beauvau,' reported the
Austrian Ambassador to Maria Theresa, 'and the weakness of
the Duc de Choiseul in following their lead, the open war he is
waging against the Favourite and his public jests at her expense
have long turned the King's heart against his Minister.' The new
Favourite, like the King, wished for nothing better than to live
and let live, to be on good terms with everyone, high and low.
She was much less inclined to vindictiveness than the Pompadour
who struck without mercy when she met an obstacle in her path.
She sent a message to Choiseul that if he wished for a *rapprochement* she would meet him half-way. Left to themselves they
might have negotiated a *détente*, but the Favourite had unwittingly
become the spear-head of the attack on the Minister by colleagues
who were jealous of his power.

The King's dislike for changes in his entourage was notorious,
and his liking for Choiseul remained intact. Distressed by the
friction between the Minister and the Favourite, and possessing
no other potential pilot of equal ability and experience, he strove
to avert a break. 'Tell your sister to be more careful or I shall
exile her,' he exclaimed to Choiseul, but the warning was in vain.
There was talk of the Duc d'Aiguillon, the nephew of Richelieu,
whom Choiseul regarded as his most serious rival; but when he
mentioned his apprehensions to the King he received a reassuring
reply.

How can you imagine that d'Aiguillon could replace you? What
good could he do, hated as he is? You manage my affairs well and
I am pleased with you. But beware of your *entourage* and of busy-
bodies. You know Mme du Barry. *Elle est très jolie, j'en suis content,
cela doit suffire.* She feels no hatred for you; is aware of your ability,
and wishes you no harm. The outburst against her has been
terrible and largely undeserved. Am I desired to take a girl of

birth? If the Archduchess was to my taste I would marry her with
great pleasure, but I should like to see and know her first. The fair
sex will always trouble me, but you will never see me with a Mme
de Maintenon.

The letter was followed by an interview between Choiseul and
Mme du Barry at Fontainebleau, but by this time the rift was too
deep. She was a good-natured woman, testifies the Duc de Croy,
and wished no harm to anyone except Choiseul, whom she hated.
'I was astonished that with his amiable nature he did not win her
over, but he almost seemed to challenge her authority.' Only
when she realised that he could not be tamed did she press the
King for his dismissal, and she was never to make such a request
again. The Minister's enemies tried to undermine his position
by charges that he was friendly to the rebellious *Parlements* and
that his devotion to the *Pacte de Famille* might drag France into
an Anglo-Spanish dispute about the Falkland Islands; but it was
the tears of the Favourite more than any political issue which
turned the scale. 'The lady no longer hides her hatred,' reported
Mme du Deffand to Horace Walpole; and the interview was a
tactical error. 'He is subjected to pin-pricks, for instance, exclusion from the little suppers in the private apartments, and
when they are partners at whist she makes faces and shrugs
her shoulders.' Without the moral support of his strong-
willed sister he might have resigned without waiting to be
dismissed.

The strongest card in the Minister's hand was the unstinted
confidence he enjoyed in Vienna and Madrid. While he was at
the helm the Empress and Kaunitz knew that the Austrian
alliance would remain intact and the King of Spain was assured
that the *Pacte de Famille* was in safe hands. So long as the colonial
rivalry with England lasted—and there was no prospect of its
termination—the maintenance of the friendship of Austria and
Spain was an axiom of French policy. No one understood this
vital consideration better than the King, and it was doubtless
this factor more than any other which prolonged Choiseul's
ministerial career by many months. Though the Seven Years
War had proved a disaster for France there was no thought of a
new orientation, for no alternative was in sight. Indeed, in view
of the emergence of Prussia as a Great Power and the apparent

invincibility of England, prudence dictated a strengthening, not a weakening, of the Hapsburg alliance.

What could be more natural than to cement the treaty by ties of blood? On the death of the Queen in 1768 Louis XV had coquetted with the idea of marrying one of the elder daughters of Maria Theresa, but such an unnatural union had only to be considered to be dismissed. For a moment the Finance Minister, Abbé Terray, dreamed of securing the Pope's assent to a dissolution of the Favourite's marriage on the ground of non-consummation, to be followed by her marriage to the King. But why should not a much more suitable match be arranged on a lower level between Marie Antoinette, youngest daughter of the Empress, and the eldest grandson of Louis XV, who was only one year her senior? The plan originated soon after the end of the Seven Years War, and discussions took place between Choiseul and the Austrian Ambassador. On her twelfth birthday a symbolic dolphin (dauphin) was presented by the French Ambassador, and on her thirteenth the Empress bade her Ambassador in Paris select a French priest to train the destined bride. 'I am impatient to know who will be chosen as the confessor of my daughter. I should also like a *friseur*, but I leave everything to Choiseul.' The choice—and there could not have been a better one—fell on the Abbé de Vermond who did his best for the warm-hearted but indolent girl who hated the sight of books. An artist was dispatched from Paris to paint her portrait, followed by a coiffeur. The marriage contract, signed on April 4, 1770, fixed her allowance and promised jewels worth 100,000 crowns. The Papal Nuncio officiated at the marriage by proxy, the Dauphin being represented by a brother of the bride. 'May your Majesty be good enough to guide her,' wrote the Empress to the King. 'She is full of good will but at her age I beg indulgence for any mistake. I commend her as the most tender pledge of the happy union between our states and dynasties.' As the Archduchess drove away from the Hofburg her mother whispered: 'Be so good to the French that they can say I have sent them an angel.' They knew they would never meet again.

The Empress furnished her daughter with a budget of counsels and commands. 'You will find a tender father who, if you desire it, will also be your friend. Love him, obey him, try to anticipate his thoughts as much as you can. It is this father, this friend, who is my whole consolation in my grief, in the hope that you will follow my advice to await his directions in everything. Of the Dauphin I say nothing. The woman is subject to her husband in everything, and she should have no other occupation than to please him and do his will. The only true happiness on earth is a happy marriage. Everything depends on the woman.' Not a word was said about the Favourite.

The bride of fourteen was welcomed at Compiègne by the King, his three daughters, his three grandsons, and Choiseul, and delighted everybody except her timid and tongue-tied *fiancé*. 'The Dauphine arrived four hours ago,' reported the King to his grandson the Duke of Parma. 'I am pleased with her, and so is my grandson. She is charming, but quite a child. The whole of her household is enraptured.' He described her as 'ma Duchesse de Bourgogne,' alluding to his mother, the Rose of Savoy. Two days later the Court drove away, halting for a brief visit to Mme Louise in her nunnery at St. Denis. The night was passed at La Muette, a small hunting lodge in the Bois de Boulogne, and in the evening the Dauphine had her first view of the Favourite of whom she had never heard. Mme du Barry had never appeared at formal gatherings, but on this occasion, to the general surprise, she sat beside the King. It was inconceivable, commented the Austrian Ambassador in his bulletin for the Empress, that he should have chosen this moment for an honour so long withheld. When the bride innocently inquired what was the function of that pretty woman, it was explained that she was there to amuse the King. She was soon to learn the truth from Mesdames. Next day the court drove on to Versailles, and on the following morning the marriage was celebrated by the Archbishop of Rheims.

'The King is most kind and I love him dearly,' reported Marie Antoinette in her first letter to the Empress, 'but his weakness for Mme du Barry—the most stupid and impertinent creature imaginable—is pitiful. She has joined in our play every evening at Marly. Twice she sat next to me but she did not speak to me, and I did not converse with her though I spoke to her when it was unavoidable. As regards my dear husband he has greatly improved. He is most friendly to me and even begins to show me confidence.' She confessed that her mother's letters brought tears to her eyes, 'quoique je suis très bien ici.' The Austrian Ambassador reported that she was adored by her entourage and the public. 'There is only one opinion about the Dauphine,' wrote Mme du Deffand to Horace Walpole: 'elle grandit, elle embellit, elle est charmante.' 'The Dauphine is always charming and livelier than ever,' reported the King to his grandson in Parma in 1771. The only shadow in the picture was the frigidity of her husband, of whom the King contemptuously remarked: 'Il n'est pas un homme comme les autres.'

While the anxious Empress was receiving cheerful letters from her daughter and reassuring bulletins from her Ambassador a bomb exploded under her feet. 'I command my cousin the Duc de Choiseul,' wrote the King on December 24, 1770, 'to place his resignation as Minister of State and of the Post Office in the hands of the Duc de la Vrillière, and to retire to Chanteloup to await my further commands.' His cousin the Duc de Choiseul-Praslin, Secretary of the Navy, received his *congé* on the same day. 'The Duc de Choiseul will only see his family and those whom I permit to go,' wrote the King to the Duc de la Vrillière, and he was to leave Paris within twenty-four hours. On receiving the letter of dismissal at Versailles the fallen Minister drove to Paris and broke the news to his wife. To the Duchess it came as a relief, but beneath the smiling serenity of Choiseul burned a fierce resentment. Observers who were closest to events were the least surprised. Choiseul, commented the Austrian Ambassador to the Empress, had dug his own grave by his indiscretions. 'His continuance in office much longer would have surprised me much more than his fall. Let us hope his successor will not be an even greater muddler.' The Empress took the news with less complacency, and the Dauphine shared her mother's regret at the disgrace of the stoutest champion of the alliance. Louis XV thought it necessary to assure the King of Spain that French policy would undergo no change. It was a revolution, declared Horace Walpole, who followed events in France more closely than any other Englishman. 'Choiseul has lost his power ridiculously,' he wrote to his old friend Sir Horace Mann, 'by braving a *fille de joie* to humour two women—his sister and his wife.' The reaction of the capital was shown by the crowd of carriages which blocked

the street in which Choiseul lived. His cheerful temperament and
lavish hospitality had won him a host of friends, and a demonstration in his favour served the double purpose of expressing
disapproval of the Favourite and the King. Still more striking
proof of his popularity was the flood of visitors to his country
home in Touraine. To go to Chanteloup, declared Mme du
Deffand, was to go to Court. 'He is not only the best of men but
the greatest of the century,' she added; 'he will bulk much larger
in history than he does today.' The ostentatious homage to a
fallen statesman was correctly interpreted by the King no less
than by his subjects as an indication of the declining prestige of
the Crown. Such a manifestation would have been unthinkable
in the reign of Louis XIV. His successor was at once too indolent
to rule and too easy-going to punish.

Under the shock of indignation Choiseul drafted a stinging
letter which on second thoughts he decided not to send.

Sire, I was appointed Foreign Minister by Your Majesty eleven
years ago without desiring or expecting it, and I obeyed with
reluctance. Since the peace Your Majesty has known how little I
have clung to office and the favour it implies. I should feel grateful
to Your Majesty for relieving me but for the fact that I have had
the misfortune to forfeit the favour of Your Majesty. I was warned
of intrigues, for there was no concealment of their plans. But I was
deceived by your good opinion of my services, and I could not
believe that Your Majesty would conceal my disgrace till the last
moment. It is quite simple that Your Majesty considers me unworthy of his confidence and unfitted for my posts. I desire for
the glory of Your Majesty and the good of the state that my successors will serve Your Majesty as well as myself. I venture to say
that I have not deserved the veto on my movements. I do not ask
for kindness to myself. But Your Majesty is just, and I beg for
my freedom of movement as the last favour I shall ever ask.

Choiseul settled down to the life of a wealthy nobleman in his
sumptuous country home. To Bernis, now French Ambassador
in Rome, who wrote to condole, he replied that he had foreseen
it for some time and had never felt happier. Yet the loss of his
highly paid offices was a heavy blow to a self-indulgent man who
had never attempted to live within his income, and even the
ample fortune of his wife failed to cover his expenditure. He

built, hunted, gambled, and filled the house with dozens of guests at a time. He had his failings, but he knew how to make and keep friends. Though d'Aiguillon, his successor at the Foreign Office, pressed his master to punish his visitors, the King replied that if he were younger he would feel annoyed, but at his age he only wanted peace. The first request for permission brought the reply that he neither forbade nor allowed visits, a formula correctly interpreted as a tacit assent. Never again was such homage to be paid to a fallen demigod till Bismarck withdrew to Friedrichruh. Perhaps some of his visitors may have speculated on his possible return to office on the accession of the Dauphin, but selfish considerations are insufficient to explain the lure of Chanteloup.

Choiseul attributed his dismissal less to the Favourite than to Richelieu and the King. Ever since the death of the Pompadour the First Gentleman of the Bedchamber had been searching for another royal mistress who, like the Duchesse de Châteauroux, would owe her position in large measure to his support. Among the early occupations of the statesman's enforced leisure was the composition of his Memoirs in which he paid off old scores.

However low my opinion of the King, I think he would never have decided on the presentation of Mme du Barry unless he had been encouraged by Richelieu, and I believe she would never have aspired to presentation without his advice. He would have been able to pass for an old debauchee still amiable in society if he had been wise enough to content himself with the only *rôle* which suited him. His intelligence, apart from certain graces, is very mediocre. He indulged in fantastic ambitions, convinced that all means were good. His embassy in Vienna was a failure, but he thought himself a great politician. He had courage, commanded armies, and thinks he was a great General. He thought himself fitted for administration. He was brought up at Court, secured a post by intrigue, and he thought intrigue could lead to the highest place. Unaware of the very narrow limits of his abilities he considered himself equal to everything, and when he missed his goal, he always attributed it to the jealousy of Ministers. He thought me jealous of him, but I was not. I think of him only as a figure of fun in all his posts. He is the hero of the degradation to which France owes the indecent elevation and extraordinary capacity for mischief of the woman du Barry. The unfortunate character of the

King would have been unable to make the kingdom groan so long
if he had not been sustained and guided by vice personified in
M. de Richelieu.

What Choiseul thought of the ungrateful monarch we have seen
in an earlier chapter. For Mme du Barry he made allowances,
recognising that such a *fille de rien* was bound to fight for her
own hand. When his request to the King to continue some of
the ample revenues he had enjoyed in his simultaneous tenure of
various posts was rejected, he appealed to her to plead his cause,
and the good-natured creature managed to save something from
the wreck. Many years later, when she too had received her
congé, she was visited by the man whose fall she had helped to
engineer. She greeted him with the words: 'It is good of you
not to have retained bitter feelings for me.' 'I never had any,'
replied Choiseul. His bitterness was reserved for the King.

The vacuum left by the fall of Choiseul was filled by his two
chief enemies at Court. The Foreign Office was assigned to the
Duc d'Aiguillon who had long coveted the post though his
qualifications for high office were few. Of very different calibre
was Maupeou, an elderly lawyer who had been First President of
the *Parlement* of Paris and was appointed Chancellor in 1768.
His first task was to take up the long-standing challenge to the
Absolute Monarchy represented by the claims of the *Parlements*.
In his Memoirs Choiseul attributes the attack solely to the selfish
desire to fortify the royal power, but there was also a case for
drastic reform. The whole system of justice was riddled with
hoary abuses, among them the purchase of posts, presents to
judges, and lack of a modernised jurisprudence. Two years
before Maupeou's appointment Louis XV had restated the claim
to autocracy in resonant phrases. 'It is in my person that sovereign
power resides; the Courts derive their power from myself alone;
to me alone belongs the legislative power. If the *Parlements* continue the scandalous spectacle of a challenge to my sovereign
power, I shall feel compelled to employ the authority received
from God in order to preserve my peoples from the tragic consequences of such enterprises.' The warning, published in the
Gazette de France, was addressed to all the *Parlements* of France.
Never had there been so vigorous an assertion of rights, but
never had the voice of the monarch produced so little effect,

for no one believed that the feeble ruler would match words with deeds. The *Parlements* continued their remonstrances, and in 1767 the *Parlement* of Paris decreed the expulsion of the Jesuits despite the secret disapproval of the King. If the royal authority was to be energetically reasserted it would have to be achieved, not by the ruler, but by a Minister backed by the royal authority and resolved to overcome all opposition. Maupeou summoned Voltaire to his aid, for, though no lover of nerveless absolutism, he preferred it to the selfish pretensions of reactionary magistrates. His last historical work *Histoire du Parlement de Paris*, published pseudonymously at Amsterdam in 1769, listed its misdoings through the centuries from the brutal suppression of the Knights Templars to the inglorious reign of Louis XV.

Maupeou's chance came in 1770 when the *Parlement* of Rennes, in union with the Estates of Brittany, censured the Duc d'Aiguillon, Governor of the Province, for continuing war taxes in time of peace. Though the King held his shield over his representative, the *Parlement* declared that he could not perform his duties till he was formally acquitted. Incensed by opposition, the King removed the registers of the *Parlement*, whereupon the magistrates declined to sit. The case was transferred to the *Parlement* of Paris, whose members approved the action of their colleagues. Though a *lit de justice*—the *ultima ratio* of the royal prerogative—annulled the decree, the *Parlement* of Paris condemned d'Aiguillon and was supported by all the *Parlements* of France. The King had always disliked the magistrates, and Choiseul's supposed sympathy with their claims was one of the excuses for his disgrace. The Chancellor's campaign against the only institutions which challenged his autocracy commanded his entire approval. On the night of January 21, 1771, all the magistrates were arrested and exiled to different parts of France. Having cleared the site, Maupeou proceeded to construct a new edifice. A *lit de justice* at Versailles imposed three edicts, the first suppressing the *Cour des Aides*, the second forbidding the sale of offices and replacing the hereditary magistrates by royal nominees, the third creating a new *Parlement* which, in the words of the King, would provide quicker and purer justice. A Supreme Tribunal was established in Paris with six *Conseils Supérieurs* in the provinces, and the members of the Provincial *Parlements* were also dismissed. The

Chancellor's triumph was brief, for the prestige of the new magistrates was irretrievably damaged when the wife of one of their number was charged with corruption and her husband was forced to resign by Beaumarchais, the most brilliant pamphleteer in France after Voltaire. Though Goezman was the only blemished sheep in the flock, the incident compromised his colleagues and on the death of Louis XV, Maupeou's work was undone. The Chancellor was dismissed, the old magistrates were recalled, and the unreformed system lingered on till the Revolution. The whole drama illustrates the inability of the Government to loosen the grip of vested interests on the rare occasions when it tried.

Having eliminated the Choiseul family, Mme du Barry was confronted with a more formidable foe in the Dauphine who at any moment might become Queen. The little Archduchess had been sent to France to keep the Austrian alliance in repair, a task which necessitated the steady favour of the King. This, in turn, demanded tolerable relations with the Favourite, who was detested at Vienna on the double ground of her origin and her enmity to Choiseul. The King preferred the vivacious Dauphine to his daughters, whose loathing for the Favourite was unconcealed; but as she grew to maturity it became increasingly difficult for him to tolerate the boycott of the only woman he loved. Though the Empress shared her daughter's disgust at the infatuation of the King, she was better able to assess the importance of the Dauphine's political *rôle*. Her intimacy with Mesdames— and there was nobody else with whom she could be intimate —was an unspoken challenge to the *maîtresse en titre*. Louis XV, the least vindictive of men, let things slide for the first year after the marriage of his grandson and then decided to act. Mme de Noailles, Superintendent of her Household, was informed that the Dauphine talked too freely and that such conduct might produce undesirable results in the Royal Family. On receiving the message Marie Antoinette consulted her aunts and her spiritual adviser Abbé de Vermond, who informed the Ambassador, who, as in duty bound, informed the Empress. Since issues of *haute politique* were at stake, Kaunitz dispatched a friendly warning.

> To fail in consideration for someone enjoying the favour of the King is to fail in consideration for him, and offensive words would be even worse. Such persons should be regarded simply as objects

of the confidence and favour of the sovereign, without inquiring whether rightly or wrongly. Prudence indicates the same tactics, for they can make mischief. I cannot believe that the Dauphine, gentle and sensible as she is, has not grasped all this, so I feel she has been blamed to excess. Since, however, the King believes it, I think she should see him at once and tell him she will do his bidding.

When the letter was read to the Dauphine she replied that an interview was needless, for she would be so careful that no further complaint could arise. This was not enough for the King, and the tension increased; for though she set a guard on her tongue her conduct was more eloquent than any words. She continued to meet the Favourite at cards, at the royal table and at balls, but not a glance indicated that she was aware of her existence. Since the timid King dreaded an interview as much as the offender herself, he summoned the Austrian Ambassador who was received in the apartments of the Favourite. Mme du Barry explained—no doubt with truth—that she felt no hostility to the Dauphine. When the King entered he remarked: 'Hitherto you have been the Ambassador of the Empress, but now I beg you to be mine for a time.' The Dauphine, he continued, was charming, but she was young, impulsive, and married to a man incapable of guiding her steps. She listened to evil counsels and mixed in all sorts of intrigues. No names were mentioned, but the ruler had his daughters in mind. The Ambassador, equally attached to the Empress and her daughter, represented to the Dauphine that the alliance was at stake and that she must make the sacrifice. A day or two later, the scene having been prepared by the Ambassador, she was about to speak to the Favourite for the first time when Mme Adelaide broke in with the words: 'It is time for us to go and await the King in the apartments of our sister Victoire.' Caught off her guard her nerve failed, and she subsequently apologised to the Ambassador, alleging her fear of displeasing her aunt. Mercy assured the Empress that his conversations with the Favourite had convinced him that, though mindless and frivolous, she was not malicious, and that a single word from the Dauphine would remove many difficulties. Her appearance and manners were reasonably refined, and, unlike the Pompadour, she had no political ambitions.

Louis XV was as hurt as the Favourite at the public snub she had received. 'Well, M. de Mercy,' he remarked to the Ambassador, 'your counsels have not borne fruit, and I must come to your aid.' But the Dauphine had a will of her own, and months passed before her surrender. The incident had brought a sharp rebuke from Vienna, for the Empress never spared the rod.

> The aunts have not won the respect of their family or the public, and you choose to follow their lead. This fear and embarrassment about speaking to the King, the best of fathers, and of speaking to persons to whom you are advised to speak! This fear of even saying *bon jour*! Even a word about clothes, about some trifle, causes you to make a wry face. You have allowed yourself to be enslaved to such an extent that your reason and sense of duty are paralysed. I cannot keep silence after Mercy's conversation with you about the King's wishes and your duty. You failed him, and what good reason can you allege? None. You must regard the du Barry merely as a lady admitted to the society of the King. As his first subject you owe him obedience—you also owe an example to the courtiers that the will of your master should prevail. No one would suggest familiarity, but some commonplace word, some little attention, not for the lady but for your grandfather, your master, your benefactor. And you fail him in such a marked manner at the first opportunity of obliging him and displaying your attachment which will not so soon recur! You made such a good start. Follow Mercy's advice.

The Dauphine endeavoured to diminish her mother's anxieties.

> I have several reasons for believing that the King does not really wish me to speak to the du Barry, apart from the fact that he has never mentioned it to me. He is friendlier than ever since he learned I had declined. If you were here you would realise that this woman and her clique would not be content with a word and would always press for more. I am in no need of being led by anyone in matters of honour. I do not say I never will, but I cannot agree to do so at a fixed time in order that she may announce it in advance and put a feather in her cap.

Far more effective than the admonitions of the Empress was the kindness of the King. One day, reported the Ambassador, he had lunched with the Dauphine, had made a long stay and seemed in excellent spirits. She knew in her heart that she would have to yield, but not for a year and a half after her arrival in France

could she be induced to raise the blockade. Learning that the
du Barry would join the ladies of the Court in paying their respects
to the Royal Family on New Year's Day, 1772, the Ambassador
hurried to the Dauphine. 'I tried every imaginable means of
persuading her not to snub the Favourite,' he reported to the
Empress, 'and it was only with great difficulty that I secured her
promise. The main thing was that Mesdames were not consulted.'

Next day, when the Favourite appeared with two other ladies,
the Dauphine looked at her and remarked: 'Il y a bien du monde
aujourd'hui à Versailles.' The deed was done, but it had been
a severe ordeal. 'I followed your advice,' she remarked to the
Ambassador; 'here is the Dauphin to bear witness.' The shy
young man whose advice, so far as we know, had never been
sought, smiled but said nothing. 'I have spoken once,' she continued, 'but there I will stop, and that woman will not hear my
voice again.' Her vow was not to be taken literally, for they
were often thrown together, but never again was a remark
addressed directly and solely to the Favourite. Her banal observation produced the desired result. The Ambassador expressed
his congratulations and advised the Empress to follow suit. The
same evening the King embraced her, while the frowning aunts
reproached her so sharply that she almost regretted her act. The
Empress, as usual, found it easier to blame than to praise.

> Your agitation after those few words and your saying it cannot
> happen again alarm me. Who can give you better advice or better
> deserve your confidence than my Minister who knows everything
> about France? His sole object is your welfare. I repeat, my dear
> daughter, if you love me, follow his advice without hesitation in
> everything. If he wishes you to repeat your attentions to the lady
> or to the Comte and Comtesse de Provence, remember that he knows
> best how to avoid trouble.

During 1772 Mercy reported the good news that the Dauphine
was shaking off the yoke of Mesdames. 'She is on terms of easy
friendship with them,' he reported in February, 'but she reflects
and decides for herself. No one leads her.' In June he added
that the King was very fond of her. The Empress was never
satisfied, and on the last day of 1772 she asked for more. 'I am
hoping to hear the result of my advice about your attitude to the

Favourite. You must not be content with abstaining from attacks.
You must treat her with courtesy and speak to her as to any other
lady received at Court. This you owe to the King and to myself;
you owe no account of your actions to anyone else.' Her mother's
scolding letters were a trial to the Dauphine, who explained that
the problem of the Favourite was complicated by the Dauphin's
growing detestation of her; but she took the counsels of her
mother to heart, and now it was her turn to urge her husband to
treat the Favourite with less disdain. He followed her advice,
and at the customary reception on New Year's Day, 1773, he
surprised the courtiers by addressing the lady in a friendly way.
On the same occasion the Dauphine spoke no word either to the
Favourite or to the two ladies who accompanied her. When the
Ambassador remonstrated, she replied that she had treated all
three alike and had therefore given no cause of complaint. The
Favourite was distressed, but when Mercy explained that the
Dauphin's *beau geste* was due to his wife she sent her a message
of gratitude. Equally incapable of hatred and of deep feeling,
she asked nothing more than to be left in undisputed command
of the King's heart.

The closing years of Louis XV were perhaps the happiest of
his life. The disasters of the Seven Years War were becoming a
dim memory, and no one foresaw that the revolt of the British
Colonies would shortly tempt France to strike another blow at
her hereditary enemy. There was no need to worry about the
succession for, though the marriage of the Dauphin as of the
Comte de Provence was still childless, the Comte d'Artois, who
married at the close of 1773, might reasonably be expected to
produce an heir to the throne. The King knew that his popularity had waned, but the rapturous welcome of the Dauphin and
the Dauphine in the capital in 1773 proved that the monarchy,
if not the monarch, retained its hold. The heir was respected for
his blameless life by all whose respect he cared to possess, and
his drab personality was in some measure redeemed by the
sparkle of his wife. The Favourite's enemies had been expelled,
and no rival was in sight. Mme Adelaide and her sisters had
never meant much to their father, and their hostility to the lady
of his choice destroyed what remained of his affection. 'The
King is ageing,' reported the Austrian Ambassador to the

Empress. 'He finds himself isolated, helpless, without comfort in his children, and there is neither affection nor fidelity in his motley entourage.' For the last five years of his life he depended for his happiness on the Favourite alone, whose unfailing spirits appealed to him scarcely less than her physical charms. That they delighted in each other's company at least as much as the King and the Pompadour there is no reason to doubt.

Early in 1774 she was informed by Morande, a French adventurer who had fled to London, that he was about to publish three thousand copies of a book entitled *Mémoires et Secrets d'une Femme publique* for export to Holland and Germany, whence they would be smuggled into France; but he would be prepared to desist if it were made worth his while. She informed the King who dispatched police agents to kidnap the blackmailer, but Morande had received a warning and could not be found. The worried monarch turned to Beaumarchais who preferred the velvet glove to the iron hand. In return for 20,000 francs cash down and the promise of an annuity of 4,000 francs, the blackmailer handed over the manuscript and the three thousand printed copies to the King's agent, and the incriminating compilation went up in smoke.

Only an exceptionally strong constitution could have stood up to the strain of decades of debauchery, but in his early sixties Louis XV began to ask himself if the pace was not too hot. Yet he might have reached the age of Louis XIV had not the dread disease assailed him which had swept his parents into the grave. On New Year's Day, 1774, the Favourite held her usual crowded reception. The first danger-signal came from the *Almanach de Liège*, an annual which catered for credulous readers by forecasting events, with the ominous words: 'In April a great lady who is fortune's favourite will play her last part.' Though she bought up and burned the offending publication, even her buoyant spirit could not eradicate the sinister impression, and she was heard to mutter: 'If only that accursed month were over!' A second danger threatened from the Lenten sermons of an Abbé whose freedom of language astonished the Court. Referring to a recent statement that the average duration of life was increasing, he reminded his hearers of the early death of the King's parents, son, four daughters, daughter-in-law, and four *maîtresses en titre*.

When he ended with the warning: 'Forty days more and Nineveh will be destroyed,' the King turned pale. The Favourite and her friends, reported the Austrian Ambassador to Maria Theresa on February 19, were worried by the tendency of the King to talk of his health and of the terrible account he would one day have to give to the Supreme Being of the way he had spent his life.

On April 27 Louis XV drove out from Trianon to the hunt, but felt too ill to mount and soon returned. Next day, shivering with fever, he was taken in his dressing-gown to Versailles, though the Favourite longed to keep him at a safe distance from the clutches of his family. We can follow the drama from day to day and at times from hour to hour in an eyewitness report by the Duc de la Rochefoucauld Liancourt published in 1846. At first the symptoms were not taken very seriously, for the King was often feverish; but the appearance of spots set all doubts at rest and for a man of sixty-four there seemed little hope. Ignoring medical advice, his daughters remained at the bedside, and the anxious faces of the doctors told the sufferer more than their words. 'You tell me I am not ill and shall soon be all right again,' he grumbled; 'you don't believe a word of it, and you ought to tell me the truth.' His terror and cowardice were beyond description, testifies the Duc de Liancourt, who heartily despised him. The excitement aroused by the serious illness of every autocrat was increased by the knowledge that his death would mean a clean sweep of the Ministers and the eviction of the Favourite. The Court was divided into two camps—those who hoped he would live and those who desired him to die: in both cases the main motive was personal advantage. Everyone believed what he wished to believe, for a man who had given so little love could count on little in return. The sick-room and the ante-chambers were crowded with officials, courtiers, and doctors, who wrangled about the treatment and speculated on coming events. The Dauphin and the Dauphine remained in their apartments owing to the risk of infection. Over fifty inmates of the palace went down with the plague and ten of them died.

When the customary bleedings proved useless the question arose whether the sufferer should receive Extreme Unction. One party argued that the revelation of mortal danger would kill him, the other that to let him die without making his peace with the

R

Church would be a crime. The King himself had no desire to confess till he felt certain that the end was near, for confession involved separation from the only person he loved. Yet the nearer the approach of death the calmer he became. Realising that his life hung by a thread he gently told her on May 3 that she must leave Versailles, gave her his portrait in miniature, and promised that he would always remain her friend. When he asked for her again two hours later the valet told him she was gone. 'Already,' he murmured, and tears rolled down his cheeks. The moment had come at last for the Church to assume control. His Confessor was summoned, heard his confession, and gave absolution. Next day, after receiving Holy Communion, he bade the Grand Almoner, Cardinal de la Roche Aymon, to announce that he repented his offences to his people. Though by this time his face was swollen and almost black and the discomfort was acute, he whispered to Adelaide that he had never felt happier and more at peace. The same evening he received Extreme Unction, kissed a crucifix, and joined in the prayers. Two days later, on May 10, after a fortnight of suffering, he passed away. The next moment the whole palace was in uproar. 'A terrible noise like thunder was heard in the ante-chamber of the new rulers,' records Mme Campan. It was the crowd of courtiers who rushed to salute the rising sun. 'The tumult announced that their hour had come, and the young couple, with tears in their eyes, instinctively fell on their knees, exclaiming, "Mon Dieu, guidez nous, protégez nous, nous régnons trop jeunes."' After a further two days the corpse was transferred to St. Denis along a route where derisory cries took the place of tears.

Louis XV had known that the sands were running out of the hour-glass. The weakest link in the chain was the virtual bankruptcy of the Treasury. 'Your Majesty's finances are in a state of terrifying collapse,' reported the Controller-General in 1769, 'expenditure exceeds revenue by fifty million francs, and every year adds to the National Debt. The most urgent liabilities are about 80 millions. Even worse is the fact that the whole of next year's revenue has already been spent. This situation cannot go on, for the moment is at hand when it will plunge the kingdom into irremediable catastrophe.' The warning, like so many earlier admonitions, was unheeded by the nerveless monarch

with whom the smiles of Mme du Barry counted for more than
the fate of France. To the charge of the Recording Angel that
he had squandered his heritage and let his country down there
is no reply. The word failure is written in big letters across the
whole record of his reign. When a ruler loses the respect of his
subjects and no constitutional remedy is at hand, revolution is
not far away.

12

THE LEGACY OF LOUIS XV

I

THE legacy of Louis XV to his countrymen was an ill-governed, discontented, frustrated France. Viewed from a distance the *ancien régime* appeared as solid as the Bastille, but its walls were crumbling for lack of repairs and the foundations showed signs of giving way. The Absolute Monarchy, the privileged *Noblesse*, the intolerant Church, the close corporation *Parlements*, had all become unpopular, and the army, once the glory of France, was tarnished by the rout of Rossbach. Though there was little thought of republicanism, the *mystique* of monarchy had almost evaporated. 'He goes to Crécy and to Choisy,' wrote a pamphleteer at the close of the reign; 'why does he not go to St. Denis?' Now he had gone, and he had taken dynastic autocracy with him in the funeral cortège. The educated bourgeoisie, which was to supply the leaders of the Revolution, resented the shackles of a caste system which barred its advance towards a position in the State commensurate with its growing numbers, intelligence, and wealth. When the Abbé Sieyès asked in his famous pamphlet in 1789 what the *Tiers État* had been and answered with the monosyllable *Rien*, he was scarcely exaggerating the political and social anomaly. The Revolution occurred because the *ancien régime* failed to make reasonable adjustments in good time, and in the era of Absolute Monarchy it is impossible to acquit the ruler of the major responsibility. No one could say that Louis XV lacked warning, for the air was thick with complaints. Though he cared less and less for appearances as he grew older, in the deeper levels of consciousness he was aware of the general malaise though not of its full volume. He knew that he was no longer loved and realised that he had never deserved the affection of his subjects. 'A complacent egoist and mediocrity, criminal only because he was a King,' is the verdict of Jobez at the close of his six stout volumes on the reign. He left France less suffering and therefore less unhappy than his predecessor but far more degraded in the eyes of the world. He had let his people down. In 1715 there had been hope of recovery, in 1774 there was little or none. 'I am far from believing that we are approaching the century of reason,' wrote Grimm in 1757. 'I almost believe Europe is menaced by some sinister revolution.' 'I see all the states of Europe rushing to their ruin,' echoed Rousseau in 1772; 'all the peoples groan.' The shrill voice of Cassandra was heard in the land. While England, Prussia, Austria, and Russia were advancing from strength to strength, France was going downhill.

The *chansons* circulated in Paris on the death of the old ruler were no harsher than those launched against him during his closing years, for that would have been impossible. Here is a specimen.

> *Sans goût, sans moeurs et sans lumières,*
> *Faible, timide, peu sincère,*
> *Voila, je crois, ton caractère.*

The comments of the two most dazzling performers on the European stage, though more measured in their terms, were scarcely less severe. 'This prince, like so many others,' wrote Voltaire to Frederick the Great, 'was little suited to his post. He was indifferent to everything except trifles of personal concern.' 'Let him rest in peace,' replied the King. 'He exiled you and waged an unjust war against me. One can feel these wrongs, but one must be ready to forgive. A man who lives in dissipation, who never gives a moment to reflection, who believes all his entourage tells him, acts as one might expect.'

Discontent had accumulated during the long War of the Austrian Succession and the almost equally prolonged struggle of the Seven Years War, and in the closing decade of the reign it had swelled into a flood. When the equestrian statue of Louis XV with his head crowned in laurels was erected in 1763 in what is now the Place de la Concorde, four figures were placed at his feet named Strength, Peace, Prudence, Justice. The irony of this juxtaposition was not lost on the capital, and placards affixed to the monument by unknown hands told a very different story.

> *Il est ici comme à Versailles.*
> *Il est sans coeur et sans entrailles.*

When this was removed another equally unflattering comment took its place.

> *Grotesque monument, infâme piédestal,*
> *Les vertus vont à pied et le vice est à cheval.*

While the official *Gazette* dutifully described the unveiling as taking place amid acclamations, Barbier recorded in his journal that none were heard.

> At Court [reported the Austrian Ambassador to Maria Theresa] there is nothing but confusion, scandals and injustice. There has been no attempt at good government; everything has been left to chance; the shameful condition of the nation's affairs has caused unspeakable disgust and discouragement, while the intrigues of those who remain on the stage increase the disorder. Sacred duties have been left undone and scandalous conduct has been tolerated.

The Church spoke with a divided voice. The late ruler was unctuously saluted as 'the best of princes' by the Bishop of Soissons in a funeral address. 'I will not speak of the great achievements of this mighty King, his successes, his victories,' echoed the Bishop of Arras; 'a prince so dear to human hearts must have been after God's heart.' Such Byzantinism rang hollow, but when a third Bishop denounced his evil example the sale of his sermon was forbidden. Anyone who exalted the discredited monarch discredited himself, for the era of conventional flattery was over.

Louis XV had made an auspicious start, for the nation looked with hope and confidence to the pretty lad after an era of almost incessant war, military disasters, and crushing taxation. How deeply rooted was monarchical sentiment appeared when he hovered for a few days between life and death at Metz in 1744. In the frequent conflicts between the crown and the *Parlements* public opinion was far from unanimous on the side of the latter. 'When the people is not downtrodden,' testified Bernis, a shrewd observer, 'and when the course of justice is not interrupted by Court tempests and the ferment of the *Parlements*, the public is always on the side of the King. The distinctive character of the nation is to love its master, respect his authority, and defend it against all comers whenever it does not play the tyrant.' There was nothing of the tyrant either in will or in deed about Louis XV, but it was hardly less fatal to the prestige of the monarchical system to have such a dissolute trifler on the throne. France lost her respect for her rulers in the eighteenth century and has never recovered it. That the machinery was worn out nobody attempted to deny. 'All the symptoms point to great changes and revolutions in government,' wrote Lord Chesterfield on a visit as early as 1753, and from 1750 the word revolution became a term in common use. At the close of the reign a placard was affixed to the Palais Royal, the residence of the Orleans branch of the Royal Family, summoning the colourless Duke to play his part. 'Show yourself, great Prince, and we will place the crown on your head.' Paris was flooded with broadsheets and satires, to which the Chancellor Maupeou replied in brochures distributed gratis in the streets and parks. The people believed that the most unpopular of the Ministers cared little about the reform of the judiciary, and his attack was attributed to his love of power and his hostility to the *Parlement*. In the closing phase of the reign there was talk for the first time of the sovereignty of the people, fundamental laws, the right of resistance, the English Constitution, and the Revolution of 1688. The roar of the avalanche could be heard in the distance.

We can trace the mounting discontent in the writings and journal of the Marquis d'Argenson, by temperament a pessimist and by loss of royal favour a disappointed man, but at the same time an Intellectual of moderate views, described by Richelieu as Secretary of State of Plato's Republic. Having had direct experience of administration and witnessed the functioning of institutions at close quarters, he was more interested in political science than most of the *Philosophes*, but no one was less of a revolutionary. The fullest statement of his critical and constructive views in the opening phase of the reign is enshrined in his *Considérations sur le Gouvernement de la France*, written in 1737, circulated in manuscript, revised after his fall, published in 1764, seven years after his death, and saluted by Voltaire as a work of Aristides. Bossuet's conception of the Lord's anointed was a paradox under a ruler destitute alike of dignity and morals, yet the idea of a republic was still far away. D'Argenson, like Montesquieu, believed in monarchy, but he realised that it must perform its duties if it was to endure. The era of uncritical acceptance of the *status quo* was over. The British Parliament, he felt, possessed too much power, and he disapproved the claims of the *Parlements* to present remonstrances, since the sovereign power, whatever it was, should be unquestioned. 'I should only leave to the governed the liberty of their own actions, with some Colleges arranging for their happiness but no general assemblies of all the governed.' Yet to consult them about taxation was desirable.

> That will content the people, who will feel they are admitted into all affairs of state as—and better than—in a republic. But this admission to the knowledge of affairs had its limits. Their consent is not necessary as in England. It is a mistake to wish for an intermediary power between the Government and the people. There need only be the protector and the protected, the former preventing anarchy, the latter enjoying the benefits and the order provided by the laws. Let the Government be at once mild, firm and beneficent and there will be no need for the balance of the three powers so highly extolled in England. The ruler should be a man of affairs, combining absolute authority with the force of reason; but in the sphere of international relations, such as the declaration of war and the cession of territory, he should not be entirely uncontrolled. Here a national senate, composed equally of all the Orders, should restrain him by the necessity of obtaining subsidies.

Till such a body came into existence the *Parlement* of Paris seemed the most suitable organ for the purpose since it appeared to be shedding many of its old faults. The *Noblesse* should fill the higher posts in the army and the administration but it should surrender its feudal privileges.

D'Argenson's creed was a strong Monarchy, an industrious ruler, a devoted *Noblesse*, the control of local affairs in town and

village by agents chosen at an annual meeting, economic opportunity rather than political liberty, priority of agriculture over
industry, a general capitation tax and equality before the law.
Since the central government was overburdened by detail, he
advocated the division of France into small units administered
by officials appointed by the Intendants from a list elected by the
communes. The Provincial Estates should be more representative. Internal tolls should disappear and foreign trade be freed
from its shackles. Though the whole programme is conceived
within the framework of enlightened autocracy and is less advanced than the teaching of Montesquieu, its implementation
would have carried the régime a considerable distance beyond
the practice of the era of Louis XV.

D'Argenson's outlook was permanently soured by his dismissal from the Foreign Office in 1747 after scarcely more than
two years at his post. Never a happy man, his tone becomes ever
more querulous during the decade which remained to him. At
the close of the year which terminated his official career he gazes
at the face of France in something like despair. 'What ruin
threatens us and indeed already assails us. The taxes and the
laws are destroying the State. The people only obey and abstain
from revolt owing to their extreme weakness, though they riot
for bread in the south.' Two years later, disgruntled because
unemployed, he thinks aloud. 'I am on my estate in Touraine.
I see only fearful misery, and not only misery but despair. They
only wish to cease having children and to die. Sometimes the
taille is three years in arrears. There is serious talk of the King
travelling round his kingdom next year. God grant that he may
thus learn to know the misery of his people and apply the remedies.' The greatest hardship, he notes in 1750, was the ravages of
game. 'The poor peasant is afraid of everything and he dare not
complain for fear of fresh vexations. Diminish the power of the
Noblesse as you have already suppressed that of the clergy, but
do not substitute that of the bloodsuckers as is the case today.
Substitute that of the commune, democracy and equality, and
you will have a good government.'

The populace spoke of the King with great contempt, records
d'Argenson, and Mme de Pompadour feared that she might be
lynched when she drove through the Faubourg St. Germain.

Everyone in high place—King, Favourite, Ministers—was hated and despised. 'I thought the *Parlement* would be exempt, but it is hated too, above all Maupeou, the First President.' The populace wanted to set fire to Versailles, and troops were stationed at the bridge of Sèvres. 'The ship of state seems totally abandoned. The sailors are as idle as the pilot. Everyone thinks only of pleasure, intrigue, plenty of money to spend in mad luxury and magnificent trifles.' Everybody, including the very rich, was deep in debt, and the King was the worst offender.

> Everyone says the King ought to reduce his expenses, and the *Parlement* has just told him so: some people think Machault advised it to do so. Even the slightest reform is difficult—in the stables, building, food, journeys, pensions: vested interests are too strongly entrenched. All the King's resources are only drops in the ocean. Every day the number of useless people increases, enriched without merit or work. Salaries are two to three years in arrears.

Louis XV inherited prodigality from Louis XIV and thought it beneath him to economise. 'He is no megalomaniac nor is he devoid of wisdom, but he is easy-going, superficial, and weak.' Instinctively adopting the line of least resistance, he let things slide.

In December, 1751, d'Argenson confided to his journal his celebrated forecast of the Revolution.

> A philosophic breeze of freedom and anti-monarchical sentiment is blowing. It affects the mind and we know how opinion governs the world. Perhaps this form of government has already taken shape in minds, to be implemented at the first opportunity. Perhaps the revolution will be made with less opposition than one expects. There would be no need for a prince and no enthusiasm for religion. All the Orders are dissatisfied. The military, dismissed directly the war was over, is treated with harshness and injustice, the clergy reviled and mocked, the *Parlements* and other corporations, the provinces, the common people overburdened and wretched, the financiers triumphant. All this is inflammable material. A riot can easily turn into a revolt and the revolt into a revolution in which real tribunes of the people would be chosen, and committees and communes, and where the King and the Ministers would be deprived of their undue power to do harm. Absolute monarchical government is excellent under a good King, but who will guarantee

that we shall always have a Henri Quatre? Experience and nature prove that we shall get ten bad ones to one good.

Louis XV was sufficiently aware of his unpopularity to avoid the capital on his summer journey to Compiègne. 'Am I to show myself to this wretched people which says I am a Herod?' The Favourite resented the attitude of the streets even more than the easy-going monarch. 'I hear Mme de Pompadour is bitter about the reception of the King in Paris,' noted d'Argenson, 'and she exclaims that all these ungrateful people should be decimated and hung. How far it all is from my ideal of a Titus on the throne and a Sully at his side!' There was bold talk among the magistrates and the Jansenists of the nation being above the King and the Church above the Pope. In 1753 a Bishop recalled the death of Charles I, adding that the *Parlement* in case of need could judge and execute the King; and a magistrate foretold that he expected the revolution to start with barricades.

A second and shorter political treatise, written in 1755 and published in 1784, registers a notable advance on the *Considéra-tions*. D'Argenson's ideas are succinctly presented in the form of a royal proclamation in thirty-four articles. All landed pro-perty was to contribute to taxation. Patents of nobility should not be bought. Thirty-two provincial assemblies should be elected, each with a President, Secretary, and Treasurer, enjoying far-reaching autonomy. They should be opened by Royal Com-missioners who would explain the assessment of taxes. Govern-ment decisions could not be challenged, but criticisms would be allowed. Though only Catholics could hold public office, tolera-tion should be complete. While the ultimate power of the Crown would remain intact, the control of local affairs would be trans-ferred to parishes, districts, provinces. D'Argenson's second plan would in practice have ended autocracy and centralisation, and admitted the people to a share in power. 'Pour mieux gouverner il faut moins gouverner.' He had seen too much of inefficient absolutism at close quarters to desire its continuance or believe it possible. Though in his plan the local bodies could not legis-late, they could present bills for the King to ratify. Radical though his proposals appeared in 1755, there is no suggestion of the sovereignty of the people or a national assembly to bridge the gap between the subject and the ruler.

On the eve of his death in 1757 d'Argenson recorded his final impressions of the reign from which in his early years he had entertained the liveliest hopes.

> The people is in dumb despair and there are plenty of channels through which the idea of resistance can reach the masses—among them the magistracy, the most estimable section of the nation by its morals and learning, and all the lower clergy who are opposed to the Bull Unigenitus. In all the provinces there is misery, a dumb discontent with the Court, an undisguised fury against the avarice of the financiers, open revolt against the Intendants, envy, poverty, hunger.

Only in one direction did he discover advance—there was more interest in public affairs. 'Fifty years ago the public was wholly uninterested in the news. Now everybody reads the *Gazette de France*. Much nonsense is talked about politics, but they are no longer ignored. England has conquered us.' If the diarist had returned to earth in the summer of 1789 he would have felt little surprise at the course of events. Louis XV himself, little though he had seen of his country and his countrymen, entertained few illusions in his later years about his unpopularity and the growing demand for a new deal. *Après moi le déluge*, though not his own phrase, expressed his attitude of resigned pessimism as accurately as *l'état c'est moi* embodied the robust self-assurance of his majestic predecessor. It is the difference between a major and a minor chord.

On learning of his accession at the age of nineteen Louis XVI pressed his wife to his heart, exclaiming, 'What a burden! At my age! And I have been taught nothing.' 'Mon Dieu,' confided Marie Antoinette to her mother, 'what will become of us? M. le Dauphin and I are terrified that we are called to the throne so young. Dear mother, help your unfortunate children with advice.' The Empress responded, but her reiterated admonitions to the frivolous little Queen were ignored. The new King, modest in his demands and austere in his morals, required no exhortations, and his selection of Turgot as Controller-General to cleanse the Augean stables was hailed with relief. 'I believe I am born to regenerate France,' exclaimed the new Minister, and Voltaire commented that if anyone could restore the franc it would be he. It was the tragedy of France that he was allowed

too short a time, for within two years he was thrown to the
wolves by the vested interests with the extravagant Queen at
their head. His eviction sounded the death-knell of monarchical
autocracy and the *ancien régime*. In the pregnant phrase of Sorel
he had proved both the necessity of large-scale reform and the
inability of the Monarchy to achieve it. After mildly encouraging
first Turgot and then Necker the ruler lost his nerve and allowed
the ship of state to drift before the storm. It was not the fault of
Louis XV that his grandson suffered from paralysis of the will
and an incurable inferiority complex, but he was directly responsible for bequeathing a situation which demanded a superman
when no superman was in sight.

II

During the reign of Louis XV the prestige of the Church
reached its lowest point since the Council of Trent. No com-
manding figure emerged after the death of Fénelon and Male-
branche in 1715, no impressive preacher, no eminent writer, no
thinker of repute. Fleury, a well-meaning mediocrity, owed his
place as First Minister to the lucky accident that he had been
appointed tutor to the boy King. Moreover the Church had
never been so sharply divided—Jesuits versus Jansenists, Gallicans versus Ultramontanes. The wealthy hierarchy, like the
Monarchy and the *Noblesse*, clung tenaciously to its privileges,
while the curé, himself a peasant, was as poor as his flock. The
ruthless harrying of the Huguenots, which continued throughout
the reign, was deplored in circles which had little or no sympathy
with their beliefs. The Jesuits had rendered themselves unpopular not only by their power and their claims but by the fact that
they took orders from abroad. The moral standard of the clergy
was good, but the savage punishments imposed in the name of
religion disgraced the Church in the eyes of the world. The
name of Calas, thanks to Voltaire, is immortal while that of
Christophe de Beaumont, Archbishop of Paris, the most prominent French ecclesiastic of his time, is known to students alone.

Every departure from traditional beliefs, including Buffon's *Histoire Naturelle*, was angrily denounced by the Church. Lip service was paid at Versailles to creeds and ceremonies, but except for the pious Queen, the Dauphin and a few other *dévots*, they were merely an incident in the daily routine.

The influence of the Church in the national life was diminished less by its lack of leaders, its intolerance and the low moral standard of many professing Catholics than by the atmospheric change which we call the Enlightenment. A wave of incredulity swept over France in the hectic days of the Regent. 'I don't believe,' wrote his mother in 1722, 'that there are a hundred people in Paris, ecclesiastics as well as laity, who hold the true faith and believe in our Saviour.' The disillusioned old Duchess was always prone to exaggeration, but the great days of the French Church were over. The cool breeze blowing across Western Europe reached its maximum velocity in the middle of the century, transforming the country of *Le Roi très Chrétien*— not merely for the moment but for generations to come—into one of the most sceptical communities in the world. Tradition and authority, the Vatican and the Sorbonne, ceased to be the final arbiters in the questionings of the human spirit. Incredulity and apathy spread through the land. 'We know as much of the attributes of God as the priests,' wrote d'Argenson in his Journal in 1757, 'and we can worship Him without the aid of these pretended *dévots* who are only drones in the hive.' For d'Argenson, as for Voltaire and Rousseau, the choice was not between orthodoxy and atheism but between 'natural religion' and superstition. Proclaiming himself a deist he adds: 'that is a title of those who have true religion in their hearts and have abjured the whole world. Nature supplies us with all we want.' The Church was as superfluous as the creeds. Sympathising with the poor he advocated the suppression of convents and the use of their property to enrich poor parishes. Looking round at the litter of broken marriages and their inescapable consequences in a land where divorce was forbidden, he expressed the hope that the institution of marriage would gradually make way for *unions libres* on the ground that fidelity was more likely under conditions of free choice. Such a flouting of tradition would have been unthinkable in the era of Louis XIV.

In the third quarter of the century both sides were fighting with the gloves off. An edict of 1737 threatened death for writing, printing, or selling any work attacking religion or the authority of the Crown. The quinquennial Church Assembly of 1765 deplored the growing licence of opinion in religion and politics. 'A multitude of rash writings have trampled underfoot human and divine laws. The most sacred truths have been obscured and the principles of Monarchy shattered. Nothing has been respected either in the civil or the spiritual order. The majesty of the Supreme Being and of Kings is outraged in the realm of faith and morals, and the spirit of the century appears to threaten a revolution involving total ruin.' At the next Assembly in 1770 the Bishops drafted a memorandum to the King on the dangerous results of liberty of thinking and printing. Throughout the reign many important books were suppressed or burned and several eminent writers imprisoned or fined. That there were some grounds for such licence never crossed the minds of the unworthy and incompetent rulers in Church and State. There were plenty of reputable dignitaries in the Church, and there were also worldly prelates such as Cardinal Rohan, Grand Almoner of France, and Talleyrand, Bishop of Autun. When Loménie de Brienne, Archbishop of Sens, was recommended for the Archbishopric of Paris in 1785, the King exclaimed: 'In Paris we must at any rate have an Archbishop who believes in God.'

Frontal attacks, however formidable, on specific dogmas, pious legends and ecclesiastical ceremonies like those by Voltaire and Diderot were less damaging to the authority of the Church than the sapping and mining by the secular spirit; for militant impiety was often disapproved by men and women who had shed their inherited beliefs. Many a cultivated sceptic was prepared to admit that the teachings of the Church were still useful for the common herd who should not be deprived of their familiar consolations. While religion in any form made no appeal to Mme du Deffand, she frowned on irreligious talk in her salon. Only in the drawing-rooms of Mme de Tencin and Mlle de Lespinasse, Mme d Épinay and Baron d'Holbach, were the *Philosophes* permitted to say whatever they liked.

The first resounding broadside of the reign was fired by Voltaire in his *Oedipe* published in 1718.

Ces organes du ciel sont-ils donc infaillibles?
Un ministère saint les attache aux autels.
Ils approchent des dieux, mais ils sont des mortels.
Pensez-vous que qu'en effet au gré de leur demande
Du vol de leurs oiseaux la vérité dépende?
Non, non, cherchez ainsi l'auguste vérité
C'est usurper les droits de la Divinité.
Nos prêtres ne sont pas ce qu'un vain peuple pense.
Notre crédulité fait toute leur science.

The same gospel of toleration was proclaimed in trumpet tones in the *Henriade*, an epic which sang the praises of the royal author of the Edict of Nantes, and in the *Lettres Philosophiques sur les Anglais* which saluted the happy land where people could believe what they liked and say what they thought.

Voltaire, declared Gibbon, his near neighbour at Lausanne, was the most extraordinary man of the century. The greatest figure in the literature of all ages, and the most representative of Frenchmen, echoed Goethe. Centuries would be needed to produce his equal, exclaimed Diderot. *Ce n'est pas un homme, c'est un siècle*, cried Victor Hugo. *Le plus bel esprit de ce siècle* was the verdict of President Hénault. While Chateaubriand complained that he had rendered incredulity fashionable, Quinet hailed him as the angel of extermination sent by God against His sinful Church. The Goddess of Reason was enthroned, and Voltaire was recognised by friend and foe as the High Priest of the cult. No Protestant had ever struck such damaging blows against the institutions, teachings and practices of the Roman Church. Though his faults were as conspicuous as his merits, the intellectual climate of France was permanently modified during his lifetime, largely by his unwearying pen. Certain things which he attacked were beyond his understanding, but many others deserved to die. 'The spirit of intolerance sank blasted beneath his genius,' declares Lecky. 'Wherever his influence passed, the arm of the Inquisition was palsied, the chain of the captive riven, the door flung open. He died leaving a reputation that is indeed far from spotless, but having done more to destroy the greatest of human curses than any other of the sons of men.' His creed is embodied as clearly in the *Siècle de Louis XIV* and the *Essai sur les Moeurs* as in the *Dictionnaire Philosophique*. Freedom of thought, encouragement of the arts and sciences, religious toleration, mild laws, sound finance, avoidance of war, above all a spirit of humanity: such was his recipe for a happier world in which man could grow to his full stature. Where Voltaire led the way a crowd of lesser men followed before the main army of the Enlightenment, captained by the Encyclopédists, swept everything before them in the third quarter of the century. Unbelief among the Intelligentsia became as fashionable as orthodoxy had been in the spacious days of Bossuet and Louis XIV. The salons were crowded with *Philosophes* for the simple reason that no other celebrities were available. Though Mme Geoffrin had no sympathy with their views and Mme Necker detested their irreligion, they knew that there was no choice. Not till the coming of Chateaubriand and Joseph de Maistre, both of them laymen, at the end of the century did orthodoxy recover a precarious footing in the intellectual life of France.

The old nobility, known as the *Noblesse de l'Épee*, which had challenged the Crown during the Wars of Religion and in the squalid intermezzo of the Fronde, finally lost its place in the political life of the nation during the long reign of Louis XIV. As the royal authority waxed under the dazzling rays of the *Roi Soleil*, the nobility faded away and in the eighteenth century it ceased to count except on the social plane. With the wealthier section dancing attendance at Court and the rest marooned by poverty on their country estates, they had little thought but to cling to their outworn privileges. Louis XV, like his predecessor, preferred to pick his agents among men who owed everything to his favour and nothing to their birth. For a century after the death of the Regent the Orleans branch of the Royal Family played little part except in the brief emergence of the regicide Philippe Égalité. The Great Condé never regained his influence after the fiasco of the Fronde, and the shoddy intermezzo of the Duc de Bourbon after the death of the Regent further discredited the family. The last of his line to play a prominent part was the Prince de Conti who collaborated in the secret diplomacy of Louis XV and vainly aspired to the Polish throne. Of the older nobility Mirabeau and Lafayette alone campaigned for a new deal. Marshal Richelieu, bearer of one of the most distinguished names in France, never fulfilled his ambition to become a Minister or a

S

member of the King's Council, and was forced to content himself
with the post of *Premier Gentilhomme de la Chambre* and the sine-
cure Governorship of Languedoc. Though the old families continued to receive the highest posts in the army and the Church
they exercised no influence on the shaping of policy. The Duc de
Choiseul, the ablest Minister of the reign, was selected not for his
birth but for his brains. *Roi fainéant* though he was, Louis XV
remained the sole fountain of honour and the grandees fed meekly
out of his hand. Their day was over and they knew it. Their
decline in prestige was accelerated through the purchase of titles
by wealthy war contractors and financiers and by profitable
unions with bourgeois heiresses. The Duc de Choiseul and the
Duc de Lauzun, for instance, were only too glad to marry the
daughters of Crozat, an army contractor who had made his pile.
The *Noblesse* fell so far and so fast that they surrendered their
ancestral privileges without a struggle when the storm broke
over their heads in 1789.

The lower section of the nobility, the *Noblesse de Robe*, possessed as little effective power as the *Noblesse de l'Épée*. In the
absence of representative institutions, the *Parlements*—above all
the *Parlement* of Paris—occasionally strove to fill the gap between
the Government and the people, not as champions of the rights
of the many, but for their own class interests. However imperfect
their system of hereditary and purchasable appointments, they
were the only institutions which dared to challenge the omnipotence of the Crown. Yet their opposition to absolutism and
their approval of Gallicanism carried them only a short distance
along the road to reform. No one can maintain that the *Noblesse
de Robe* made any serious effort, either within their Order or as
independent citizens, to avert a catastrophe by personal sacrifices
or constructive statesmanship.

III

The outstanding features of the era of Louis XV were the
waning of authority and the rise of the bourgeoisie. These two
historic processes were closely connected. While the prestige of

the old nobility and the Church was rapidly declining, the middle-class bankers and contractors lawyers, industrialists and high-brows elbowed their way towards the centre of the stage. Though La Bruyère denounced the greed of the *nouveaux riches* as vigorously as the arrogance of the *Noblesse*, Samuel Bernard, the first large-scale financier of the century, was far too wealthy to be ignored; and the Paris brothers helped to finance the State for a generation after the death of Louis XIV. The prosperity of England, where social stratification was less rigid and where success in commerce and industry was ungrudgingly recognised, was an object-lesson to her more backward neighbour. When Louis XV ascended the throne England was little known in France except as the most formidable of her foes, which Bossuet denounced as a guilty nation. The *Lettres sur les Anglais et les Français* by the Swiss Protestant Muralt, published in 1725, had attracted some attention; but the most persuasive interpreter of the island kingdom was Voltaire whose experiences and reflections during his three happy years in London were embodied in his *Lettres Philosophiques sur les Anglais*, published in 1733. Though the England of Hogarth was no earthly paradise and the portrait was a little flattering, he was justified in his contention that his countrymen had a great deal to learn from her neighbour's way of life. A single generation had produced Newton and Locke, the Glorious Revolution of 1688, and the inauguration of Limited Monarchy. Liberty of utterance and religious toleration made a special appeal to his heart and mind and earned his undying respect. The sojourn in England transformed the *littérateur* into a *Philosophe*. The sparkling little book, at first sight merely a pleasant *causerie* on a foreign land, fulfilled the deeper purpose of holding up the mirror to his less privileged countrymen. Compared with France, England was a free and happy state. The era of 'Anglomania' had begun.

The second authoritative interpretation of the English system was provided in the *Esprit des Lois*, an encyclopaedic survey of political institutions, past and present, published in 1748. Montesquieu, like Voltaire, had studied England on the spot, and his eulogy of the separation of powers was an oblique rebuke to the monolithic system of his native land. Detesting absolutism and clericalism, and arguing not from abstract principles but

from historic study and personal observation, this liberal conservative, himself a lawyer, pleaded for a limited Monarchy and
the rule of law. Standing midway between Voltaire, who was
satisfied with the principle of enlightened autocracy, and Rousseau,
who proclaimed the sovereignty of the people, Montesquieu was
the spiritual father of Mirabeau, the Anglophils and the moderates
in the Constituent Assembly of 1789. Of all the political critics
of the *ancien régime* he was the most impressive.

The popularisation of English institutions and ideas by Voltaire
and Montesquieu was followed by a stream of distinguished
visitors from beyond the Channel. *La Ville Lumière* was the
natural starting-point of the Grand Tour considered almost
obligatory for the sons of the nobility, but the English Milord
made little impression abroad except as a living demonstration
that he came from a wealthy land. Far deeper was the impact
produced by three leading Intellectuals, Horace Walpole, Gibbon,
and Hume, all of whom had mastered the language and were
lionised in the salons. No better bridge-builders could have been
found than the son of the first English Prime Minister, the writer
of a best-seller History of England, and the author of the *Decline
and Fall of the Roman Empire*. Though the two nations were
often at war during the eighteenth century there was little
popular hostility, and indeed the land of free institutions, religious
toleration, an independent judiciary and commercial success
excited admiration far beyond the select circle of the Intelligentsia.
Yet there were limits to the aspirations of the French admirers of
the English way of life. What they desired was religious toleration, decent government, fair taxation and an upright judiciary,
not full political self-determination.

Autocracies, dynastic or otherwise, have no use for a free
press, and foreign journals required at any rate tacit permission
to circulate. The official *Gazette de France* recorded the doings of
the Court and provided as much or as little information as the
Government thought fit to supply. France, like other countries,
remained largely illiterate till the middle of the nineteenth century,
and the supply of newspapers was even more limited than the
demand. Paris had to be content with the *Mercure de France*, an
organ of information not of political discussion, for the editor
was an official nominee. Under Marmontel it became a little

kinder to the *Philosophes*; but the hand of the censor lay heavily
on authors, editors and publishers alike, since in theory every
book had to be submitted to the Director of Publications. Action
was rarely taken unless the Church was attacked or some prominent official, courtier or ecclesiastic felt himself aggrieved. Even
when permission had been secured from the Director, the
Parlement or the Sorbonne might intervene, the author being
consigned to the Bastille by a *lettre de cachet* and his writings committed to the flames. To avert such disasters many works were
published abroad, usually in Holland, sometimes under a *nom de
plume*. Contributions to the *Encyclopédie* were mutilated by the
timid printer without consulting the editor. The pressure of the
censorship varied with the zeal or opinions of the Director of
Publications. With the appointment in 1750 of Malesherbes,
himself something of a *Philosophe*, as *Directeur de la Librairie*, the
danger of punishment was reduced. Without Malesherbes, testifies Diderot, the *Encyclopédie* might never have seen the light.
Had Damiens used a larger knife and brought the Dauphin to
the throne it would have remained a torso. Louis XV was no
zealot, and the Pompadour was painted with a volume on her
lap. After his early experience in the Bastille Voltaire decided to
pitch his tent near or beyond the frontier, since his passion for the
Enlightenment was not matched by zeal for a martyr's crown.
Diderot was imprisoned for his *Lettre sur les Aveugles*. So great
was the dread of penalties that in some cases authors confided
their message to handwritten copies which circulated among a
trusted *clientèle*. Under these circumstances criticism was confined
to the salons and to the anonymous *chansons* and broadsheets
which fluttered about the capital like autumn leaves. As the
saying went, the government of France was despotism tempered
by epigram. The venerable *Journal des Savants* catered for high-
brows and left politics alone.

The sentiments of the Paris bourgeoisie during the reign of
Louis XV are mirrored in the journals of Marais, Buvat, Barbier,
Hardy and Bachaumont, who stood midway between the tradi-
tionalists and the *Philosophes*. While occasionally criticising
the extravagance of the Court they accepted the Monarchy
without a thought of serious change. Uninterested in ideas, they
were mildly anti-clerical and disliked the Jesuits. For the manual

worker they cared as little as for the grandees. The ideology of the unofficial lawyer class is most fully revealed in the voluminous journal of Barbier which spans the years from 1718 to 1763. A man of fair intelligence and cool temperament, unambitious and hating extremes, his impressions of the passing scene are presented in a dry and unemotional style. While disliking abuses he recognised the need of a strong executive to avert mob violence which he feared beyond everything. His ideal was Fleury, the champion of economy and peace: most of the Ministers he regarded as *fripons*. As a lawyer, though not a magistrate, he liked the *Parlements* to stand up for their traditional rights, but he frowned on their claims being pressed to a serious clash with the Crown. Temperamentally a man of the right centre, he moved cautiously towards the left as the reign advanced. Though he never dreamed of the States General, his comments display growing dissatisfaction with the governance of France.

He records his surprise at a demonstration in 1750 against the impressment of young vagabonds in order to people 'our Mississippi', since the Parisians in general were easy-going folk and no such sedition had been witnessed for forty years, even in the seasons of dear bread. He admitted, however, that there was a loud outcry against the extravagance of the King, above all his mania for building royal residences. Even worse was the fact that taxation was not reduced on the return of peace in 1748 and that he had recently borrowed fifteen million francs at five per cent without announcing the purpose of the loan. Moreover there was sharp resentment against Mme de Pompadour through whom alone, it was said, posts could be obtained, and then only for cash. 'She ought to be content with entertaining the King who is so bored wherever he finds himself, and she should not interfere in matters of State, at any rate in internal affairs. She would be just as rich and she would not make so many enemies.' The grandees hated her, but they were just as bad themselves. 'Everyone is talking of the immense expenditure by the King who is robbed by all his entourage,' he writes in May, 1751, 'especially in his frequent journeys to his different residences. It is said that his revenues for 1752 are being spent in the present year.' When the Royal Family drove to Notre Dame in September, 1751, for a thanksgiving for the birth of a Dauphin there

were no longer cries of 'Vive le Roi', and the attendants had to
order the people to cheer. No wonder, comments the diarist,
for not a single tax had been taken off, and the price of bread had
risen. A year later he describes the popularity of a pamphlet
ridiculing the Bishops and adds that people were beginning to
scoff at sacred things. He himself was totally indifferent to
religious beliefs and practices.

Barbier records a final flicker of interest in the Court when
Damiens stabbed the King on January 5, 1757. When the news
reached Paris next morning there were few dry eyes. Special
services were held, and the officiating priests could scarcely pro-
nounce the words *salvum fac regem* owing to their sobs and those
of the congregation. Though he seems to have been little
affected, he admits that at the moment of the attack the royal
victim behaved like a hero. A year later he records that the
Favourite's stock stood higher than ever. 'The Ministers report
everything to her before discussions in the Council. She concerns
herself with the army and all matters of State. She has plenty of
brains, but is she not undertaking too much? That is the way to
make influential enemies in such a large Court.' Once again we
are struck by the mildness of judgment which distinguishes
Barbier from d'Argenson. Feeling no responsibility for events,
holding no office and cherishing no ambitions, he surveys the
scene with a detachment unique among the diarists and memoir-
writers of the reign. In no direction could he discover any statesman or institution capable of giving France the decent government and moderate reforms which she craved. Like most of the
bourgeoisie he stood nearer to Montesquieu than to any other
publicist in his preference for a system in which no man and no
group of men should possess unchallenged power. Shortly
before laying down his pen in 1763 he confesses his anxieties.
'If the authority and the pretended rights of the *Parlements* are
diminished, there will be no obstacle to entrenched despotism.
If on the other hand the *Parlements* combine in forceful opposition,
that will involve a general revolution which would be very
dangerous and might serve as a pretext to England and other
Powers to declare war.' Though Barbier's colours are drab
enough we would gladly have listened to his comments on the
closing years of the reign. His place as Parisian chronicler was

partially filled by Bachaumont, who covered the years 1762–71 in a rather colourless chronicle continued by other hands. Better off, with a wider range of intellectual interests, and running a salon with the aid of his mistress, he was more of a *Philosophe* though equally little of a radical. In his jottings, as in those of Barbier, the aura of Monarchy has vanished into thin air. For him and his circle the Court and its doings had ceased to count, and he resented institutions and precepts which tended to prevent him from doing what he liked.

While the Court continued to live in the past, the capital was moving briskly towards the century of the common man. The most eloquent expression of the attitude of the bourgeoisie towards *les grands* at the close of the reign is to be found in the plays of Beaumarchais, the most incisive of dramatists since Molière; though *The Barber of Seville* was not performed till 1775 it was written in 1772. 'Because you are a Grand Seigneur,' exclaims Figaro, 'you think yourself a great genius. Nobility, fortune, rank, office, makes you so proud—you merely gave yourself the trouble to be born: otherwise you are a very ordinary person, while I, lost in the crowd, have had to display more skill and resource merely to exist than have been used for a century in the government of Spain.' The barber was thinking not of Spain, where intellectual life was like a stagnant pond, but of France. Figaro is Beaumarchais himself. 'Detestable,' commented Louis XVI after witnessing a performance at the palace; 'this man attacks everything which must be respected in a government.' Despite the frowns of the ruler the play was performed to enthusiastic audiences at the *Comédie française*. The octogenarian Marshal Richelieu, the sole survivor of the Court of Louis XIV, noted the atmospheric change in conversation with the young King.

LOUIS XVI: You have seen three centuries.
RICHELIEU: Three reigns, Sire.
LOUIS XVI: Well, what do you think about it?
RICHELIEU: Under Louis XIV no one dared say a word. Under Louis XV people spoke in whispers. Under Your Majesty they talk out loud.

How far did the rise of Freemasonry contribute to the decline and fall of the *ancien régime*? While latter-day Monarchists and right-wing Republicans such as Madelin reply 'to a considerable extent', left-wing Republicans like Mathiez deny its political significance. Bernard Fay takes it much more seriously than Mornet, the most comprehensive explorer of the intellectual origins of the Revolution, who dismisses it as a social rather than a political phenomenon. The earliest lodge was founded in Paris in 1727 and it quickly became fashionable, the element of mystery adding to its appeal. In 1737 Barbier, who detested novelties, noted in his journal that the meetings were a danger, and he approved the Cardinal's veto. Next year membership of a lodge was condemned by the Vatican, which has always frowned on secret societies and detected a vein of anticlericalism in the latest variety. In 1740 d'Argenson records the exile from the capital of M. de Mailly, husband of the reigning Favourite, for arranging meetings in his house. Though police raids occasionally occurred only moderate penalties were imposed, for the Government was much more zealous in harrying Jansenists and Protestants than in molesting citizens who made no trouble. By the middle of the century the lodges had a free hand and spread throughout the country despite their condemnation in 1763 by the Sorbonne, now a powerless institution. The movement had not begun to alarm the *Noblesse* or the Church very seriously, for aristocrats and a few priests and the Protestant Necker were members, and in 1773 the Duc de Chartres, later Philippe Égalité, became Grand Master. Nothing appeared more socially respectable or less revolutionary. That feminine lodges were formed seemed further evidence that the whole movement was unpolitical. Though a few prominent Freemasons, among them Montesquieu and Diderot, were political liberals as well as *esprits forts*, the great majority were obedient subjects. Hundreds of the members of the Constituent Assembly were masons, but no key to the Revolution is less plausible than its attribution in large measure to the machinations of secret societies.

IV

Though not every cultivated *roturier* was an *esprit fort*, the *Philosophes* who filled Europe with their fame from the middle of the century may be broadly described as the voice of the French Intelligentsia. Their interest in the unseen world was slight since their minds dwelt on the empirical plane. A sense of liberation, of exploration, of something approaching intellectual intoxication, stirred in their blood. What might not reason, the noblest of human facilities, achieve when the shackles of centuries were struck off! The seeds sown in Bayle's *Dictionnaire historique et critique*, Fontenelle's *Pluralité des Mondes* and Montesquieu's *Lettres Persanes* ripened to harvest in the third quarter of the century in Voltaire's *Dictionnaire Philosophique* and the *Encyclopédie*. The study of institutions and societies, the natural sciences and creeds, was approached from an anthropocentric standpoint as distant from the theocentric presuppositions of Bossuet, the last echo of the Middle Ages, as if the writers were inhabitants of different planets. The secularisation of thought, which had begun at the close of the fifteenth century and had been carried on by the *Libertius* of the seventeenth, swept forward with a rush. A new religion, fashioned not by Church Councils, Popes or metaphysicians, but by historians, sociologists and economists, found ever-increasing acceptance among the professional classes, anchored in an optimistic conception of human nature and a robust belief in the capacity of the free mind to explain the past, reform the present, and plan the future. Once the dead hand of tradition, embodied in autocracy, feudalism and clericalism was removed, mankind, master of its fate, could march ahead with open eyes and head erect towards the Promised Land. That the acid test to be applied to institutions and beliefs was no longer their antiquity but the happiness they tended to produce was proclaimed by Helvétius. The notion of human depravity originating with a legendary Fall of Man was rejected as a libel both on God and man. While Voltaire believed in reason as a safer guide than the heart, Rousseau trusted the generous instincts of the common man; yet they agreed that the race was entitled to a better life than it had ever enjoyed and they never doubted that it might be achieved. 'Almost everyone in Paris is a *Philosophe*,' reported Horace Walpole in 1765, by which he meant a blend of rationalism and optimism. Voltaire's *Écrasez l'infâme* was aimed, not at the *Être Suprême* in which he sincerely believed, nor at Christian ethics, which he held in deep respect, but at ecclesiastical intolerance and intellectual obscurantism, the torture of bodies and the burning of books. 'You have no idea of the influence which Voltaire and his great contemporaries possessed in my youth,' declared Goethe to Eckermann half a century later, 'and how they dominated the whole civilised world.'

The notion of limitless progress formulated by the Abbé Saint-Pierre under the Regency, developed by Turgot, and elaborated by Condorcet amid the turmoil of the Revolution, filled the *Philosophes* with pride in the achievements of mankind. While the builders of Utopias from More and Campanella onwards never seriously believed that their ideal commonwealths could be brought down from the clouds, the *Philosophes* were convinced that their plans for an enlightened, tolerant, warless and therefore happy world were well within the compass of human endeavour. Voltaire expected little from a change of institutions, but he was almost alone in this view. 'I would rather obey a lion,' he explained, 'than two hundred rats of my own species.' Montesquieu came much closer to the ideas of 1789 in his plans for Limited Monarchy, and Diderot in his claim that nature had made neither servant nor master. Rousseau, who spoke for the common man with greater authority than any eighteenth-century pundit, exclaimed 'Je hais les grands.' The time of crises and the century of revolution were drawing near, he wrote in 1762. 'The French are late for everything,' declared Voltaire in 1764, 'but they do arrive. The light has been so spread that the explosion will soon come and there will be a great upheaval.' 'During the last fifteen years,' he added in 1767, 'there has taken place a revolution in the minds of men which will produce a great epoch. A man of my age will not see it, but we shall die in the hope that men may become more enlightened and more gentle. The world is having its wits sharpened.' The more the subjects of Louis XV fretted over the present, the more ardently they dreamed of a golden age not very far ahead. Optimists and pessimists alike, friends and foes of the Enlightenment, agreed that vast changes were at hand.

The reign of the *Philosophes* may be said to begin with the publication of the *Esprit des Lois* in 1748 which evicted theology from political science as firmly as the *Leviathan* had banished it a hundred years earlier in England; and Montesquieu's massive treatise, with its epoch-making assertion of relativity in the analysis of institutions, may be regarded as an antidote to Bossuet's *Politique tirée de l'Écriture Sainte*. We find ourselves not only in a new century but in a new world. A still more formidable attack on tradition and authority was launched by the *Encyclopédie*, a battering-ram in seventeen folio volumes, each containing nearly one thousand double-column pages. 'Not a book but an act,' exclaims Nisard. The first comprehensive survey of the whole field of knowledge available in the middle of the eighteenth century—far more complete than Bayle or the recently published *Chambers's Encyclopedia*—expounded a doctrine of progress on the basis of the unaided achievement of *homo sapiens*. 'La raison,' declared Bayle, 'est le tribunal suprême et qui juge en dernier ressort et sans appel de tout ce qui nous est proposé.' His confidence in reason as the best and indeed the only guide was fully shared by Diderot and d'Alembert, who gathered round them a team of experts and exhorted their readers to think for themselves, searching for truth in science and history, not in the Bible or the Church. In the political sphere, on the other hand, there was nothing in the *Encyclopédie* more radical than dislike of autocracy, a demand for civil liberty, and the removal of the abuses of feudalism: Rousseau's contributions dealt with music, not with political science. The novelty of the enterprise lay in the uninhibited approach and the testing of laws, institutions, and creeds by their effect on human happiness. Man was conceived as potter's clay, to be shaped by a master hand, infinitely teachable, capable of the highest achievements if he were set on the open road with all artificial barriers swept away. Since he had created civilisation, what limit could be set to the march of the human spirit? Though Voltaire's contributions were few, the *Encyclopédie* breathed his inquiring spirit. That he was a Deist and Diderot an atheist, like Lamettrie, Helvétius and Holbach, made little practical difference, since, like Buffon, he confined the activity of the *Être Suprême* to the creation of the world and the gift of reason, after which mankind had to make its own way. The teachings of the Church were not merely rejected but despised: nature provided all that was needed. 'Oh nature,' exclaimed Diderot, a far more radical thinker both in politics and religion than Voltaire, 'sovereign of all beings, and you, her admirable daughters, virtue, reason, truth, be and remain our sole divinities. To thee are due the incense and homage of the world.' The fighting spirit of the Crusaders had returned to earth under a different flag. The old conflicts of Rome with Wittenberg and Geneva faded into insignificance in view of the empirical approach of the *Encyclopédistes* to the problems of history and society, life and mind. Voltaire spoke with pride of *notre église* of which he was the High Priest. The Reformation was a feud between the churches, the *Aufklärung* a running fight between traditional beliefs and various phases of unbelief.

The *Encyclopédie* was planned in 1745, announced by Diderot in a prospectus in 1751, and published between 1751 and 1765. The first two instalments were denounced by the Church and suppressed as hostile to authority and religion. Booksellers were forbidden to sell them, but no veto on the continuation of the enterprise was imposed. A volume appeared each year, the seventh coming down to G in 1757. Beginning with 2,000 sub-scribers, the sales rose to 4,000, but the opposition kept pace with the success. In 1759 the Government forbade the sale of the seven volumes and the printing of any more. 'His Majesty has recognised that they contain several maxims tending to destroy the royal authority, to establish the spirit of independence and revolt, irreligion, and incredulity.' At this stage d'Alembert withdrew, for the worry had worn him out. The tougher Diderot carried on as sole editor, contributing many articles himself. Offers of shelter arrived from Berlin and St. Petersburg, but the enterprise, with its large staff, was too bulky to transplant. The ten remaining volumes appeared *en bloc* in 1766, followed by ten more of plates, the latest appearing in 1772. Owing to the ban the copies were privately distributed, but the purchasers were ordered to surrender them to the police. Despite official sabotage the work was reprinted at Geneva and Lausanne. Half-hearted in everything, the Government failed to check the flowing tide.

Though Diderot has ceased to be read, since he lacked the magic of style, he ranks with Montesquieu, Voltaire, and Rousseau among the makers of nineteenth- and twentieth-century France —individualist, anti-clerical, utilitarian, democratic. Diderot, declared Goethe in old age, was unique, and anyone who derided him was a Philistine. Like Voltaire he was interested in everything, and his best writings were on art. Reformers, not revolutionaries, the *Philosophes* voiced the demands of the bourgeoisie for efficient government and the reign of law. On the eve of his death Voltaire proudly declared that France—and indeed all Europe—had become Encyclopedist. There was little exaggeration in his claim, for the Romantic movement was still in its infancy and the conception of organic development was slowly taking shape in Herder's capacious mind. That the *Philosophes* created discontent is a fable, for the sufferers did not need telling where the shoe pinched. The only revolutionary of the reign was the Abbé Meslier, virtually unknown in his lifetime, author of an unpublished treatise denouncing the Monarchy, the Church, and the institution of private property. Compared with this ruthless iconoclast the *Encyclopédists* were cautious conservatives.

The gospel of the *Encyclopédie* was expounded in the celebrated *Discours Préliminaire* of d'Alembert and was summarised in a single sentence: *Il faut tout examiner, tout remuer, sans exception et sans menagement*. His hero is Bacon, founder of the inductive method. Though the criticism of Church and creeds had to be kept within limits by fear of reprisals, the empirical ideology of the *Philosophes* shines through the contributions. 'The mind can only accept what we think good, the heart only love what seems to us good,' we read in the article on Intolerance. 'Instruction, persuasion, and prayer are the only legitimate means of extending religion. Conscience is the universal guide of our actions. Work out your own salvation and pray for mine. Anything further is an abomination in the sight of God and man.' No item aroused so much controversy as the article on Geneva, widely attributed to Voltaire and indeed saturated with his spirit, but actually the work of d'Alembert. The Genevese pastors, he declared, were exemplary in their morals, avoided disputes on matters beyond our understanding, and differed from one another without mutual persecution. In few countries were ecclesiastics less prone to

THE LEGACY OF LOUIS XV

superstition, and many of them rejected the divinity of Christ. Intolerance and superstition merely increased incredulity. Among the educated classes religion had been reduced to Deism in its simplest form. An elaborate article entitled *Mages* took a bolder line, analysing the discrepancies in the Synoptic Gospels and arguing that the record of Christian origins was saturated with legend. 'There is a wide difference between the truth of religion and the truth of history,' concludes the author with his eyes on the censorship; but readers had little difficulty in guessing which was to be preferred.

Though neither Diderot nor d'Alembert regarded himself as a political thinker, political science received a generous allowance of space. No editorial lead was provided, but the general message was clear from the assumptions of natural right and the social contract, since there were no precedents in the history of France to which appeal could be made. The political articles indeed might have been signed by Locke, for Limited Monarchy is presented as the system most conformable to common sense. The standpoint of the *Encyclopédie* may be defined as a little to the left of Voltaire and far to the right of Rousseau. Though Montesquieu passed away a year after the publication of the first two volumes, his spirit of cautious liberalism hovers over the scene.

The fullest discussion of political science is to be found in the article *Autorité Politique*.

No man has received from nature the right to command others. Liberty is a gift from heaven, and every individual of the same species has a right to its enjoyment on reaching the age of maturity. The only natural authority is that of the father, which has its limits and ceases when the children grow up. All other authority derives either from violence or voluntary contract. In the latter case a man cannot and should not surrender himself unconditionally to another: that would be idolatry and treating him as God. All legitimate power has limits, and the prince is limited by the laws of nature and the state. Hereditary government is not a possession and it can never be taken from the people to whom it belongs in full right. If the contract is broken by the ruler he forfeits his authority. The state does not belong to the prince but the prince to the state. He has no right to change the constitution. In the words of Sully, Kings have two sovereigns, God and the law.

A similar message of ordered liberty is proclaimed in the

articles on Monarchy, Fundamental Laws, and Representation. 'Liberty of the citizen means that he does not fear any other citizen.'

> Fundamental laws are conventions between the people and him or them to whom it allots sovereignty. Strictly speaking they are not laws but conventions; yet since they are binding on the contracting parties they have the force of laws. To ensure the success of limited monarchy the whole nation can reserve the legislative power and the nomination of its magistrates, entrusting to a Parliament the granting of subsidies, to the monarch—among other prerogatives —the military and executive authority.

The article on Limited Monarchy pronounces it the best system. Such was the government of England—a blend of liberty and royalty, in which the three organs of power balanced each other. The aim of the monarch should be to earn popularity, and he should feel flattered by the approval of the meanest of his subjects. The article on Representation went further. Since the rights of constituents, like the rights of the nation, were inalienable, their representatives could be disavowed if they abused their mandate. Here for once the *Encyclopédie* passed beyond the axioms of Locke and Montesquieu and moved in the direction of the sovereignty of the people, a conception almost unknown in France before 1789. Rousseau had many readers, but *Le Contrat Social* aroused far less interest during his lifetime than *La Nouvelle Héloise* which inaugurated the Romantic Movement in France.

The demand for reform during the second half of the reign of Louis XV proceeded on parallel lines. In politics the desire was for a modest share in the tasks of government, in the ecclesiastical field for the toleration of minorities, in the economic sphere for a new approach to the problem of agricultural production. One of the gravest offences of the *ancien régime* since Colbert was its neglect of agriculture, the principal source of national wealth before the Industrial Revolution. In the eyes of the Physiocrats France resembled a vast, encumbered and undeveloped estate awaiting the touch of a magician to raise the whole standard of life. The state was a tree of which agriculture was the root. The Physiocrats campaigned under the banner of Quesnay, the trusted physician to the King and Mme de Pompadour, and of the Marquis de Mirabeau, familiarly known as *Ami des Hommes*.

While the main interest of Colbert and the Mercantilists was the development of industry and commerce, the Physiocrats argued that the first concern of every government was the land, and that everyone possessed a natural right to a share in the bounty of nature. Feudal privileges were not merely a denial of fundamental rights but an obstacle to the increase of national wealth; and natural rights, above all personal freedom and the control of one's property, possessed higher sanction than the laws of man. While Quesnay and Mirabeau *père* never dreamed of a social revolution, their gospel of natural rights threatened the integrity of great estates.

Though they placed the fostering of agriculture in the forefront of their programme, the Physiocrats also demanded decentralisation, decontrol of industry and commerce, the taxation of land and of income from investments, the end of class immunity from taxation, and the abolition of feudal privileges and tithes. New taxes should not be imposed without some form of consent by the taxpayers. Uncultivated or badly cultivated land belonging to the Crown, the clergy, or the communes should be sold in order to enlarge the property of the little man. Though their teachings produced no immediate effect their books were widely read and strengthened the forces which were clamouring for a new deal.

The crusade began with the publication of *L'Ami des Hommes: Traité de la Population* in 1756, which ran through many editions and was translated into several languages. The population, which had declined during the later decades of Louis XIV, must be increased in the interest of the power and progress of France, but more mouths required more food. A Ministry of Agriculture should be created, burdens lightened, small cultivators encouraged, interest on loans reduced; large landowners should reside on their estates and increase the production of food. The Preface describes the book as 'la voix de l'humanité qui réclame ses droits'. Mirabeau reminds the King that the cultivators of the soil were the most useful of his subjects and asked nothing from him except peace and protection. 'It is with their sweat and blood that you gratify all the useless people who tell you that the greatness of a prince resides in the value and numbers of favours he divides among his courtiers and the nobility.' Though Mirabeau *père* was a domestic tyrant and was to earn unenviable celebrity by his

T

quarrels with his greater son, he combined an original mind with a sincere desire for the public weal extremely rare among members of his class.

Among his most attentive readers was Quesnay, who expressed a desire for his acquaintance. When they met in 1757 the Marquis recognised the intellectual superiority of the bourgeois physician who had propounded similar ideas in the *Encyclopédie*. In the article *Fermiers* Quesnay attributed the poverty of rural France to the flight of young folk to the towns in the hope of a better life and in order to escape liability to the *corvée* and the militia. Stable prices and moderate taxation were the first necessities for agriculture. The argument was developed in the article *Grains*. The yield of the soil, declared Quesnay, could be enormously increased. The decline of population was an ominous sign, and many of the King's subjects were living in penury. Freedom to sell their produce, improvement of transport and the application of capital would effect an agricultural revolution. His *Tableau Économique*, privately printed at Versailles in 1757 and subsequently published, pleaded for a single moderate tax on land, based on the annual yield, which would enable all other taxes to be dropped and the vast expanse of collection saved. A later work, entitled *Physiocratie*, provided a philosophic foundation for his economic demands. Natural law demanded opportunity to develop one's faculties in liberty and peace. Though the State must be strong enough to guarantee the security of the citizen, it must be kept from wrong-doing by the pressure of public opinion. Quesnay took less interest in history and philosophy, religion and science, than the *Philosophes*, but he had more to propose in the sphere of concrete reforms. His dislike of restrictions and his belief in individual enterprise won approval from Adam Smith who would have dedicated the *Wealth of Nations* to him had he been alive in 1776.

Quesnay's teaching was developed in a series of publications from the busy pen of Mirabeau. His *Théorie de l'impôt*, published in 1760, denounced the farmers-general as parasites, and argued that taxes should be collected by representatives of the taxpayers. A short term of imprisonment at Vincennes as a penalty for the book failed to quench his ardour, and he renewed the attack in his *Éléments de Philosophie rurale* published abroad in 1767. The weakness of the Physiocrats was their indifference to industry and commerce, as the weakness of the Mercantilists lay in their neglect of the agriculturist. Their hour seemed to have struck when Turgot was appointed Controller-General on the death of Louis XV, but his reforms were scrapped when he was thrown to the wolves two years later at the bidding of vested interests. So France drifted towards the abyss, not for lack of storm signals and expert advice, but because the resistance of the privileged classes proved tougher than the nation-wide but unorganised clamour for reform, and because intervention in the American War struck the final blow at the tottering financial edifice.

A sombre picture of the closing years of the reign of Louis XV as they appeared to a young aristocrat is painted in the Memoirs of the diplomatist Comte de Ségur. The King, he declares, was overpraised in his youth and too severely blamed in his old age, for he was never guilty of an act of cruelty. He cared for nothing but repose, the courtiers only for money. 'We young nobles walked on a carpet of flowers which covered an abyss.' Respect and hope were reserved for the portion of the palace where lived the Dauphin and his wife, but there was not the slightest thought of revolution. On a visit in 1785 Jefferson described the country as the richest but the worst governed in Europe. The chief beneficiaries of the *ancien régime* were the principal victims of the new deal. The full extent of the damage wrought by Louis XV became apparent in the failure of his successor's half-hearted attempt to avert a catastrophe. 'The sins of the fathers are visited on the children to the third and fourth generation.' While the constitutional struggles in seventeenth-century England illustrated the Hegelian definition of tragedy as the conflict not of right with wrong but of right with right, the collapse of the Bourbon Monarchy is the drama of discredited minorities clinging like limpets to their privileges till the tornado broke over their heads. An explosion lay in the logic of history, though the subsequent phases through which the revolution passed were conditioned by such unpredictable events as the flight to Varennes and the Brunswick Manifesto. The long inglorious reign of Louis XV and the brief intermezzo of his virtuous grandson confirm Lord John Russell's homely aphorism that there is nothing so conservative as progress. It is the diehards, crowned and uncrowned, who make revolutions inevitable. The seeds of decay had been sown in the later years of Louis XIV, but there had been plenty of time to cut out the dead wood and pull up the tares. The *ancien régime* was doomed to collapse, not by the pen of the *Philosophes* who merely encouraged their readers to think for themselves, but by the obstinate refusal of the Crown and the privileged classes to sanction the moderate changes which would have averted an ocean of blood and tears. France was still monarchist in sentiment in 1789, but the authority of the Crown was waning from day to day. Once set in motion by the summoning of the States-General the avalanche could not be arrested and the revolution had to run its course.

BIBLIOGRAPHICAL NOTES

CHAPTER 1

L'Histoire de France, ed. Lavisse, vols. VII and VIII, supersedes all earlier surveys except Voltaire, *Le Siècle de Louis XIV*, and Ranke, *Französische Geschichte*. The best short studies of the reign are by David Ogg and Maurice Ashley. John Lough, *Introduction to Seventeenth-Century France*, describes the social stratification. The Memoirs of Saint-Simon should be read in the superb edition of de Boislisle, 42 vols. Chéruel, *Saint-Simon considéré comme historien de Louis XIV*, discusses their value. Dangeau's Journal, 19 vols., though indispensable, is little more than a Court circular. Louis XIV, *Mémoires pour l'instruction du Dauphin*, 2 vols., were published by Dreyss in 1860. We come nearest to Mme de Maintenon in her voluminous correspondence. The best biography is by St. René Taillandier. *Souvenirs sur Mme de Maintenon*, ed. Comte d'Haussonville and G. Hanotaux, 3 vols., contain the Memoirs of her secretary Mlle d'Aumale and the correspondence in her old age with her niece Mme de Caylus. Comte d'Haussonville, *La Duchesse de Bourgogne*, 4 vols., is the best account of the closing phase of the reign. For the champions and critics of absolutism see Lanson, *La Politique de Bossuet*, Paul Janet, *Fénelon*, and Michel, *Vauban*. For the Church see Abbé Brémond, *Histoire littéraire du sentiment religieux en France*, and Pastor, *Geschichte der Päpste*, vols. XIV and XV; for the Jansenists Sainte-Beuve, *Port Royal*, 5 vols., Charles Beard, *Port Royal*, 2 vols., and Gazier, *Histoire du Mouvement Janséniste*, 2 vols. The best short history of the Huguenots is by A. J. Grant. Ronald Knox, *Enthusiasm*, Hazard, *La Crise de la Conscience Européenne*, and Hanotaux, 'La Théorie du Gallicanisme' in *Sur les Chemins de l'histoire*, vol. I, are useful. Petit de Julleville, *Histoire de la Langue et de la Littérature Française*, vol. V, is the best survey of seventeenth-century writers.

CHAPTER 2

The volumes of Saint-Simon on the Regency are more authoritative, though not more impartial, than those on Louis XIV. Duclos, *Mémoires*

277

secrets sur le règne de Louis XIV, la Régence et Louis XV; Buvat, *Journal de la Régence*, and Mathieu Marais, *Journal et Mémoires sur la Régence et le Règne de Louis XV, 1715-37* [with a long Introduction by Lescure] are contemporary recorders. The best surveys of the Regency are in *Histoire de France*, ed. Lavisse, vol. VIII, Part 2 [by Carré]; Funck-Brentano, *La Régence*; and E. Bourgeois, *Le Secret de Dubois*; Arvède Barine, *Madame, Mère du Régent*; Lescure, *Les Maîtresses du Régent*; and Barthélemy, *Les Filles du Régent*, describe his private life. For the Duchesse du Maine see Maurel, *La Duchesse du Maine*, the Memoirs of Mme de Staal-Delaunay, and W. H. Lewis, *Life and Times of the Duc du Maine*. The best biography of Montesquieu is by Albert Sorel, of Abbé Saint-Pierre by Molinari, of John Law by H. Montgomery Hyde.

CHAPTER 3

The fullest accounts of the shoddy intermezzo of the Duc de Bourbon are in Piépape, *Histoire des Princes de Condé au XVIIIe siècle*, vol. I, and Thirion, *Mme de Prie*. The Memoirs of Marshal Villars, 6 vols., illustrate the youth of Louis XV. For his marriage see Gauthier-Villars, *Le Mariage de Louis XV*; Nolhac, *Louis XV et Marie Leczinska*; Marquise de Réaulx, *Le Roi Stanislas et Marie Leczinska*; Maugras, *Le Roi Stanislas et la Cour de Lunéville*. Nolhac, *Le Château de Versailles sous Louis XV*, writes with the authority of a Curator. Coxe, *Memoirs of Horatio, Lord Walpole*, vol. I, provides extracts from the dispatches of the British Ambassador.

CHAPTER 4

The best survey of the France of Louis XV is in Lavisse, *Histoire de France*, vol. VIII, Part 2. Comprehensive narratives are provided by Perkins, *France under Louis XV*, 2 vols., and Jobez, *La France sous Louis XV*, 6 vols. Voltaire, *Le Siècle de Louis XV*, and his *Histoire du Parlement de Paris*, are useful. The system of government and the structure of society are described by Carré, *La France sous Louis XV*; Funck-Brentano, *L'Ancien Régime*; Tocqueville, *L'Ancien Régime et la Révolution*; Taine, *L'Ancien Régime*; F. L. Ford, *Robe and Sword* (Harvard Historical Studies, 1953); Sée, *Histoire économique de France*. Lecky, *History of England in the Eighteenth Century*, chapter 17, is excellent. Gaxotte, *Le Siècle de Louis XV*, defends the *ancien régime*. Sorel, *L'Europe et la Révolution Française*, vol. I, surveys the whole century. For the Church see Jervis, *History of the Church of France*, vol. I.; Regnault, *Christophe de Beaumont*, 2 vols.; and Preclin, *Les Jansénistes du 18e siècle*, 3 vols., Sainte-Beuve's *Lundis*, 29 vols., are a gold-mine.

CHAPTER 5

E. and J. de Goncourt, *La Duchesse de Châteauroux et ses Soeurs*, remains the fullest account of the de Nesle sisters. The correspondence between the Duchess and her cousin the Duc de Richelieu is printed in the *Mémoires de la Duchesse de Brancas*, ed. E. Asse, 1890. The best biography of Richelieu is by d'Estrée. His memoirs, edited after his death by his secretary Soulavie, include doubtful material.

CHAPTER 6

We watch the King through the unfriendly eyes of the Marquis d'Argenson, *Journal et Mémoires*, 9 vols., and the friendly eyes of the Duc de Luynes, *Journal*, 1735-58, 17 vols.; the Duc de Croy, *Journal*, 4 vols.; the *Mémoires* of Duport de Cheverny, 2 vols.; and the *Souvenirs* of Marquis Valfons. For the Queen see the Journal of the Duc de Luynes; President Hénault, *Mémoires; Lettres Inédites du Roi Stanislas à Marie Leczinska*, ed. Boye; *Lettres Inédites de la Reine Marie Leczinska et la Duchesse de Luynes au Président Hénault*. For the Dauphin and Dauphine see E. de Broglie's eulogy, *Le Fils de Louis XV*, and Stryienski, *La Mère des trois derniers Bourbons*. For the unmarried daughters see Stryienski, *Mesdames de France*, and Mme Campan's Memoirs. The King is seen at his best in *Lettres Inédites de Louis XV à son petit-fils l'Infant Ferdinand de Parme*, and in Léon de la Brière, *Mme Louise de France*. Vrignault, *Les Enfants de Louis XV: Descendance illégitime*, 1954, and Émile Dard, *Le Comte de Narbonne*, supplement Comte de Fleury, *Louis XV intime et ses petites maîtresses*.

CHAPTERS 7 AND 8

Four biographies of Mme de Pompadour are of value: Edmund et Jules de Goncourt; Campardon (*Mme de Pompadour et la cour de Louis XV*); Nolhac, and Nancy Mitford. Nolhac's second volume, *Mme de Pompadour et la Politique*, shows her influence on foreign policy to have been less than was believed. *Correspondance de Mme de Pompadour* (1875) reveals her affection for her family. Marquis d'Argenson, *Autour d'un Ministre de Louis XV, Lettres Intimes*, contains many letters to Comte d'Argenson relating to favours for her protégés. The Memoirs of Mme du Hausset, her lady-in-waiting bring us very close to her. Marquiset, *Le Marquis de Marigny*, describes the honourable career of her brother. Edmond and Jules de Goncourt, *La Peinture au dix-huitiéme siècle*, 2 vols., discusses the artists of whom she was a generous patron.

CHAPTER 9

Choiseul's *Mémoires* cover only portions of his career; Gaston Maugras, *Le Duc de Choiseul*, 2 vols., describes the whole. Maugras, *Le Duc de Lauzun et la Cour*, and the *Correspondance de Mme du Deffand*, 3 vols., the bosom friend of the Duchess, light up the triangular Choiseul *ménage*. Pierre Calmette, *Choiseul et Voltaire*, contains their political correspondence. Choiseul's foreign policy, particularly the Austrian alliance, is described in the Duc de Broglie, *l'Alliance Autrichienne*, and Bernis, *Mémoires et Lettres, 1715–58*, 2 vols., with a lengthy Introduction by Frédéric Masson. For the Austrian side see Arneth, *Maria Theresa*, vol. IV. The conflict with the Jesuits is fully described in Pastor, *Geschichte der Päpste*, vol. XVI, and Masson, *Le Cardinal Bernis depuis son Ministère*.

CHAPTER 10

Correspondance de Louis XV et du Maréchal de Noailles, 2 vols., with a long Introduction by Camille Rousset, covers the middle years of the War of the Austrian Succession. For the King's private diplomacy see Boutaric, *Correspondance Secrète de Louis XV*, 2 vols.; Duc de Broglie, *Le Secret du Roi*, 2 vols.; Vandal, *Louis XV et Elizabeth de Russie*. For his agents see Homberg et Jousselin, *Le Chevalier d'Éon*; Lhermier, *Le Mysterieux Comte de St. Germain*; Preedy, *The Courtly Charlatan*; Loménie, *Beaumarchais et son Temps*, vol. I; Pouget de Saint-André, *Le Général Domouriez*; Marsagny, *Vergennes, son Ambassade à Constantinople*. The best brief survey of foreign policy is in Émile Bourgeois, *Manuel historique de politique étrangère*, vol. I, ch. 14. Butterfield, *The Reconstruction of an Historical Episode*, summarises the controversy on the origins of the Seven Years War.

CHAPTER 11

The earliest biography of Mme du Barry, by Edmond and Jules de Goncourt, is the most hostile, that by Claude Saint André the most lenient. Fauchier-Magnan, *Les du Barry*, deals with the family, above all with her patron Jean du Barry. The struggle with the Parlement is described in the massive monograph of Flammermont, *Le Chancelier Maupeou et les Parlements*. The account of the death-bed of Louis XV by the Duc de la Rochefoucauld-Liancourt is in Sainte-Beuve, *Portraits Littéraires*, vol. III.

CHAPTER 12

For the plight of France on the death of Louis XV see Marquis de Ségur, *Au Couchant de la Monarchie*, 2 vols.; B. Fay, *Louis XVI*; Madelin *Le Crépuscule de la Monarchie*; Salvemini, *The French Revolution*. The political opposition is described in Rocquain, *L'Esprit révolutionnaire avant la Revolution*, and Aubertin, *L'Esprit Publique au dix-huitième siècle*. English influences are explored by J. Churton Collins, *Voltaire, Montesquieu and Rousseau in England*, and Texte, *Rousseau et le cosmopolitisme littéraire*. For the intellectual movement see Mornet, *Les Origines Intellectuelles de la Révolution Française*; John Morley, *Diderot and the Encyclopedists*, 2 vols.; Kingsley Martin, *French Liberal Thought in the eighteenth century*; Roustan, *Pioneers of the French Revolution*; Lanfrey, *L'Église et les Philosophes au dix-huitième siècle*; Hazard, *La Pensée Européenne au 18e siècle*; Bury, *The Idea of Progress*; Cassirer, *Die Philosophie der Aufklarung*; Sée, *L'Évolution de la Pensée politique en France au 18e siècle*; Fay, *La Francmaçonnerie et la Révolution intellectuelle du 18e siècle*. Lough, *L'Encyclopédie* contains a selection of articles with a useful Introduction. Higgs, *The Physiocrats*, discusses Quesnay, the elder Mirabeau and their school. The best detailed biographies of Voltaire are by Desnoiresterres and Georg Brandes, the best short studies by Gustave Lanson and Brailsford. F. C. Green's study of Rousseau (1955) supplements but does not supersede John Morley's well-known volumes. Petit de Julleville, *Histoire de la Langue et de la Littérature Française*, vol. VI, and Faguet, *Le Dix-huitième Siècle*, are useful.

INDEX